The Second Journey

The Second Journey

Visions and Voices on
First- and Second-Half-of-Life Spirituality

Robert P. Vande Kappelle

WIPF & STOCK · Eugene, Oregon

THE SECOND JOURNEY
Visions and Voices on First- and Second-Half-of-Life Spirituality

Copyright © 2020 Robert P. Vande Kappelle. All rights reserved. Except for brief quotations in critical publications or reviews, no part of this book may be reproduced in any manner without prior written permission from the publisher. Write: Permissions, Wipf and Stock Publishers, 199 W. 8th Ave., Suite 3, Eugene, OR 97401.

Wipf & Stock
An Imprint of Wipf and Stock Publishers
199 W. 8th Ave., Suite 3
Eugene, OR 97401

www.wipfandstock.com

PAPERBACK ISBN: 978-1-7252-8310-7
HARDCOVER ISBN: 978-1-7252-8311-4
EBOOK ISBN: 978-1-7252-8312-1

Manufactured in the U.S.A. 07/22/20

Unless otherwise noted, Bible quotations are from the *New Revised Standard Version of the Bible*, copyright © 1989 by the Division of Christian Education of the National Council of the Churches of Christ in the United States of America. Used by permission.

Two roads diverged in a wood, and I–
I took the one less traveled by,
And that has made all the difference.

—ROBERT FROST

Contents

Preface | ix

1. Introduction | 1
2. Biblical Spirituality | 19
3. Early Christian (Proto-Orthodox) Spirituality | 42
4. Gnostic Spirituality | 58
5. Ancient Wisdom Spirituality | 82
6. Christian Gnostic Spirituality | 99
7. Augustinian Spirituality | 116
8. Christian Mystical Spirituality | 129
9. Sectarian Spirituality | 154
10. Liberal Protestant Spirituality | 176
11. Christian Existentialist and Neo-Orthodox Spirituality | 191
12. Current Progressive Spirituality | 214
Epilogue | 227

Appendix: A Typology of Spirituality | 231
Bibliography | 237
Index | 241

Preface

OCCASIONALLY, IN CONVERSATION WITH adults on matters of faith and spirituality, I encounter someone who tells me, "I am Buddhist," or "I am Daoist." At first I am intrigued, because they are not ready to worship with Daoists or join a Sangha (Buddhist monastic community). More recently, I sense that they seem to be using the concepts of Taoism or Buddhism as code words for a progressive or newly found spirituality. Daoism, as taught by its original practitioners, and Buddhism, as taught by the Buddha, are remarkably holistic traditions, building on solid first-half-of-life principles designed to lead to second-half-of-life spirituality.

The Human Identity

What does it mean to be human? we ask. What makes a person unique? Does biology have priority? Are personality and spirituality equally significant factors? What about race, gender, and social class? To what extent are we shaped by our upbringing or education, by our friends and loved ones? What roles do our jobs and accomplishments play in our self-image and identity?

When our Western forebears thought of personhood, they searched the realm of art and drama for guidance, settling on the term "person" as definitive. The word "person" comes from the Latin word for "mask" or for the actor's role in a drama. The Judeo-Christian tradition builds on this idea, viewing human personhood as an organic participation in the one personhood that is God. In other words, the human self has no meaning or substance apart from the Selfhood of God. God's personhood, however, is not a mask, but the face behind all masks. We humans are the masks of God, and we play out God's image in myriad ways.

The problem we face in a secular society is that we do not know we are the masks of God. Hence, we are compelled to create our own significance, our own masks and personhood. This makes us—like atoms—inherently unstable. When we do not see our lives as a participation in Another, we are forced to manufacture our own private significance. Needing a word for this phenomenon, modern psychology chose the Latin word for "I," or "ego." This is the atomized self (the small or false self), which does not really "exist" at all. In such a state of insecurity, it overly defends and overly defines itself. This imperial ego becomes the basis for all illusion and evil. It is Adam and Eve trying to survive outside of the Garden, something they cannot do.[1]

Impoverishment of Soul

It is no secret that our world is in a state of crisis. The prognosis is bleak and the conditions may be irreversible. The tip of the iceberg, evident to almost everyone nowadays, is the environmental fate of our entire planet. During the second half of the twentieth century we learned that deterioration in the quality of the air we breathe, the water we drink, and the soil in which we grow our crops seriously threatens our continued life and well-being on this earth.

In addition to environmental degradation and anticipated ecological factors such as unpredictable weather patterns, increasing number and severity of storms, and sea-level rise, we can add pandemics and the outbreak of new diseases, species extinction, malnutrition and widespread famine, terrorism, violence and crime, the breakdown of the family, increased addictive behavior, unemployment, corporate scandals, an increasing income gap between rich and poor, religious fanaticism and sectarian wars, and the list goes on and on.

The current crisis involves many factors: ecological, political, economic, sociological, and ethical. At its core, however, the problem is spiritual. The crisis of spirit, dubbed "the impoverishment of soul" by Matthew Fox, one of today's leading spiritual teachers, is particularly evident in our Western civilization today. Modern societies are characterized by imbalance, or more accurately, by dissociation between the spiritual and physical realms of life.

---

1. Rohr, *What Mystics Know*, 24–25.

Preface

Ecotheologian Thomas Berry believes our situation today as an earth community is so desperate that we must dream the way forward. We must summon, from our unconscious, ways of seeing with which we are unfamiliar, visions that emerge from deeper within us than our conscious rational minds. As John Philip Newell suggests, reconnecting with our inner depths "will demand a fresh releasing within us of the world of dreams, myths, and the imagination. Whether as individuals or collectively as nations and religious traditions, new beginnings will be born among us when we open to the world of what we do not yet know or what we have forgotten deep within."[2]

The *Second Journey* is an invitation into this liminal reality between the known and the unknown, so that we might learn how to move forward as individuals and as communities and nations. It requires melding the visions of those who lived before us with our own contributions and efforts today, embracing the known and the unknown, the visible and the ineffable.

Whether the current crisis is curable is debatable, but it clearly requires massive cultural reorientation. More importantly, it requires a transformation of the human spirit and a commitment of will. Only a relationship of genuine harmony with nature and a love of nature's God can transform humans from consumers to caretakers. When historians look back at the start of the twenty-first century, it is hoped that they might remember it most for two commitments: as a time when the peoples of the world made a profound commitment to one another and made an equal commitment to nature. It is thus that we demonstrate our love for God. This book is about spirituality, itself primarily an expression of the human longing for—and our dependence upon—God. This innate sense of dependence on God, explored by many of the personalities we examine in this study, is well summarized by Augustine's famous assertion, "You have made us for yourself, O Lord, and our heart is restless until it rests in you."

In this regard, the most outstanding of the medieval Jewish rationalist philosophers and codifiers of Torah, Maimonides (1135–1204), sees the intellectual love of God as the ultimate aim of religious observance. In his *Mishneh Torah* (Code of the Law), he compares love of God to romantic lovesickness, arguing that humans should pine for God's love constantly. This, he believes, is the true meaning of the phrase "for I am

---

2. Newell, *Rebirthing of God*, 89.

faint with love" in Song of Solomon 2:5, viewing the whole of the Song as a parable to illustrate this theme. In this regard, he views the entirety of nature, meaning the *physical* universe, as God's garment that, while concealing God, also reveals God's glory. This idea is not pantheistic, but rather panentheistic, that all is *in* God.

The Task at Hand

While *The Second Journey* discusses religious and theological issues, particularly from a progressive Christian perspective, our focus is on spirituality.[3] Spirituality, traditionally defined by Christians as "life in the Spirit," encompasses the journey of life from a distinct perspective. Spirituality is the journey of life "from God, to God, and with God." As a result, it is also a journey toward Self. In other words, the process of coming to know or to experience God is also the process of knowing oneself. Through this process, one comes to differentiate between one's temporary or false self, which we call the ego, and one's permanent or True Self, that part of us made in the image of God and made for ongoing or everlasting relationship with God. In the end, we discover that we know God by being known, much like one loves by being loved.

This book is not a handbook on spirituality, not a step-by-step instruction manual on how to be more spiritual. Spirituality is the journey of a lifetime. While it requires effort, it is also effortless, in that it requires letting go. In the journey of spirituality, progress is expected; there are steps forward, certainly, but also many more backward. The goal of spirituality is always God, and while God makes the journey interesting, it is never easy. Orthodox or traditional spirituality—what we call first-half-of-life spirituality—is formulaic and instructional; in other words, it can be taught. Second-half-of-life spirituality is more caught than taught, for there are no clear steps to follow or learn. This book, while dealing with orthodox Christianity's struggle for supremacy, focuses on rebels and free thinkers, on those who may not necessarily have reached their goal of union with God but come to understand that somehow the journey is the goal.

Using technical language when necessary, our intent is to speak of spirituality as something helpful and valuable for ordinary people. There is be little or no emphasis on the kind of spirituality that we ordinarily

---

3. For a typology of spirituality, associated with personality types, see the appendix.

associate with institutional worship, sacramentalism, or extreme piety. While we examine monasticism, mysticism, Pietism, revivalism, and the Holiness Tradition, the goal is to discover there guidelines for everyday spirituality rather than the hyper-spirituality common to esoteric behavior and practice. Hence, we avoid focusing on visions, ecstasies, miracles, charismatic practices, stigmata, meditative techniques, devotional practices, seclusion, or withdrawal from society. This book is written for sinners, not saints. It is not intended to convince readers of the truth of specific doctrines, beliefs, or ways of life. Rather, the focus is on relinquishing fears and concerns and on finding ways to think and live more holistically and nondualistically. Once our soul comes to its True Self, it can be almost anything except selfish or separate, and that sort of thinking and living is primarily what holistic and unitive spirituality entails.

As you read this book, you will undoubtedly come across ideas with which you may disagree, ideas you will accept wholeheartedly, and ideas you have never heard before, ideas that may keep you thinking late into the night. Expect to be challenged, perplexed, and frustrated, but also to grow spiritually and intellectually in ways you never imagined.

The central defining characteristic of spirituality is an individual's sense of connection to a greater whole. At its heart, spirituality involves an emotional experience of awe and reverence. Such experience is highly desired, fervently sought, endlessly disagreed upon, and thoroughly fascinating. Why did our ancestors have such a wonderful idea of God? Because they lived in an awesome world. They wondered at the magnificence of whatever it was that brought the world into being. This led to a sense of adoration. This adoration, this gratitude, we call religion. Now, as the outer world is diminished, our inner world is drying up. The task of spirituality is to help us regain our sense of awe and reverence, beginning with a profound commitment to nature and continuing with an equal commitment to the whole of humanity and every living creature. If we do not love what is visible around us, how can we love God, whom we cannot see? (1 John 4:19–20).

Overview

The Second Journey follows a natural progression, historically and theologically. To make vivid visions and voices from the past, we contemporize historical individuals and movements whenever possible, using the historical (narrative) present to personalize their message. For second-half-of-life thinking and living, the eternal present is the dominant reality.

Chapter 1 introduces the topic of spirituality, defining terms such as religion, theology, and spirituality. This chapter describes the first and second halves of life, distinguishing between first- and second-half-of-life thinking and living. Second-half-of-life spirituality, we discover, is more about unlearning and unknowing than about learning and knowing. Chapter 2 provides focus to our primary task, examining the nature and development of Christianity-based spiritualities, starting with its conception in the biblical tradition. While exemplifying first-half-of-life spirituality, the Bible embraces the promise and hope entailed in second-half-of-life living and thinking. Chapter 3 describes early Christian orthodox spirituality, focusing on the spiritual and theological boundaries established for the early Christian movement by the New Testament and by the efforts of two second-century Christian apologists, Justin Martyr and Irenaeus. Distinguishing between orthodoxy and heresy, they provide the parameters for traditional Christian orthodoxy.

Chapter 4 examines Gnostic theology and spirituality, noting how Christian and non-Christian *gnosis* (wisdom or knowledge) expand upon orthodox spirituality, paving the way for second-half-of-life spirituality. Chapter 5 examines the contributions to spirituality of several ancient Greek philosophical schools—including those associated with Plato, Aristotle, Zeno, and Plotinus—as well as the religious literature associated with the god Hermes and with the mystical Jewish Platonist Philo of Alexandria. Chapter 6 reviews the theological contributions of two influential gnostic Christians, Clement and Origen, both associated with an important Christian intellectual academy in the city of Alexandria, Egypt, advocates of the Alexandrian school of Christian theology and spirituality. While non-Christian Gnostics see God as remote and inaccessible, known only through intermediaries and emanations, Clement and Origen understand God as accessible through the human powers of intelligence and love.

Chapter 7 examines the theology of Augustine, one of medieval Christianity's most influential thinkers, focusing on his doctrine of grace and its relation to faith, reason, free will, predestination, and the reality of evil in the world. Chapter 8 explores Christian mystical spirituality, focusing on Eastern Orthodox spirituality, particularly the veneration of icons, their power based on the Transfiguration of Christ. Here readers explore kataphatic and apophatic spirituality, learning that knowing God involves both light and darkness, usually in that order. Chapter 9 introduces the notion of immediacy in spirituality, an aspect of Protestant spirituality associated with Baptists, Quakers, Pietists, and Revivalists.

We conclude our study of Christianity-based spirituality examining individuals and movements that engage with the modern ethos and its turn to experience as the pathway to knowledge and truth. Chapter 10 examines Protestant Liberalism, particularly the spirituality of the influential Romantic thinker Friedrich Schleiermacher. Chapter 11 explores Protestant existentialism, as charted by the Danish theologian Søren Kierkegaard, and its impact on such twentieth-century Neo-orthodox theologians as Karl Barth, Emil Brunner, and Paul Tillich. Chapter 12 examines progressive spirituality as witnessed by two of its leading contemporary figures, Matthew Fox and Richard Rohr.

Note for Leaders and Participants

The Second Journey is useful for individual or group study. As you read this book, consider journaling as a way to grow spiritually. A good place to start is with your hopes and dreams. As you reflect and write, be honest with your thoughts and feelings, without ignoring your fears. Transparency facilitates the process of becoming healthy and whole.

Each chapter concludes with questions for discussion or reflection. Write the answers to each question in your journal, in addition to the questions below, which are appropriate for each chapter. If you are reading this book in a group setting, be prepared to share your answers to the following questions as well as those at the end of each chapter with others in the group. Leaders may select questions from these lists that they deem most helpful for group discussion.

1. After reading this chapter, what did you learn about first-half-of-life spirituality?
2. After reading this chapter, what did you learn about second-half-of-life spirituality?
3. In your estimation, what is the primary insight gained from this chapter?
4. *For personal reflection*: Does this chapter raise any issues you need to handle or come to terms with successfully? If so, how will you deal with them?

1

Introduction

THIS BOOK ARISES OUT of the need for untrained laity—folks in ordinary (unreligious) careers or ways of life who may or may not have been exposed academically to religious or theological studies—to be more creative in thinking about spirituality by engaging broadly with the Christian tradition. Like every discipline, spirituality and its subset Christian theology have technical terminology and unique mindsets. Hence, when introducing technical terms, we define them.

We begin with a common disclaimer. How often do we hear people say, "I love religion, but I hate theology," or better yet, "I am spiritual, but not really religious." This attitude is widespread and is often based on astute discernment. Religion can be impractical, and theology complicated and boring. But the answer to complicated religion is understandable religion, and the antidote to poor theology is good theology. While we cannot speak of spirituality without religious language or apart from theological concepts, the answer to impractical religion and complicated theology is not poor religion or no theology, but rather clear theology leading to holistic spirituality.

To understand spirituality, specifically Christian spirituality, we begin by defining religion and theology. If religion is central to culture, there should be agreement among scholars on a definition of religion, but no consensus exists. In order to provide distinction between religion and non-religion, some scholars appeal to a distinction between two realms of reality, the sacred and the secular, arguing that human involvement with the sacred defines the essence of religion.

The notion that religion can be defined as human interaction with the sacred has a long legacy in the West. This view, based upon a sacred-secular dualism, divides the world into two domains, the one containing all that is sacred and the other all that is profane. This distinction, based on an antiquated dualistic perspective long entrenched in the Western mindset, provides insuperable problems for many modern individuals, whose experience leads them to conceptualize the sacred (and therefore the supernatural, the spiritual, the metaphysical, and the nonmaterial) as a projection and/or an extension of society, thereby collapsing the sacred into the profane (the natural, physical, and material). Incidentally, the sacred-profane dualistic worldview is not a universal idea, but rather a particularly Western construction.

While it is true that many societies do not draw a clear line between culture and what scholars would call "religion," this does not mean that religion doesn't exist. What it does mean is that even when we think we have a handle on what religion is, we might be off base. Perhaps the most helpful starting point in understanding religion and its role in society is to examine the etymology of the word.

The classic explanation of the word religion, traced to the first-century BCE Roman orator Cicero, derives religion from the Latin word *relegere* (*re* + *lege*), which means "to read over again," in the sense of "consider carefully." Thus *religio*, the nominative of the Latin *religionem*, means such things as "respect for what is sacred, reverence for the gods, sense of right, and religious observance." In Roman society, religious law maintains the proprieties of divine honors, sacrifice to the gods, and proper ritual. Incorrect ritual and improper sacrifice are *vitia* (translated as "vice" in English), and the improper use or search of divine knowledge is *superstitio*. Neglecting the *religiones* (plural of *religio*) owed to the traditional gods is considered atheism, a charge leveled by ancient Romans at Christians as well as at Jews and Epicureans. The reason is clear: any moral deviation from acceptable religious norms is not only perverse, but it can bring harm to the state.

Another possible origin of "religion" is the Latin word *religare*, which means "to tie or to bind fast." Many modern writers favor this etymology, on the assumption that it helps to explain the power inherent in religion. Modern scholar Joseph Campbell favors a derivation from *ligo* (bind, connect), probably from a prefixed *re* (again) + *ligare*, meaning "to reconnect," a correlation made prominent by Augustine. The question immediately arises, to what should one reconnect? The answer is not clear. To theists, *religare* means to reconnect to God and to God's will for our lives. To polytheists *religare* implies reconnecting to the higher powers around us, and to the values espoused by social and religious leaders. To nature-based cultures, *religare* means to revere nature's ways, and to find one's place in the natural order. In each case, finding harmony with that which is considered to be ultimate in power and reverence, whether natural or supernatural, and with other human beings, is essential and mandatory. For monotheists, *religare* is best expressed in the double-love command, also known as the Great Commandment: "You shall love the Lord your God with all your heart, and with all your soul, and with all your mind, and with all your strength . . . and your neighbor as yourself" (Mark 12:30–31; cf. Deut. 6:4; Lev. 19:18).

A third possible origin of the term "religion" is the Latin word *religiens*, meaning "careful," in contrast to *negligens*, its opposite. In this sense, religion is a way of life lived thoughtfully and mindfully, not neglecting duties or devotion.

Because all three definitions are instructive, I recommend that you take a few moments to personalize their meaning by pondering the following questions:

1. What do I hold sacred in my life? How do I show respect for the sacred in my life?
2. What do I consider to be "ultimate" in the universe in terms of power and reverence? How can I find harmony with this power?
3. Am I living thoughtfully and mindfully? How do I fall short of that mark? How can I live more intentionally? Am I lacking in discipline or devotion?

The attempt to define religion is a relatively recent phenomenon. As scholars are divided on the etymology of religion, so also they disagree on its definition. Some find the task to be impossible, arguing that attempts to define religion comprehensively inevitably fall victim to the bias of a particular religious or non-religious point of view. Others maintain that given the basic diversity among cultures and religions, no single definition encompassing all religions is possible.

Definitions of religion suffer either from being too narrow, excluding many belief systems that most agree are religious, or from being too vague and ambiguous, suggesting that practically anything qualifies as religion. A good example of a narrow definition is the common attempt to define "religion" as "belief in God," effectively excluding non-theistic views and ignoring the multiple conceptions of God held by people throughout history and even today. A good example of a vague definition is the tendency to define religion doctrinally, as a perspective or worldview. Here again it would be hard to draw a line between what qualifies as "religious" ideology or as non-religious ideology, and once again we fall into the dualistic dilemma to which we alluded earlier.

In my approach to religion, I am not concerned with a definition that might be acceptable to everyone or applicable universally, for such a definition does not exist. Rather I employ a definition by William A. Young: "*Religion is human transformation in response to perceived ultimacy.*"[1] This definition views the role of religion to be dynamic rather than static and radically this worldly in scope and orientation. Notice that his definition involves two distinct phenomena: belief and behavior. Stated differently, what people believe has consequences for the way they act.

While this definition seems excessively broad, in that "ultimacy" can apply to non-religious areas of concern such as political, economic, and cultural pursuits, that is not Young's intention. His use of the concept of ultimacy carries specific meaning: "The ultimate is the center of life; it conditions and gives meaning to all of existence."[2] Other authors define religion in supportive ways. William A. Christian defines ultimate reality as something that is "more important than anything else in the universe,"[3] and Paul Tillich famously defined religion as that which is of "ultimate concern."

Young, Christian, and Tillich converge in their understanding of religion as that which leads to personal and social transformation, and that is my approach as well. The definition of religion as a "means toward ultimate transformation," initially formulated by Fred Streng in 1973, views religion as a way of life oriented to a common goal, the goal being to reach a state conceived to be the highest possible for individuals and societies.[4] "Religious" persons are said to acknowledge that life is under threat (often called sin or evil), whether by illusion, ignorance, chaos, oppression, self-destruction, or death. Whereas "religious" persons are said to acknowledge these threats because they see themselves as only

---

1. Young, *World's Religion*, 3.
2. Ibid., 5.
3. Christian, *Meaning and Truth in Religion*, 60.
4. Streng et al., *Ways of Being Religious*.

potentially human, "non-religious" persons tend to think of their humanity simply as given.

In this definition, the phrase "means toward" refers to the various ways by which people seek to become changed into that highest state, individually and communally, including ethical, social, economic, mystical, and aesthetic practices and pursuits. Likewise, the phrase "ultimate transformation" implies that human life presents us with a quest or comprehensive task (often called salvation, enlightenment, liberation or fulfillment), something non-religious persons disavow.

The term "theology" is much easier to define. It comes from two Greek words, *theos*, meaning God, and *logos*, meaning "word" or rational thought. Theology, or more specifically Christian theology, then, is Christian thought about God. Of course, the word "God" cannot be defined exactly, but as we note above, it is normally used to represent whatever is believed to be the Ultimate Reality, meaning the source of all things, the highest of values, or the source of all other values. God is that which is deemed worthy of being the goal and purpose of life. In light of this, it seems self-evident that human beings cannot live without theology.

While we can define religion or theology with some degree of meaning and specificity, the word "spirituality," properly understood, is used with little or no clear meaning, or with a wide and vague significance, yet the term is essential for our study, and I can think of no better single word to describe our subject. In antiquity, the word is not used, and when first introduced in the English-speaking world, it refers to the clergy, specifically to the ecclesiastical vocation, as distinct from secular or temporal vocations. From this sixteenth-century usage, the term comes to describe things of the spirit as distinct from things of matter, including such things as spirits, ghosts, or souls.

The meaning of a religious way of life, notably one's piety or acts of religious devotion, comes still later, although its use in Ignatius Loyola's *Spiritual Exercises* refers to the practice of piety and more specifically, techniques of devotion. When first used in the French-speaking world, the term "spirituality" is a term of reproach, associated with mystical or ascetical devotion such as used by Pietists and related sects and movements not in the religious mainstream. In this respect, spirituality represents an excess of striving after the purely immaterial.

By the nineteenth century, the term is no longer one of reproach but simply a description of ways of prayerful piety, with a view toward the practices of ascetics or mystics. At times spirituality comes to be associated with the "inner" or "interior life" of humans in general. In the first half of the twentieth century, the terms spirituality or spiritual theology is applied to ascetic or mystical theology, as opposed to dogmatic and moral theology.

In nineteenth- and twentieth-century Protestant Liberalism, with the advance of biblical criticism and widespread skepticism on matters of faith, pious people focus on religious practice (*lex orandi*) over against the vicissitudes of historical belief (*lex credenti*), and "spirituality" expresses what is sought. In the late twentieth century, the word "spirituality" finds wide usage yet goes undefined, having a vague association with living holistically, contemplatively, fully, and harmoniously with nature, others, and all of life. This latter perspective, that all life has a spiritual aspect, is associated widely with spirituality, and the term becomes disengaged from theology in general or religion in particular.

Such lack of specificity, however, makes the concept so universal as to lack value. For our purposes, then, I reconnect the term with its root meaning, that is, with Spirit, or as the ancient Hebrews did, with the "wind" or "breath" of God. To be spiritual, then, is to breathe deeply and harmoniously with Reality (Infinity). Spirituality, then, is a Spirit-filled way of living, walking a hopeful, creative, life-filled path. In using the term "path," I distinguish this way of living from a highway, for spirituality must be personal. By necessity, to choose one path is to reject another. Unlike a highway, a path is not goal-oriented, for spirituality implies choice and even mystery. To quote Matthew Fox, spirituality is

> the way itself, and every moment on the way is a holy moment; a sacred seeing takes place there. All who embark on a spiritual path need to be willing to learn and to let go; to know that none of us has all the answers, and yet that none of us is apart from deity . . . What is common to all paths that are spiritual is, of course, the Spirit—breath, life, energy. That is why all true paths are essentially one path—because there is only one Spirit, one breath, one life, one energy in the universe. It belongs to none of us and all of us. We all share it. Spirituality does not make us otherworldly; it renders us more fully alive. The path that spirituality takes is a path away from the superficial into the depths; away from the "outer person" into the "inner person"; away from the privatized and individualistic into the deeply communitarian.[5]

---

5. Fox, *Creation Spirituality*, 12.

Introduction

In his public lecture "The Seven Spiritual Laws of Success," the prominent Indian-American physician and philosopher Deepak Chopra defines success as "the progressive realization of worthy goals." Humans are goal-seeking organisms. Because worthy goals involve the ability to love and be compassionate, harmful addictive behavior qualifies as unworthy. From this perspective, a requisite quality for goal-seeking is the ability to hear one's inner voice, to be in touch with the Spirit within, one's true self and creative center. Living out of one's core, one's innermost being, Chopra believes, is what humans mean by "spirituality." Spirituality, simply defined, is "Self-awareness." You will notice I capitalize the word "Self," for this is both intentional and essential to a proper understanding of the concept.

Because it is easy to fall into a simplistic or merely humanistic view of spirituality, let me clarify what I mean. When I think of spirituality, I have in mind the account of Jesus healing a victim of blindness in Mark's Gospel. According to Mark 8:22–26, when Jesus heals a blind man in the town of Bethsaida, the healing occurs in three stages. First, the man is blind. Next, Jesus lays hands on him, using saliva to anoint the man's eyes. However, the man's vision is blurry and indistinct. Lastly, Jesus again lays hands upon the blind man's eyes, whereupon his sight is fully restored, enabling him to see everything clearly.

The same pattern can be applied to spirituality (its three stages also understood as three distinct types of spirituality):

1. *self-consciousness.* This stage of awareness—the first-half-of-life-phase—denotes "self-awareness," a selfish, self-centered, egocentric state. Characterized by allegiance to the ego or false self, this stage represents deception and spiritual idolatry. In this stage, a false and dream-like state, humans are in the dark, unaware, and self-deceived.

2. *God-consciousness.* This phase, a transitional phase, is still idolatry, or, more accurately, monolatry, for as commonly understood, it represents institutional allegiance, attachment to ethical and man-made religious belief systems. This phase of spirituality, evident historically in salvation by effort approaches, can be likened to sleepwalking. In this stage participants are striving to make progress, but they are still in the dark. They are serving external requirements, pleasing an authoritarian deity.

3. *Self-consciousness.* This stage of awareness—the second-half-of-life phase—is entered through realization, by awakening. Those thus connected to their soul or core being are now "in the light," connected finally to their higher power, to pure consciousness. Such awareness—such living and thinking—are gifts of grace. This state of awareness cannot be earned, but, like the biblical pearl of great price, it can be found through diligent search and desire.

These stages represent the journey from darkness to light, illustrated in nature by the three phases of the twenty-four-hour day: night, twilight/dawn, and day.

The Second Journey

A journey into "the second half of life" awaits us all. This "further journey" is not chronological, nor do we magically stumble upon it at midlife or in times of crisis, though these often serve as catalysts. The second journey is largely unknown today, even by people we consider deeply religious, since most individuals and institutions remain stymied in the preoccupations of the first half of life, establishing identity, creating boundary markers, and seeking security. The first-half-of-life task, while essential, is not the full journey. Furthermore, we cannot walk the second journey with first-journey tools. We need a new toolkit.

How can we know we are entering the second half of life? The following road markers are quite reliable: when we

- experience new urges
- sense a new vision
- are ready to let go of old securities
- are ready to risk giving up the patterns of the past for the promise of the future
- are as focused on the "inner" life as on the outer dimension of life

While individuals can describe their experience of the second journey and even serve as mentors, they cannot define or outline the journey for others. This is due both to the uniqueness of the journey and to a subtle factor, known by generations of mystics and spiritual masters but elusive to many of our contemporaries: we do not choose this second journey; rather it chooses us. It finds us by means of our soul, our personal center and true home, the source of our true belonging. The soul comes to our aid through dreams, deep emotion, love, the quiet voice of guidance, synchronicities, revelations, hunches, and visions, and at times through illness, nightmares, and terrors. This identity defines us, aligning us with our powers of nurturing, transforming, and creating, and with our sense of presence and wonder. The soul guides us, preparing the way and declaring us ready for this further journey.

If we haven't acquired conscious knowledge of our soul, we haven't yet learned of its power. To experience this power, which serves as a bridge to the second half of life, we must first get to know more thoroughly the place in life we already inhabit. This place consists of our relationships and roles in both society and nature. We achieve this knowledge and intimacy through the practice of mindfulness, learning to dwell deeply in the present moment.

This talk of the first and second half of life is not new. It is embodied in the scriptures, tales, and experiences of men and women who find themselves on the further journey. We find it, for example, in the anonymous fourteenth-century classic *The Cloud of Unknowing*, with its distinction between active and contemplative spiritualities, interdependent yet distinct, and in the nineteenth-century existentialist philosopher Søren Kierkegaard's distinction between Religiousness A (a natural form of religious life concerned with ethical standards) and Religiousness B (an ethical life lived in relation to God).

In this second half of life, we are less interested in judging or punishing others, or in harboring superiority complexes. By now these things have shown themselves to be useless, ego-based, and counterproductive. Daily life now requires discernment more than kneejerk response toward either the conservative or liberal end of the spectrum. In the second half of life we focus less on commandments and precepts and more on changing our attitude, on forgiving others rather than criticizing or finding fault.

Life is more spacious now, the boundaries of our lives having been enlarged by the addition of new experiences and relationships. This may be what Ken Wilber means when he says "the classic spiritual journey always begins elitist and ends egalitarian." In the second half of life we are less concerned with mastery of independent dance steps and more with just being part of the general dance. Such people have no need to stand out, make defining moves, or be better than others. Life is more participatory than assertive, and there is less need for self-assertion and self-definition. In the second half of life people live in the presence of

God. In that reality, the brightness comes from within, a reflection of the divine that is more than adequate.

Those who live in the presence of God no longer have to prove that their ethnicity is superior, their group the best, their religion the only one that God approves, or that their place in society deserves special treatment. They become less preoccupied with amassing goods and services and focus instead on giving back to others a portion of what they have received. Their concern is no longer to have what they love, but rather to love what they have. When we meet such a shining person, we know that he or she is surely the goal of humanity and the delight of God.

The second-half-of-life journey is likened to the postcritical phase of life or a second simplicity. Paul Ricoeur speaks of it as a second naiveté or a second childhood. Whatever we call it, I believe this condition is the very goal of mature adulthood and mature religion. First naiveté (precritical living and thinking) is the earnest and dangerous innocence we sometimes admire in young zealots, but it is also the reason we should not elect them or follow them as leaders. It is probably necessary to be impetuous when we are young, taking risks and eliminating most doubt. In the long run such approaches to life are not wise. Mature wisdom is content to live with mystery, doubt, and "unknowing," and in such living ironically resolves that very mystery to some degree. It takes a great deal of learning to finally "learn ignorance," as so many religious sages discover. As T. S. Eliot puts it in the *Four Quartets*: "We had the experience but missed the meaning." This means, at least in part, that people in the second half of life need not expect to have the same experiences as others; rather, simple meaning now suffices.

This new coherence, a unified field that embraces paradox, is precisely what gradually characterizes a second-half-of-life person. It feels like a return to simplicity after having learned from all the complexity. Finally we understand that "everything belongs," even the sad, absurd, and futile parts. In the second half of life we can devote ourselves to integrating even the painful parts of our life into the now unified field, including people who are different or marginalized. If we can forgive ourselves for being imperfect and falling, we can do it for just about everyone else.

Some people seem to miss the joy and clarity of the first simplicity, perhaps avoiding the interim complexity, and finally losing the great freedom and magnanimity of the second simplicity as well. We need to hold together all of the stages of life, and for some reason it all becomes quite "simple" as we approach our later years. However, to embrace second-half-of-life spirituality, we must first experience a full and healthy first-half-of life spirituality, for the two are related and progress in that order. The transition is not clear and practically undefinable, although generally speaking, elements of the second journey are present in the first journey, and elements of the first journey continue in the second. Ultimately, it is love and not knowledge that enables us to reach God in this life.

In the sixteenth-century, Teresa of Ávila speaks of finding God, not through our intellect or understanding, but rather through divine grace, which suspends the human intellect, shifting it from understanding toward love. Thus, Teresa writes, "The important thing is not to think much but to love much," an experience she likens to entering one's "interior castle," a sort of inner structure of the soul that one must enter to find God. The result is what she describes as spiritual marriage, the soul's permanent union with God in love. An earlier mystic, Julian of Norwich, agrees that the focus of one's encounter with God is love, describing the meaning of her "showings" or visions thus: "Do you want to see your Lord's meaning? Learn it well: Love was his meaning. Who showed it to you? Love. Why did he show it to you? For love. Hold fast to this and you will learn and understand more and more. But you will never learn or know anything else throughout eternity."

As previously noted, the transformation that brings us to the second half of life is often more about unlearning than learning. Perhaps it is simply a more profound learning. Life is more spacious now, the boundaries of the container having been enlarged by transformative experiences and relationships. For many people, the second half of life is characterized by seven transformational qualities:

1. Less fear and therefore less hostility. Because we have less need to eliminate the negative or fearful from our lives, there is less need to punish other people. Superiority complexes are shown to be useless, ego based, counterproductive, and often entirely wrong.

2. Less combative. By the second half of life we learn that most frontal attacks simply add to the amount of evil within. Along with an inflated self-image, they incite retaliation from those we attack.

3. Less need of attention. When "elders" speak, they need few words to make their point. Second simplicity has its own kind of brightness and clarity, but much of it is expressed nonverbally, and only when needed. In the first half of life, we are defined through

differentiation; now we look for commonality. We do not need to dwell on the differences between people or exaggerate the problems. Creating dramas is boring.

4. Less assertive. In the second half of life it is good just to be a part of the general dance. We do not have to stand out or be better than others; life is more participatory than assertive, and there is no need for strong or further self-definition.

5. Less self-concerned. At this stage we no longer have to prove we are the best, that our ethnicity is superior, our religion the only one accepted by God, or that our role and place in society deserve special treatment.

6. Less dogmatic. At this stage we are less condemning. We no longer see God as small, punitive, or tribal. Having defended signposts, now we arrive where the signs point. Our growing sense of spaciousness is no longer found mostly "out there" but especially "in here." The inner and the outer become one. In the second journey, we have less final opinions about things and people as we allow them to delight or sadden us. We no longer need to change or adjust other people in order to be happy ourselves. Ironically, we are more than ever before in a position to change others—but we do not need to—and that makes all the difference. Now we aid and influence others simply by being who we are.

7. Less possessive. At this stage we are no longer preoccupied with accumulating additional goods and services; rather, our desire and effort are to pay back to the world some of what we have received. Our concern is not so much to have what we love, but to love what we have—here and now. This is such a monumental change from the first half of life that it is almost the litmus test of whether we are in the second half of life at all.

Such transformation requires six steps: (1) forgiveness (repudiating retaliation or "getting even"); (2) prayer (learning to listen in silence); (3) changing one's attitude ("unlearning"); (4) quiet persuasion (becoming an elder statesman); (5) becoming an agent of change (which starts with actively working for peace); and (6) influencing events (indirectly rather than directly, by modeling the transformative qualities of the second simplicity).

Introduction

If unlearning is a way to deeper spirituality, the following pathways represent "paradigm shifts," attitudinal transformations, in the journey from the first to the second half of life:

- Impatience to greater patience
- Critical to more accepting
- Pessimism to optimism
- Stoical to joyful
- Independent to dependent
- Aloof to affectionate
- Self-centered to other-oriented
- Frugal to generous

Again, these observations do not represent precepts to be followed or new commandments to be obeyed. The second half of life is not about precepts or commandments, for there is only one guideline for the second half of life: to love the Lord your God with your entire mind, heart, soul, and strength, and your neighbor as yourself. The rest is commentary.

The great difference between transformed and nontransformed people is that transformed people live to serve, not to be served. It is a perspective good parents exemplify. Many of the happiest, most generous and focused people are young mothers. Whole people see and create wholeness wherever they go.

Asking my wife Susan, a second-half person, to identify her tasks for the second journey, she responds succinctly yet profoundly:

1. Identifying and affirming my core self
2. Deepening friendships
3. Accepting my death
4. Redefining my belief system

"What about God," I ask? "Where is God in this process?" "God is in all of these," she replies, agreeing with Paula D'Arcy that God comes to us disguised as our life.

Spirituality is like breathing—breathing deeply. When you breathe in, you are experiencing or replicating first-half-of-life spirituality. When you breathe out, you are experiencing or replicating second-half-of-life spirituality. To further clarify, I invite you to take three deep breaths, focusing on four elements of the breathing process. First, breathe in fully and hold your inhalation for a while, as long as comfortable. Then exhale and hold the exhalation for as long as comfortable. Do this three times at your own pace, paying attention to each nuance of your breath as you inhale, hold, exhale, and hold. Focus particularly on the empty space at the end of your exhalation.

In this moment, you have nothing to do, nothing to accomplish. For a time, you are giving yourself the gift of being fully present, fully alive, and fully expectant. Rest right here, fully in the moment, ready to receive, then ready to give. Welcome to second-half-of-life spirituality! Receive it, embrace it, and rest fully in its risky fragility. This is the meaning of faith. If inhalation represents belief—walking by sight, clarity, affirmation, and certainty—exhalation represents faith—ambiguity, uncertainty, and unknowing. This is second-half-of-life knowing and living, second-half-of-life spirituality.

Spirituality and Theological Unlearning

The perils of theology, this zealous endeavor to convert a liquid into a solid, are not widely acknowledged, yet they must be confronted and supplanted if we are to grow spiritually. If spirituality is more about unlearning than about learning, the first theological dogma we need to unlearn is the doctrine of heaven and hell. We have learned that heaven is where good people—the "saved," namely God's beloved—spend an eternity with God, and that hell is where bad people—often non-Christians and even Christians "unsaved," according to in-group definitions—spend an eternity without God. It is far better to take these terms, as Jesus does in John's Gospel, as references to present experiences. The false self makes religion into an "evacuation plan for the next world," as Brian McLaren puts it, but the True Self knows that heaven is now and that its loss is hell now. In that respect it might be said that religion is for those afraid to go to hell, while spirituality is for those who have been there.

A person who finds his or her True Self has learned how to live in the big picture, as a part of deep time and all of history. This change of frame and venue is called living in the Kingdom of God by Jesus, and it necessitates that we let go of our own smaller kingdoms, what Earl Jabay calls "the kingdom of self," which people in the first half of life do not want to do. Life in the Kingdom of God is both practicing for heaven and living in heaven. When we do not know our True Self, we push all enlightenment into a possible future reward and punishment system, within which hardly anyone wins. When we live in God's Kingdom, we envision a more hopeful eternity.

Heaven is the state of union both here and later. As now, so will it be then. No one is in heaven unless he or she wants to be, and all are in heaven when they live interdependently. That is biblical truth. People are in heaven when they "abide in Christ," living in love with one another, making room for fellowship with the divine, and thinking and living inclusively. The larger and more inclusive our house is, the bigger our heaven. Perhaps this is what Jesus means by there being "many rooms in my Father's house" (John 14:2). If we go to heaven alone, wrapped in our private worthiness and narrow selectivity, it is by definition *not* heaven. The more we exclude, the more hellish and lonely our existence is. How can we enjoy heaven knowing our loved ones are not there, or are being tortured for all eternity? If we accept a punitive notion of God, who eternally punishes and tortures those who do not love him, then we have an absurd universe where most people on earth end up being more loving than God. Why would Jesus' love be unconditional while he is in this world, and suddenly become conditional after his death? How can Jesus ask us to bless, forgive, and heal our enemies, which he clearly does (Matt. 5:43–48), unless God is doing it first and always? Be assured, no one is in hell unless that individual chooses final aloneness and separation.

The second theological dogma we need to unlearn is the doctrine of sin and salvation. John 3:16, the most quoted verse in the New Testament, sums up the message of Jesus by reiterating the salvific dimension of Jesus' death, but moves the argument forward with its reference to God's love. This passage indicates that God's love is directed toward "the world," a term generally associated with that part of humanity that is at odds with Jesus and God. In John 3:16–18, called the "Gospel in miniature," we learn that Jesus' purpose in coming is not for the purpose of passing judgment, but rather for the purpose of turning people to God. The context makes clear that Jesus is God's gift of love to everyone, though only believers accept the gift.

The reason that Jesus does not come to pass judgment is because people judge themselves by their response to Jesus. This interpretation is seen in the story of the healing of the blind man in John 9, in crucial ways an exposition of 3:16–21. This story is not simply about the restoration of natural sight. Rather, the author uses this healing story to portray the process of spiritual decision-making. Light and darkness are no longer merely concepts, but are embodied by the characters portrayed in the story. In the blind man's journey from physical blindness to spiritual sight, readers are able to watch as someone comes to the light and is given new life. In the Jewish authorities' passage from physical sight to spiritual blindness, readers are able to watch as the religious authorities close themselves to the light and place themselves under judgment. The dramatic structure of this passage intensifies the profound theological irony: the authorities, who position themselves as judges of others, finally bring themselves under judgment as sinners.

The presentation of sin in John 9 is pivotal to the understanding of sin in John, where the self-righteousness of the Pharisees becomes the basis for their judgment as sinners: "If you were blind, you would not have sin. But now that you say, 'We see,' your sin remains" (John 9:41). In its deepest and most illuminating sense, sin in the Bible is defined not by what we do or don't do, but almost exclusively by our relationship to God. In the New Testament, believers are asked to recognize the transformative power of the love of God and to shape their lives accordingly. To reject Jesus is to reject the love of God in Jesus and so to pass from the possibility of salvation to judgment. The blind man's words in John 9:25 offer eloquent testimony to the transforming power of God's grace in the hymn "Amazing Grace": "I once was blind, but now I see."

The third and final theological dogma we need to unlearn concerns the person of Jesus Christ, the doctrine known as Christology.[6] For all practical purposes, the dualist mind is not able to accept the orthodox teaching that Jesus is both fully human and fully divine simultaneously. Rationalist thinking splits and divides, with the result that it understands Jesus as *only* divine and understands humans as *only* human, despite all scriptural and mystical affirmation to the contrary. The doctrine of the Incarnation is designed to overcome this divide, but the practical results for individual Christians, as for Christianity, are disastrous.

The application of the "I Am" title to Jesus, central to the Fourth Gospel, so thrills early Christians that they forget the continued need to balance this discovery with Jesus' even more strongly proclaimed humanity. In the Synoptic Gospels, virtually Jesus' only form of self-reference is "son of man," meaning "son of the human one." The prophet

---

6. This segment on Christology is adapted from Rohr, *Naked Now*, 67–79.

Ezekiel uses this same phrase repeatedly with reference to his mortality and humanity. Early Christian theologians know this, but they favor an obscure passage in Daniel 7:14 as background, a difficult apocalyptic text with symbolic meaning. When Jesus speaks of himself as "son of man," he clearly emphasizes his humanity.

Our Christology influences our anthropology, meaning that our view of Jesus impacts how we view ourselves. Since Christians mostly think of Jesus as having only a divine nature (for that is how they explain Jesus' ability to perform miracles), they miss a major point he makes about himself. Because dualist minds are unable to balance humanity and divinity in Jesus, they are unable to put it together concerning themselves. This is a powerful point, with major implications for Christian thinking and living. If our conception is limited to either one view or another, eliminating the possibility that it can be both, the result is that we think of ourselves as mere humans trying desperately to become "spiritual," and of Jesus as a divine being trying to look human. The Christian truth is quite different: we are already spiritual (we bear God's divine image), and our task is to become more fully human. Jesus models the full integration for us and, in effect, tells us that divinity looks just like him, even though he looks ordinarily human to others.

Such mystery is the ultimate paradox, and each Christian and all humans struggles with it anew, both in themselves and in Jesus. Over time Christians are unable to hold this mystery of Jesus intact, with the result that they fail to see, honor, and reconcile the mystery inside themselves and in others. Nondualist thinking allows us to affirm "the infinite mystery of Jesus and the infinite mystery that we are to ourselves. They are finally the same mystery."[7] What Augustine says about God, "If you understand, then it is not God," we can say about Jesus and about ourselves: "If we understand the Mystery, then it is not so."

In a remarkable statement, addressed both to Pharisees and to his disciples—and therefore to outsiders and insiders simultaneously—Jesus states that the Kingdom (the Ultimate Reality) is "not here and not there" but rather "within you" (Luke 17:21). What Jesus is saying, in effect, is that God's actions and presence cannot be limited to sacred times or sacred places, as we understand them, for the ultimate sacred reality is within us!

---

7. Ibid., 70.

We must never forget that God loves us because God is good, not because we are good. That changes everything.

Questions for Discussion and Reflection

In addition to the questions listed at the end of the preface, answer the following questions, writing your answers in a journal. If you are in a group study, be prepared to share your answers with those in the group.

1. What positive—or negative—thoughts come to mind when you think about being religious versus being spiritual? Which term best describes your approach to God or to your deeper Self? Explain your answer.
2. Of the various definitions of religion given in this chapter, which do you find most helpful? Explain your answer.
3. What do you hold sacred in your life? How do you find harmony with this power?
4. If you were to create a hierarchy of values, what value would you place at the top? Explain your answer.
5. In one sentence, define spirituality.
6. Do you consider yourself to be in the first or second half of the spiritual journey? Explain your answer.
7. Of the eight pathways or "paradigm shifts" listed in this chapter, which attitudinal shift do you find most compelling at this point in your life? Explain your answer.
8. If spirituality involves unlearning, which theological dogma(s) do you need to unlearn? Explain your answer.

2
———

Biblical Spirituality

THE BIBLE IS PERHAPS the world's greatest and best resource for spirituality. It provides a two-thousand-year record of humanity's relationship with God, including numerous examples of the human quest for transcendence. Intended initially for corporate worship but gradually, as literacy grew, for individual spirituality as well, the Bible, in its entirety, provides one continuous liturgical resource. Think of the accounts of creation in Genesis. The original setting of those passages—widely gleaned by modern creationists for historical and scientific truths—is not a laboratory, a classroom, or private study, but rather corporate worship.

The setting of the creation-faith within worship is clearly evident in Psalm 24, a three-part liturgy once used during great pilgrimage festivals celebrating Yahweh's kingship. The Psalm was undoubtedly used originally in connection with a processional bearing of the ark of the covenant into Jerusalem. The opening words of the Psalm, which announce that Yahweh is creator, function as an introit: "The earth is the Lord's and all that is in it, the world, and those who live in it; for he has founded it on the seas, and established it on the rivers" (24:1–2). The second part, in question-and-response format (24:3–6), is a liturgy for admission to the temple, and the third, an "entrance liturgy" (24:7–10), is to be sung antiphonally in the presence of the ark, understood to be Yahweh's throne-seat. In this liturgical setting, the function of creation language is to set the stage for praising God. Thus in the book of Psalms, known as the hymnbook of Judaism, the affirmation that God is the creator is a call to worship.

Psalm 8, related to the Priestly creation account in Genesis 1, is an eloquent witness to the meaning of creation-faith in the liturgy of Israel's worship. This hymn begins and ends with an exclamation of praise to God's glory and majesty, which, to the eye of faith, are evident in nature. The psalmist knows that we sometimes take this world for granted, and yet he knows too that praise is the sign that we are alive, that we are fully human. Creation-faith focuses upon the relationship between God and humanity: "When I look at your heavens, the work of your fingers, the moon and the stars that you have established, what are human beings that you are mindful of them, mortals that you care for them?" (Ps. 8:3–4). It is not simply that humans, in contrast to God, are finite. As the book of Ecclesiastes shows, the awareness of the gulf fixed between creature and creator can prompt a feeling of futility and desolation (Eccl. 1:12–14; 3:16–22; 6:1–2). Rather, creation-faith provides context for understanding existence, the awareness that our relationship with God is one of incomprehensible grace.

Including the Psalms, about one third of the Hebrew Bible is poetry. Awareness of this feature of Israel's liturgical and literary expression is invaluable for reading and interpreting scripture. The same can be said about the book of Revelation, which ends the Bible. Worship and doxology are central to this book. Revelation contains at least fifteen hymns and songs of praise. No other book of the Bible, except perhaps the Psalms, has shaped Christian music as much as has Revelation. Framed in liturgy, from the opening setting "on the Lord's day" (1:10) to the Eucharistic closing (22:17), Revelation overflows with songs and heavenly choruses praising God and exhorting worshippers to sing through their struggles. The conflict of sovereignties is often portrayed in Revelation by references to worship. In the conflict of sovereignties, the lines are drawn between those who worship the beast (a form of political, social, and economic idolatry from which more narrowly religious idolatry is inseparable) and those who worship God. In Revelation, every stage of God's victory in chapter 7 through 19 is accompanied by worship in heaven.

The New Testament contains numerous letters, written by Paul and other early Christian leaders, primarily to churches. Given the low level of literacy in the first century,[1] we may assume that most early Christians experience the New Testament only through public readings, primarily

---

1. In the first century, the literacy rate is around 10 percent for the Roman Empire and around 5 percent in Judea. Literacy is limited mostly to the governing class, scribes, and the wealthy in the empire, and primarily to the priestly class in Judea. In rural Judea and Galilee, the literacy rate approaches zero percent.

in the context of worship. In time, much of the New Testament, as is the case for the Jewish scriptures, acquires a liturgical function.

Viewed traditionally, the Bible represents divinely inspired truth. According to Christian tradition, the Bible consists of two testaments—two covenants between God and believers—one reflecting the ancient Hebraic-Jewish experience and the other the primitive Christian experience. The Hebrew scriptures—known by Christians as the Old Testament—come first. They represent the foundation—historically, ethnically, and culturally—upon which the first Christians build their faith and understanding of God, the cosmos, and the human experience. When the two testaments are placed together, as in the Bible, how are they related? If, as Gentile Christians posit, the Old Testament has an anticipatory or promissory role, fulfilled by Jesus and the New Testament church, does the first testament simply pave the way for the second, or does it stand on its own, fully intact, containing within itself both promise and fulfillment? Are the two equal, or is one somehow inferior to the other?

What, then, of the New Testament? Are Christians expected to see in its teachings and perspectives the fulfillment of prophecy, as bringing to closure the inspired biblical tradition? Is this the meaning of the term "gospel" in the New Testament, the "good news" of the Christian proclamation, that the ministry and teaching of Jesus—including his death and resurrection—represent the climax and fulfillment of revelation, the basis of the church's belief and practice, beyond which Christians need not, indeed, should not go? Or, does the New Testament, like the Old, represent both promise and fulfillment—beginnings, endings, and new beginnings? If this latter possibility is valid and true, what would those new beginnings look like, what promise and hope do they contain for our living and thinking, for what we call second-half-of-life "spirituality"?

It is our contention that the Bible anticipates and embraces such promise, such spirituality. The good news of early Christianity is not supersessionist, meaning that a new religious and cultural institution is born to replace an earlier religious and cultural institution—the church instead of the synagogue or temple—but rather that each religious and cultural institution is valid when it embraces as vital this possibility of ongoing newness and growth, when it is fueled by transformative possibilities, which enable it to progress or evolve through first- to second-half-of-life spiritualities.

The Hebraic religion, represented by the Old Testament, contains both promise and fulfillment, evidence of both first- and second-half-of-life spirituality, but when it focuses organizationally on the former, for reasons of identity, security, and control, it produces figures such as Moses and David, whose task it is to build lasting theocratic institutions. However, the holistic impulse within these institutions gives birth to mystical, prophetic, wisdom, and apocalyptic figures and movements such as Jeremiah, Isaiah, Daniel, the authors of counter-cultural wisdom writings such as Job and Ecclesiastes, the Essenes, Philo, and the Zohar, but also Jesus and Christianity.

The Christian tradition, as witnessed by the books of the New Testament and church history, also grows and develops, demonstrating within its scriptures and its developing mystical and dogmatic theologies elements of both first- and second-half-of-life spirituality, focusing and returning regularly to the former, as occurs in the Hebraic and Jewish tradition.

Today, the Western Christian church is in decline, both numerically and in social influence. Like the cosmos, there are signs of newness and growth in some circles, but overall, the Western church seems caught in a vast entropy, a loss of energy and vitality. I believe this loss can be slowed and even reversed, not by a return to institutional and dogmatic conservatism—that is, by a return to its first-half-of-life spirituality and identity—but by institutional and individual rediscovery of their second-half-of-life heritage.

While knowing that no one in the modern world reads the Bible in a "pure" way, since people can only assimilate its insights through their own interpretative traditions and lenses, we select four Old Testament events for their promise for second-half-of-life living and thinking and two from the New Testament. From the Old Testament we examine the account of creation, the call of Abraham, the Exodus, and the paradoxical encounters of Moses and Elijah with God on Mount Sinai. From the New Testament we select specific teachings of Jesus and the apostle Paul.

Old Testament Spirituality

If by spirituality we mean the spiritual life of individuals, rather than the corporate expression of religious practice better classified as "liturgy," then we find that much of our study of spirituality in the Old Testament is extremely limited. While the Bible introduces numerous noteworthy individuals, the emphasis is not on individualism but on "corporate personality." The Bible portrays Israel as God's people, not simply as a collection of individuals but as a divine company ("a priestly kingdom and a holy nation"; Exod. 19:6; 1 Pet. 2:9). Out of families, clans, and tribes God forms a nation, with a corporate personality: When one person suffers, everyone suffers; when one person is blessed, the people enjoy the benefits; when one person sins, the whole nation participates in the judgment; when one person receives a promise, he or she does so on behalf of the nation.

Americans today live in a pluralistic society, with diverse cultures, religions, and societal values, and we are taught to be tolerant. Ancient societies are quite the opposite; they are homogeneous, with little tolerance or diversity, and with no such thing as freedom of religion. The concept of corporate personality provides Israel with stability, solidarity, and unity during the period of its ascendency. These qualities enable Israelites to maintain social and religious cohesion in a sea of paganism. Their laws, rituals, and values provide them with a distinctive way of life, which preserves them to this day.

To understand the biblical concept of community, we must go back to the story of Abraham: God starts with one family, declaring a promise so wondrous yet absurd as to engender laughter, creating something in Sarah's womb when she is unable to conceive: "Is anything too wonderful for the Lord?" (Gen. 18:14). From Isaac comes Jacob, and from him the twelve tribes of Israel. They take his name, his personality, his style of life, and the covenant he has with God. They call themselves "*bene Israel*," sons of Israel. The doctrine of election is not arbitrary. Rather it reminds them that they are beloved, God's intentional creation. They are not one nation *out of* many, but one nation *for* many. In such unity there is resolve, resilience, and strength.

Despite this emphasis on corporate personality, the God Israelites worship is concerned for the needs of the individual as well as the group; powerful enough to grant their requests; angry with sin yet willing to forgive it; amenable to reasoned argument; glorious yet terrible, deserving of praise but dangerous to behold; reliable, yet not predictable; merciful but just. Above all, they portray and worship God as a person, though clearly as a larger-than-life person, whose absence is acutely painful even if his presence can be far from comfortable.

The God-Shaped Vacuum in Every Human Heart: The Garden of Eden

Religion involves the sense of God, of the human, and of creation. These aspects belong together, and they cannot be treated separately. We would have no sense of the divine without creation. Speculatively, we could talk about God as being prior to or outside creation or independent of creation, but in actual fact there is no such being as God without creation.

There is something very important about the origin of the universe as we now know it: everything is derived from the same source. Science indicates that, and so does theology. If that is so, then everything in the universe is cousin to everything else. There is literally one family in the universe, one bonding. And if our planet is a single community of existence, then all living beings are interconnected and all things are vital. In a universe where everything is related by origin, nothing is unimportant, nothing is marginal.

The book of Genesis begins with the well-known words: "In the beginning God created the heavens and the earth." And God creates without compulsion, for no reason other than love. Therefore, the Bible might well begin with the words: "In the beginning was . . . Love!" Love is the act of will that at the beginning of time brings forth life. Love—God, energy, Being—is the primal force in the universe. Without love, nothing can exist; however, with love, all is possible.

In the second account of creation (found in Genesis 2–3, the so-called "J account of creation"), the author focuses on two sets of relationships: theological (issues related to the vertical relationship between humans and God) and sociological (issues related to the horizontal relationship between humans). The primary thrust of the story is vertical, having to do with the rule of God and the nature of human destiny. Both agendas belong together. The first part of the story, the "pattern of creation" (described in Genesis 2:3b–25 and central to the theological agenda) represents harmony between humans and God, nature, others, and self.

The second part of the story, the "pattern of the fall," (described in Genesis 3:1–24 and central to the sociological agenda), shows the distortion of human community that comes from human autonomy, that is, human rebellion against the pattern of creation. The result is disharmony with God, nature, others, and self. Disobedience (the "pattern of the fall") represents a reversal of the pattern of creation, disharmony between humans and God, nature, others, and self. The Bible describes the nature of the human spiritual condition thus: God creates us for love and freedom, attachment hinders us, and grace is necessary for our salvation (the transformation necessary for our release from attachment to first-half-of-life thinking and living).

The famous French mathematician and philosopher Blaise Pascal speaks inspirationally when he declares: "There is a God-shaped vacuum in the heart of each person that cannot be satisfied by any created thing but only by God the Creator, made known through Jesus Christ." Psychiatrist Gerald May agrees with Pascal when he writes, "I am convinced that all human beings have an inborn desire for God. Whether we are consciously religious or not, this desire is our deepest longing and our most precious treasure . . . Some of us have repressed this desire, burying it beneath so many other interests that we are completely unaware of it. Or we may experience it in different ways—as a longing for wholeness, completion, or fulfillment. Regardless of how we describe it, it is a longing for love. It is a hunger to love, to be loved, and to move closer to the Source of love. This yearning is the essence of the human spirit, the origin of our highest hopes and most noble dreams."[2]

There is a pathetic grandeur in the picture of Adam reaching to taste the fruit of the tree of knowledge of good and evil. Knowledge is humankind's capacity. Freedom to leave the innocence of childhood is precisely what elevates humans above the animals. But when humanity's capacity for knowledge becomes the occasion for arrogant power and self-exaltation, inevitably it results in a fall from the life of trust and goodness that God intends. We cannot recover the mythological innocence of Adam, nor can we return to a Garden that is a figment of the religious imagination. Nevertheless, through revelation humans know there is a better way, the way life can and should be.

While the pattern of the fall ends with the expulsion of Adam and Eve from the Garden, there is good news here. Graciousness appears in the narrative in 3:21, where God clothes the hapless couple, mercifully shielding them from their shame and giving them a new start, for they get to live and try anew. The ending is hopeful, for it represents a new beginning.

---

2. May, *Addiction and Grace*, 1.

God's Love for All Humanity: The Call of Abraham

In the Bible, the prototypical model for the journey of faith is found in the patriarchal stories of Genesis 12–50, starting with the story of Abraham. For Jewish readers and listeners gathered for worship in synagogues to hear these accounts, the underlying significance of chapters 12–50 is not the accounts of the individual patriarchs and matriarchs but the story of Israel's self-understanding. At the time this material is put into writing, the main question is not, "Who are Abraham, Isaac, Jacob, and Joseph?" but "Who is Israel?" Israel is grappling with her identity, her self-understanding as a people called by God. The theological answer is found in the doctrine of election, the notion that the people of Israel are chosen by God.

But what does election mean? Is God racist, favoring some people over others? The Bible answers this question with a resounding "No." The covenant God establishes with Israel should not be regarded as an expression of divine preference for Jews over others, or as divine commission for one group to rule others, or as reward for good conduct on Israel's part. As the history of Israel demonstrates, the establishment of the covenant is not followed by good conduct. Moreover, the Bible portrays the covenant people as sinful, stiff-necked, stubborn, and singularly inept at learning from their experiences. In fact, in the Bible the Israelites are punished repeatedly, and more severely than others are. Nevertheless, God does not nullify the contract or make it void. The biblical answer to election is given in the portrayal of Abraham, Isaac, and Jacob, patriarchs whose lives are characterized by the following traits:

1. They *live by faith in God*. In Abraham, Israel understands something about herself, that she has been called into existence by God himself, that she has been created by God's initiative and preserved by God's grace.

2. They are *called to be a servant people*. Election does not mean that some people are chosen because they are better than others, but rather that they are called to spread God's grace. God's purpose is seen in Genesis 12:3 ("in you all the families of the earth shall be blessed"); it is a universal purpose, one that moves from particulars to universals, from individuals to communities and nations. In Abraham, God brings one person of faith into existence in order that God's blessing might be extended to all humanity. This is the Bible's

stress on election, that when God calls a people, they are called to service, and the rest of the Old Testament, and then the gospels and epistles, show what it means to be a servant people. In the Bible, the election of a people becomes the basis for good news, what the New Testament calls "gospel." This is the message of Genesis 12–50, and it is transported to a higher key in the New Testament.

3. They are *called to a life of pilgrimage*—a life of mobility, movement, and change. Biblical faith is a calling faith, a calling to go forth, to be on the way, to be moving in God's direction, to be pioneers of faith. Abraham is told to break his ties with his land and his former security, a way of life that up to that point had been deeply rooted to the land. Like Abraham, God's people are called to a nomadic consciousness. We see this clearly in the prophetic consciousness, a stance that could be counter-cultural in the sense that one could be both an agent of change and a critic of the established order. The prophetic message is that God is doing a new thing. As we see in Abraham, faith is not so much consent or agreement as something dynamic, manifested in movement. The story of Abraham and the patriarchs is the story of God on the move with his people.

God's Presence with Humanity: Moses and the Exodus

The presence of God is one of the central themes of the Old Testament. The Torah (the first five books of the Bible) sets out the terms on which God will be with the people of Israel; the historical writings show from concrete examples how God's presence can be forfeited, and how gracious God is, who never allows absence from an unworthy people become permanent; the prophetic writings look forward to the day when God will never seem absent again; and the Psalms reflect on all aspects of presence and absence as they affect both the worshipping community and the individual at prayer.

The earliest global civilizations, whether Asian, Indian, or Middle Eastern, are religious, and their religions precede and give rise to their cultures. This principle particularly exemplifies the Egyptians and the ancient Semitic empires of the Middle East. From the first, these cultures conceive of the problem of life on earth as dependent on the larger reality of the cosmos and the transcendent. We know of no time when humans in this region are conscious of themselves but not yet of the divine.

As early as the fourteenth century BCE there is an Egyptian monarch (Akhenaton; also known as Amenhotep IV) who conceives of a god who is the creator of the world and of all humankind.

About a century later, an Israelite named Moses leads a captive people out of slavery toward a new land of settlement. This event, known as the Exodus, is marked by a wilderness encounter with deity that results in a new self-understanding and identity for the people. Moses and his Israelite followers define their religion in terms of that experience. Their God is the one "who brought them out of the land of Egypt, out of the house of bondage" (see Exod. 20:2). This becomes the first statement of belief in the Judeo-Christian tradition; like all those that follow, it is an affirmation that something significant happened in the past.

When we seek to understand the meaning of our individual life stories, we do not actually begin with birth or infancy, even though written autobiographies might start there. Rather, we view early childhood in the light of later experiences that are formative or pivotal. Likewise, Israel's life story does not begin with the time of Abraham or even the Creation, although the Old Testament starts there. Rather, Israel's history has its true beginning in a crucial historical experience that creates a self-conscious historical community—an event so decisive that earlier happenings and subsequent experiences are seen in its light. That decisive event—the great watershed of Israel's history—is the Exodus from Egypt. Through the ages, the story of the deliverance of slaves from bondage, and their march through the wilderness toward a Promised Land, has had a powerful appeal to the religious imagination of many oppressed groups and individuals. It is the paradigmatic biblical story of salvation and deliverance.

Exodus 1–24, a passage that speaks of the Exodus and the birth of the nation of Israel, is less concerned with what happens historically and more concerned with the meaning behind these events. This is not to say that the narrative does not describe actual events, but to emphasize that it describes them theologically. While providing interesting stories about Moses and the Israelites, the exodus account focuses not so much on Moses as liberator of the people but on God's redemptive role. God, not Moses, is the primary actor. The broader story—beginning with the classic account of deliverance from Egyptian slavery and including the covenant enacted on Mount Sinai and the subsequent wilderness experience that led to the conquest of the Promised Land—is not recorded for its own sake. Rather it provides a clue to who God is and how God acts toward humanity, particularly toward those who are downtrodden and oppressed.

Despite his upbringing in Pharaoh's court, Moses identifies with the Hebrew slaves, an impulse that leads to his slaying an Egyptian taskmaster. Forced to flee, Moses takes refuge in "the land of Midian," an area of the Sinai Peninsula occupied by shepherds. There he marries the daughter of a Midianite priest. While tending the flocks of his father-in-law, Moses comes upon "the mountain of God." His encounter with the God of the ancestors (Exod. 3:13) in that sacred place and his role in the ensuing encounter with the pharaoh is one of the masterpieces of religious literature. It is in the Midianite wilderness that God discloses essential aspects of the divine nature, including (1) God's personal name (Yahweh), which, literally untranslatable, has come to be associated with *God's creative activity* ("I am", "I cause to be") and (2) *God's redemptive activity* ("I will be with you"; see Exod. 3:12) on behalf of Israel.

Yahweh appears to Moses with memorable words: "I have observed the misery of my people . . . I have heard their cry . . . I know their sufferings, and I have come down to deliver them . . . and to bring them to a good and broad land, a land flowing with milk and honey . . ." (Exod. 3:7–8). In a fundamental declaration of faith, the ancient Israelites affirm that their history originates in a marvelous liberation from oppression, declaring climactically the mighty deeds of God on their behalf. The verbs of the narrative sweep to a climax: God hears, God sees, God rescues.

The primary purpose of the Exodus narrative is to glorify the God of Israel, the "divine warrior" whose strong hand and outstretched arm wins the victory over Pharaoh and his armies. The text heralds five interlocking biblical themes: (1) *divine love* (when things on earth get bad, God's love is greater still); (2) *divine mercy* (God is always "for us," never "against us"); (3) *divine initiative* (God always takes the initiative in restoring that which is broken, forgotten, or lost); (4) *divine sovereignty* (God is completely in control, even to the point of hardening Pharaoh's heart); and (5) *divine freedom* (while disclosing the divine name, God nevertheless retains the divine freedom that eludes human control: "I will be gracious to whom I will be gracious, and will show mercy on whom I will show mercy. But you cannot see my face; for no one shall see me and live"; Exod. 33:19–20).

The Hiddenness of God: Moses and Elijah

Biblical talk about God is paradoxical. Because God is a person who is alive and active and yet has an awesome, even overwhelming personality, friendship with God is both a privilege and yet elusive. While it is difficult to live with God, it is impossible to live without God. Yet the hiddenness of God—perhaps even God's absence—seems the dominant reality for many seekers throughout history.

A helpful place to examine this conundrum is 1 Kings 19, a passage that records a memorable experience of the prophet Elijah on Mount Sinai. Elijah (his name means "Yahweh is my God"), persecuted by Jezebel (King Ahab's Phoenician wife) for his faithfulness to Yahweh, flees to Mount Sinai, where he prepares for an encounter with the divine: "Now there was a great wind, so strong that it was splitting mountains and breaking rocks in pieces before Yahweh, but Yahweh was not in the wind; and after the wind an earthquake, but Yahweh was not in the earthquake; and after the earthquake a fire, but Yahweh was not in the fire; and after the fire a sound of sheer silence" (1 Kgs. 19:11–12; these last few words are traditionally translated "a still small voice").

Elijah's experience on Mount Sinai reminds us of the climactic experience of Moses with God at the same location, the vision of God in darkness described at Exodus 33:17–23. If even Moses sees only God's back, is there any hope that anyone else can see God's "face" and live? For practical purposes, the God of the Old Testament is a hidden God, hidden yet everywhere present. Yet, according to the prophet Isaiah, the God who is hidden can be known by the person who does not seek to "see" God, but rather to obey God's will: "I dwell in the high and holy place," says the Lord, "and also with those who are contrite and humble in spirit" (57:15).

In the book of Jeremiah, the prophet speaks of two epochs: the time of the Mosaic covenant, which ends in human failure, and the time of the new covenant, when the divine Torah (law, teaching) is written on the heart, resulting in such personal knowledge of God that religious teaching would no longer be necessary. This vision of the restored community of Israel is profoundly expressed in Jeremiah's prophecy of the new covenant (Jer. 31:31–34), a prophecy that eventually gives the name to the canon of Christian writings ("New Testament" means "New Covenant"). In the New Testament, God is said to be fully with us in Jesus. As we read in John 1:18, "No one has ever seen God. It is God the only Son, who is close to the Father's heart, who has made him known."

New Testament Spirituality

For Christians, the relationship between the Old and New Testaments is one of continuity and discontinuity. Like two partners joined in marriage, neither is a substitute for the other, nor are they independent of one another. Rather there is relative independence, whereby they complement one another. For Christians, the gulf between the testaments is bridged by Jesus Christ, whose person and work establishes a deep discontinuity with Israel's scripture and, at the same time, a deep continuity in the purpose of God.

Until the emergence of the historical and critical study of the Bible in the eighteenth and nineteenth centuries, the Bible is sought as sole authority for Christian practice and belief. For a time, Christians seek to identify "*the* theology of the New Testament" behind all the writings, believing that scripture contained one divine revelation, which and inspired and therefore not contradictory. Modern scholarship reveals a quite different picture, recognizing a plurality of theologies within the New Testament. Consequently, less attention is placed on "spirituality," except as it is implicit in "theology," but it is now equally clear that we can no longer expect to find only one spirituality or *the* spirituality of the New Testament, and have every reason to detect many. In that respect, we can speak of a Markan spirituality, but also of a Matthean, Lukan, Johannine, and Pauline spirituality.

When we read the Bible, there are two dangers we cannot avoid but must guard against, namely (1) to interpret it uncritically, that is, subjectively or out of context, and (2) to read it as a rule book or as an easy-step instruction book. When we let it go as a modern answer book, we get to discover it for what it really is, a book that tells us who we are and what our story is. While the Bible provides individual wisdom and guidance, it calls us to create a community that becomes a catalyst for doing God's work in the world.

Jesus and the Second Journey

The central theme of the New Testament is a person, Jesus of Nazareth, a wandering preacher of the first century who changes the course of history. Whether Christian or not, all who live in the Western world are influenced by the teachings and life of this individual. Early disciples envision Jesus as the climactic historical figure, the Messiah who brings the long-awaited messianic Kingdom of God, a rule that by ending evil and suffering ushers in an age of bliss. Later followers and even unbelievers understand Jesus' historical role as pivotal, representing its midpoint. Ernst Renan, famous nineteenth-century scholar, affirms this view when he writes: "All history is incomprehensible without Christ"; also Napoleon, who confesses toward the end of his life: "This man, Jesus, vanished for eighteen hundred years, still holds the character of men as in a vise"; and H. G. Wells, who declares: "I am an historian. I am not a believer. But I must confess, as an historian, that this penniless preacher from Galilee is irresistibly the center of history."

Although we cannot be precise about the length of his life or even the duration of his ministry, scholars maintain that Jesus is born around 4 BCE, shortly before the death of Herod, and that he dies by crucifixion around 30 CE. Jesus begins a brief itinerant ministry in rural Palestine that lasts from one year to no more than three years. It reaches a limited number of people and ends in apparent failure, with his crucifixion by Roman authorities. The New Testament is a response to Jesus of Nazareth, whom Christians call Christ, and to a cluster of events scholars call the "Christ event," centered on his birth, death, and resurrection.

As we examine the Gospels, the sources for the life, teaching, and character of Jesus, we recognize that these are entirely *Christian* documents. They are not the work of neutral observers, but of those already committed to Jesus as the Christ and Son of God, and above all, to his resurrection. Though they record pre-Easter events, they are post-Easter documents. And they are written, not for a purely historical purpose, but for the edification and instruction of fellow-believers. Furthermore, our aim must be to give some record of Jesus and his teaching that takes seriously his Jewish roots and character, and yet also explains his position at the center of Christian worship and preaching, leaving room for a certain originality or distinctiveness on his part.

When we think of Jesus, I suggest we think of the historical human being who represents for Christians the ideal universal person, the embodiment of the highest and best in us all. At this point in our discussion, then, we focus on the Jesus of history, the one who bears the ideal of normality and universality simultaneously.

The human Jesus must have been a figure of great power and originality. In him a force of immeasurable magnitude begins to operate in this world, unleashing a movement that lasts through twenty centuries and is on the rise globally. When a person of such eminence appears, who can apprehend that person totally? One observer sees one aspect, another a different aspect; and even the collection of their observations cannot yield the whole person. Of course, no one can know another person completely. Even after years of marriage, husbands and wives often discover aspects of one another's being of which, up to that moment, they are ignorant. This being so, it is not surprising that, when Jesus of Nazareth appears, no single mind can encompass the whole of him, no single artist can paint the definitive portrait. What we have in the New Testament is a collection of fragments of memory and interpretation concerning Jesus, extruded through longstanding Jewish hermeneutical processes. Early Christians, believing that in Jesus all of God's promises are fulfilled (2 Cor. 1:20), add to this tradition, searching the Hebrew scriptures for passages that can be interpreted christologically.

Like the Hebrew prophets, Jesus claims knowledge of God, from which his teaching derives and upon which it is based. What he hears from God—more on the level of inner experience than on the level of head knowledge—is his to pass on. For that reason he adopts the term "Amen," a beautiful and powerful expression of Jewish affirmation placed at the end of prayer. Yet Jesus, a devout Jew, puts it at the beginning of everything important he says. When Jesus says "Amen, Amen" (often translated as "Truly" or "Verily"), he seems to be making two affirmations: (1) that his teaching is based on what he hears from God, and (2) that his message is based on divine authority.

Like good disciples, in loving relationship with God and in communion with Jesus, we too must live in confidence to also say, as it were, "Amen, Amen." What Jesus hears from God is now ours to pass on. "Let the same mind be in you," Paul writes in Philippians 2:5, "that you have in Christ Jesus." This is the truth of the Christian tradition, what it truly means to be a disciple of Jesus. We are called to recognize, surrender to, and ultimately be identified with the mystery of God utterly beyond understanding.

We need to acknowledge that Jesus says nothing to us that he hasn't somehow heard from God. Jesus has a familial relationship with God, whom he calls Abba, and it is out of that relationship that he teaches, heals, blesses, and nurtures the spiritual family we call the church. To be disciples of Jesus, we need to let ourselves be loved as he did. It is in receiving that love that we find our insight and strength.

For Jesus, discipleship is about being in an intimate, loving, and challenging relationship, much like that between parent and child. There is a unique nature to the healthy parent-child relationship, and each person has a role to play. Ideally, the parent employs the gifts of experience and knowledge to care for, nurture, and protect the child. In turn, the child depends on and trusts the parent for sustenance, well-being, and guidance in a world of unknowing. Discipleship follows that sequence. First, we learn how to be God's children, allowing ourselves to receive love, to be loved, to be cared for, and believed in, so that we can be entrusted to go about our "Father's business" as Jesus did (Luke 2:49 KJV).

In the beginning, Jesus steps into his ministry as a child of God, not as the parent or authority figure. Rather, he lets himself be the recipient, and he trusts God to lead him. Because Jesus is always listening to God and experiencing God's presence, God continually teaches him. Jesus doesn't begin his life full of power and authority. He is born helpless and vulnerable, like all of us, but throughout his life he continues to grow in love, wisdom, and maturity (see Luke 2:52). Like every true disciple, Jesus comes into the fullness of his being by faithfully following and listening to his divine Teacher, who is forever true, the source of all wisdom and knowing.

Had Jesus no other legacy, he would be remembered as one of the world's master teachers. Jesus, however, does not come on the scene to conform to anyone's preconceived expectation about sages, or for that matter, about prophets or messiahs. His subject, essentially, is threefold: he makes known something about God, something about humankind, and something about their interrelationship.

Apart from the tradition of Judaism, however, the life or teaching of Jesus is incomprehensible. In Jesus' day there is a vast human quest for God, wrapped up in piety and legalism (Judaism), and in idolatry and superstition (Gentiles). The Jews are monotheists and have a central temple in Jerusalem, dedicated to sacrifice and rituals. Much of their worship is motivated by duty and regulated by tradition. However, no code of laws can deal with the variety of human beings. While Jesus affirms the value of Jewish law in many of his actions and teachings, he regularly points beyond the law. According to Jesus, each of us has individual value and our own unique journey to God.

While Jesus changes the way we understand God, the God of the Old Testament has been speaking to humanity through an entire history of dialogue with Israel. As Walter Brueggemann indicates in his *Theology of the Old Testament*, the God that Jesus incarnates is already seen to be "merciful, gracious, faithful, forgiving, and steadfast in love" (Exod. 34:6–7). This "credo of adjectives," positive and relational in nature, announces the character of God, indicating God's intense solidarity, loyalty, and commitment to those with whom he is related.[3]

Much as we need to unlearn harsh and damning views of God, we also must unlearn many of the ways we have been taught about dealing with other human beings. There seems to be only one demand that this God of love lays upon those who receive love and forgiveness, namely, to treat those around them as they have been treated by God. That is the litmus test of all spiritual transformation.

When the institutional element dominates religion, there is often an obsession with the organization and with the details of its regulations. Blind obedience is required. This often results in institutional rigidity and sterility. When religion becomes only a matter of outer rules and rituals, then those who deviate from the accepted practices and beliefs are not tolerated. Such religious prejudice drives thoughtful people away from the institutional church. The implications of Christian teaching can be ignored if we accept tradition by rote. Hence, it takes eighteen hundred years before Jesus' teaching of the equal value of all human beings results in the abolition of slavery. It takes even longer before women are accorded the place that Jesus gives them. Cultural accretions quite at variance to a religion often creep into religious tradition to corrupt and dilute it. For that reason tradition needs ongoing experiences of God, continuous reflection on what makes us human, and transformative love. Without them religion becomes destructive and oppressive.

Paul and the Second Journey

One of the heroic figures in the life of the early church, the apostle Paul emerges from being an arch-persecutor of Christians into an unrelenting missionary of the gospel. The impact of Paul upon the church is both widespread and permanent. His influence is fourfold:

---

3. Brueggemann, *Theology of the Old Testament*, 215–28.

- The first great theologian of the church.
- The first full-time missionary to the Gentiles.
- The founder of numerous congregations in Asia Minor, Greece, and Macedonia.
- The author (actual or alleged) of a group of letters that now comprise one-fourth of the bulk of the New Testament.

Paul is sometimes called the second founder of Christianity. As the first great theologian of the church, he is both a practical theologian—in that he addresses specific needs arising in the church—and a task theologian. To him belongs the unique task of developing or disclosing a theology for the Gentile church, indicating how Gentiles are brought into full participation in the fellowship of Christ, what Paul refers to as "the body of Christ" (Rom. 12:5; 1 Cor. 12:13, 27; cf. Col. 1:18; Eph. 4:4) and "the Israel of God" (Gal. 6:16; cf. Rom. 11:25–26).

The first full-time missionary to the Gentiles, Paul helps bridge the gap as the church becomes less Jewish and more Gentile in its makeup. Jesus had performed a revolution in religion, recognizing in Judaism a rich spiritual treasure, resulting in a distinct system of worship, a religious way of life, and a high ethical outlook. Yet that treasure is not available to everyone, for Judaism is an ethnic and deeply exclusive faith. As Paul sees it, Jesus is not simply a teacher of truth but the Messiah, through whom God's eternal purpose for Israel and the nations are fulfilled. Up to that point, Jesus' task of liberating the spiritual treasure of Israel's faith for humanity is limited to Jews, and his faithfulness to God leads to the cross. Now, the work of Christ is entrusted to his followers, who are empowered by the Holy Spirit to continue the mission Jesus has begun. It is in Paul and his work that we see the task being accomplished. Paul takes the work of Christ and sets it free from possession by any one ethnic group, sect, or clique. In so doing, Paul remains the classic exponent of the idea of freedom in Christ and of the universality of God's plan for all humanity (see Rom. 3:29–30; Gal. 3:14; 5:1; cf. Eph. 3:6).

Paul also founds new congregations during his missionary travels, providing exhortation, encouragement, and support through letters and personal visits. He helps heal doctrinal and moral difficulties in his churches, providing a form of moral instruction known as *paraenesis* (see, for example, 1 Thess. 4:1–12), such as one might expect to see in the philosophical letters of his day. His letters to the church of Corinth deal with numerous practical issues they are facing, helping later Christians more fully understand the nature of the Christian life.

While not all of Paul's letters remain, by the end of the first century they are preserved through a collection that marks the church's initial Christian canon (see 2 Pet. 3:15–16). As part of scripture they become the most famous and influential set of letters ever written, influencing every major Christian thinker and practically every major revival. Central in the conversion of Augustine and Luther, they hold a critical place in their life and teachings. During the Reformation, Calvin patterns his famous *Institutes of the Christian Religion* on Paul's letter to the Romans. While Paul has no idea he is writing scripture, there is no denying that he considers his writings to be invested with special authority, and furthermore, that he expects his readers generally to recognize this as factual (1 Cor. 2:16; 7:17; 14:37–38; cf. 2 Thess. 3:14).

Aside from Jesus, Paul is the most distinctive individual in the New Testament. While it is easy to focus on his many unique insights, he is not entirely idiosyncratic. Though a pioneer of the church's Gentile mission, he is an apostle with the other apostles (see 1 Cor. 15:1–11), and he seeks to work in fellowship with church leaders in Jerusalem (Gal. 1:18—2:10). He is not antinomian, despite his strong rejection of the Jewish Torah when regarded as a means of self-justification, for he asserts its moral precepts and Jesus' summary of them (Gal. 5:14; Rom. 13:8–10).

Paul's argument in his letter to the Galatians about the relation of the law principle (Hebrew Torah) and the faith principle (Christian Gospel) seems to anticipate our model of the two halves of life. Paul begins his argument in chapter 3 by calling his listeners "foolish Galatians," for they have seemingly regressed from the second journey (living by faith: "the only thing that counts is faith working through love"; 5:6) to the first journey (living by "works of the law"; 3:5, 10). Having begun their Christian experience with freedom, trust, and the Holy Spirit (with the "second half of life" task), that is, with the presence of the living Christ (see Rom. 8:9–11), the Galatians have regressed to life in the flesh, that is, to legalistic efforts (to "first half of life" tasks). Their regression forces Paul to clarify the role of the Old Testament law (Torah) and its relation to the "law of Christ," by which he means the law of love: "The whole law is summed up in a single commandment, 'You shall love your neighbor as yourself'" (5:14).

In Galatians 4:21—5:1 Paul speaks of two covenants or ways of life—the way of slavery and the way of freedom—concluding that we should choose the latter: "For freedom Christ has set us free. Stand firm, therefore, and do not submit again to a yoke of slavery." What is this yoke of slavery? I submit it can be seen as the first phase of the journey, characterized by adhering closely to life-shaping laws.

The rule of moral and religious laws is important, Paul argues in Galatians 3:19–24, for the Old Testament laws come from God and are given to provide moral, civil, and practical guidance. Those laws, however, have a temporary and intermediary role, to bring us to maturity and faith in Christ. Before Christ comes (Gal. 4:4), the law has a custodial role, functioning as a "disciplinarian" or tutor (Gal. 3:24), much as a household slave who supervises the discipline of the child. But now that faith has come, we are no longer under this slave, but have become adults, full members in the household of God. Spiritual maturity sets us free to embark on the "further journey."

Paul's spirituality flows from his fundamental theology, in turn the result of his "conversion." Whether it be termed a conversion is questionable, since his spiritual and intellectual transformation is not the result of a change from one religion to another but rather a transformative understanding of his own faith tradition. Whether Paul's conversion is technically a call rather than a conversion, the result is his transformation from an adversary to an advocate of Christianity. With astonishing suddenness, the persecutor of the church becomes the apostle of Jesus to the Gentiles (Acts 9:15; Gal. 1:15–16). What caused this transformation? His own repeated explanation is that he saw the crucified Christ now exalted as the risen Lord: "Have I not seen Jesus our Lord?" he asks when his apostolic credentials are questioned (1 Cor. 9:1). When, in 2 Corinthians 4:6, he says that "God . . . has shone in our hearts to give the light of the knowledge of the glory of God in the face of Jesus Christ," his language implies a reminiscence of his conversion, described in Acts as having occurred on the way to Damascus, when about midday "a light from heaven flashed around him" and he fell to the ground, hearing a voice say: "Saul, Saul, why do you persecute me?" When Saul[4] asks who is speaking, he hears the reply: "I am Jesus, whom you are persecuting" (Acts 9:3–5). This experience of Jesus has a profound and lasting effect on him.

While, in his letters, Paul never describes a Damascus road experience, the story of his conversion is central to the book of Acts, where it is given three full treatments (Acts 9, 22, and 26). In his letters, Paul refers

---

4. Saul is Paul's pre-conversion name (see Acts 13:9).

to his own conversion and apostolic commission on two occasions (1 Cor. 15:8–13 and Gal. 1:15–16).

Paul's conversion represents a radical shift in his thinking about Jesus and the church. At his conversion Paul learns two things about Jesus: that he is not dead, but alive, and that Jesus is not cursed, but blessed by God. Hence the cross, rather than discrediting Jesus as an imposter, is truly God's provision for humanity, as well as the fulfillment of the promise that through Abraham all nations and peoples would be blessed (Gal. 3:6–9). Jesus is indeed the expected Messiah, but also the "Son of God." This discovery becomes the subject of his preaching in Damascus (Acts 9:20). As a Christian, he still believes in only one God, but he is convinced that God can only be fully known through Jesus (2 Cor. 4:6).

At his conversion Paul also learns that Christians are not heretics, but God's people. He discovers that in persecuting Christians he has been persecuting Christ (Acts 9:5). That correlation leads him to one of his most profound insights, that the church is neither a building nor a sect but the "body of Christ" (1 Cor. 12:27). Theologically, the church is a microcosm of the transformation that God's new order brings for the whole world. To be in the church is to have a foretaste of life in God's kingdom. Socially, the church in the Roman Empire is an alternative society, based on the new freedom and fellowship that Jesus announces: freedom to love God and to love and serve others (Mark 12:29–31). It must have taken Paul some time to process his new understanding about Jesus and the church, but as far as he is concerned, it is in Damascus that the essential core of his faith as a Christian is first revealed to him.

In a famous autobiographical passage (Phil. 3:3–11), Paul contrasts his former Jewish life as between legalism ("having a righteousness of my own") and faith ("the righteousness from God based on faith"); he also describes this righteousness as "knowing Christ and the power of his resurrection and the sharing of his sufferings by becoming like him in his death, if somehow I may attain the resurrection from the dead" (Phil. 3:10–11). This principle of incorporation into the double act of salvation—death of the false self and resurrection of the True Self—Paul applies to wide areas of Christian life (see 2 Cor. 5:14–15; Rom. 14:7–9; Gal. 2:19–20; 6:14) and with utter realism (2 Cor. 1:3–7; 11:23—12:10).

In Philippians 3:12–14 we find a further picture of the present phase of resurrection life: "Not that I have already obtained this or have already reached the goal, but I press on to make it my own, because Christ Jesus has made me his own. Beloved, I do not consider that I have made it my own; but this one thing I do: forgetting what lies behind and straining forward to what lies ahead, I press on toward the goal for the prize of the heavenly call of God in Christ Jesus." As Paul understands it, the resurrection life leads believers toward invisible and inscrutable realities such as we describe in second-half-of-life spirituality. Perhaps the best description of such spirituality is found in 1 Corinthians 1:18—2:16. Paul's message to Corinth, focusing on weakness, suffering, and relinquishment, goes against current wisdom. Talk of second-half-of-life spirituality has the ring of nonsense to legalists and libertines, and yet to those guided by the wisdom and power of God (see 1 Cor. 1:24–25), it represents the "mind of Christ"—the mindset and perspective that makes Jesus the exemplar of spirituality par excellence.

How, then, should believers live? With hope and courage. As Paul indicates in 1 Thessalonians, believers should progress in love for each other and to all (3:12–13), for a life of love, as modeled by Christ, never fails (see 1 Cor. 13). Already children of light (1 Thess. 5:5), believers must not be restless or neurotic, but calm and industrious (4:11–12; see also 2 Thess. 3:6–15). Second-half-of-life practitioners realize the transient nature of all things on this earth and thus are not overly attached to them (1 Cor. 7:29–32a). Outward affliction can affect only our external and false self. Meanwhile, renewal is occurring within (the resurrection of our True Self), infinitely more weighty and precious, for what is being born is eternal rather than temporal (2 Cor. 4:16–21).

In his letters Paul applies these principles to his followers, encouraging those who are "strong" (see Rom. 15:1–6), that is, those who have arrived at maturity (see 1 Cor. 2:6) or deeper insight (*gnosis*),[5] not to scandalize or cause offence to weaker brethren (those still living according to first-half-of-life religious standards and regulations). Here we find a basis for later Christian *gnosis*, a topic we take up in chapter 6.

Questions for Discussion and Reflection

In addition to the questions listed at the end of the preface, answer the following questions, writing your answers in a journal. If you are in a group study, be prepared to share your answers with those in the group.

---

5. On deeper *gnosis* in Paul—what we are calling second-half-of-life insight about religious rules and regulations—see 1 Cor. 2:6–7; 8:1, 7, 10.

1. If the Bible is originally intended for liturgical use, assess the advantage (or disadvantage) of reading it privately or studying it in small-group settings?
2. If the Bible consists of two sets of scripture, one Jewish and the other Christian, how do they relate?
3. In your estimation, does the modern emphasis on individualism distort the intended biblical message? Why or why not?
4. Assess the merit of Blaise Pascal's statement concerning the "God-shaped vacuum in the human heart."
5. Assess the biblical emphasis on election; what does it mean then, and what does it mean for us today?
6. If you were to write the story of your spiritual journey, where would you begin and end, and what event would you consider most decisive, that is, the watershed event?
7. Assess the meaning of the following statement: "While it is difficult to live with God, it is impossible to live without God."
8. What do you consider Jesus' greatest teaching on spirituality? Explain your answer.
9. What do you consider Paul's greatest teaching on spirituality? Explain your answer.

3

Early Christian (Proto-Orthodox) Spirituality

THERE IS AN IRONY underlying the emergence of any new or different movement, whether cultural, political, social, economic, scientific, or religious, that it is not really novel. It is essentially a reaction against, or a reinterpretation of, a preexistent tradition, movement, or ideology. This holds true not only for the emergence of new beliefs, but also for beliefs that are said to arise in experience.

As religious scholars are discovering about religious movements said to be dependent on experience, including charismatics, revivalists, and evangelicals—with their emphasis on the "Spirit's leading"—such experience is itself dependent upon doctrine, scripture, or some other residual element of Christian tradition. Christians, let us remember, could not have emerged apart from Judaism, or developed apart from movements such as Gnosticism, Valentinianism,[1] Marcionism, and cultural influences from Platonism, Stoicism, and other philosophical groups prevalent in the Greco-Roman environment. Neither would Augustine have developed his thought apart from Manichaeism and Neoplatonism,

---

1. Valentinians are followers of Valentinus (c. 100–c. 160). We know very little of Valentinus's early life, but he may have spent his early years in Alexandria, Egypt. By around the year 140, he is a popular and effective teacher in Rome. Some of his students become important Christian theologians. In his lifetime, he is never declared a heretic, and while many Christian teachers consider his views wrong, he has a substantial following. Later church authorities condemn him as a heretic, and due to his condemnation, nearly all of his writings are lost. His writings possibly include the *Gospel of Truth*, found by modern scholars among the ancient Gnostic writings at Nag Hammadi.

Aquinas apart from Augustine, Protestantism apart from Catholicism, Liberal theology apart from orthodox theology, and Neo-orthodoxy apart from Liberalism.

The crucial irony is that the Protestant turn to experience, or the nineteenth-century Liberal turn to experience, depends on experiences created by doctrines, beliefs, or behaviors they no longer accept. Even modernity, as represented especially by the eighteenth-century Enlightenment, conceives itself as coming of age, that is, as a revolt against the tutelage of antiquated authority and irrelevant tradition. Ironically, while modernity disavows the authority of traditions, postmodernism arises to challenge the claims of modernity.

Such examination brings us to a peculiarity of the topic of spirituality, for what we are calling second-half-of-life spirituality has no definition or meaning apart from first-half-of-life spirituality. It is from this latter perspective that we examine the emergence of early Christian (catholic) orthodox spirituality.

The term "orthodoxy," when applied to an ideology or a religious movement such as Christianity, invariably stirs emotion.[2] For traditional or mainline believers, whether regarding politics, religion, cultural norms, or patterns of behavior, orthodoxy is the standard of belief, the ticket of admission. To be unorthodox is to be mischievous, devious, or erroneous, a troublemaker and hence akin to being evil or incorrigible. To others, orthodoxy is lamentable and deplorable, akin to being stale, unoriginal, or simply dull. Overall, North Americans often have been heterodox—progressive, they might call it—making new orthodoxies of being unorthodox.[3]

In this book, when I apply the term "orthodox" to Christianity, I do not, of course, mean Eastern, Greek, or Russian Orthodoxy, but something purely descriptive. Orthodox Christianity, then, refers to that form of Christianity that won the support of the overwhelming majority of Christians and that is expressed by most of the official proclamations or creeds of Christian groups. While it is accurate to speak of orthodoxies

---

2. While the term "orthodoxy" means "right belief," in the early church it comes to mean the true understanding of Christianity. When speaking of early Christians who hold beliefs later recognized as conforming to the creeds developed at Nicaea and subsequent ecumenical church councils, it is appropriate to call such groups proto-orthodox.

3. Instead of the pejorative term "heretical," it is better to call individuals or groups holding alternative views "heterodox," meaning "other belief."

instead of orthodoxy when addressing each of the denominations and divisions within Christianity, there is a central core of Christian doctrine that unites most Christians.

The search for Christian orthodoxy begins with the New Testament, though its roots go back to the Old Testament and the Hebraic-Israelite-Jewish movement that culminates in early Judaism. The first Christians do not have a Christian orthodoxy in the sense of a neatly formulated system of thought. All are Jewish, initially, but as we now know, first-century Judaism is incredibly diverse. While modern critical scholarship on the Bible identifies numerous theologies within the New Testament, it also finds beneath these variations a common faith. The various theologies are the attempts of early Christians to think out and express to others this common faith. Twenty centuries have not been enough to work out all of the implications present in the basic faith of the New Testament.

The core faith of the New Testament writers is that in the life, death, and resurrection of Jesus, God encounters humanity in a decisive way. This is why early Christians face persecution and death to spread their "Good News." While the first followers of Jesus, together with most first-century Jews, look for a political Messiah powerful enough to free them from Roman imperialism, as the days pass, Christians realize that Jesus is their Messiah not for achieving what they hope he can accomplish politically, but for achieving something better. He frees them from the chains that bind them to sin and death, chains that hold them in fear. Jesus reveals that the power of good is greater than the power of evil. Though evil remains, the decisive battle is won.

The disciples go out into the pagan world with the message that God has spoken, acted, and revealed his nature to humanity. Humans need no longer climb the treacherous mountain path that leads to knowledge of God; God has taken the initiative, coming down from the mountain to transform humanity through the revelation of divine love. This revelation, they believe, occurs in Christ. As a result, Paul states, "From now on . . . we regard no one from a human point of view; even though we once knew Christ from a human point of view, we know him no longer in that way. So if anyone is in Christ, there is a new creation: everything old has passed away; see, everything has become new. All this is from God, who reconciled us to himself through Christ, and has given us the ministry of reconciliation; that is, in Christ God was reconciling to world to himself" (2 Cor. 5:16–19). That, in brief, is Christian spirituality, that in Christ believers are reconciled to God, to one another, and to their inner self.

Paul, the leading interpreter of Christianity during the New Testament period, leads Christianity in its earliest battle—against legalism. Every religion, including Christianity, tends to become legalistic. That is, it teaches that humans must obey certain rules and regulations to win the favor and rewards of God. This is first-half-of-life living and thinking, characteristic of organized religion generally, and both Jesus and Paul fight against legalism. In place of legalism, Jesus and Paul emphasize salvation by grace through faith (that is, freely and universally, though it requires acceptance). Biblically speaking, faith does not mean, "believing something," although of course some belief is involved. Likewise, faith in God or Jesus does not mean believing that there is a discernible, definable God, or believing some doctrine about Jesus. It means commitment to God or Jesus, which changes one's perspective. The moment of clarity, if it comes, is unplanned and "out of the blue," and when it comes, it results in a new way of living and thinking, focused more on others than on self, and, by implication, on caring for all of life as an extension of self. This is the simple core of faith upon which Christian orthodoxy is built.

Unlike other world religions, Christianity is a faith tradition more than a way of life. Hence, its primary focus is on doctrine rather than on legal requirements or religious law. The very idea of doctrine (a Latin word meaning "teaching"), with its implication that there is a decisive difference between truth and error, that is, between sound doctrine and heresy, is a characteristically Christian notion. Paganism, with its roots in myth and its tolerance for alternative forms of ritual, has little need of doctrine. Likewise Judaism, from which Christianity emerges, has little interest in doctrine, focusing its intellectual energies on questions of how to live more than of what to believe.

Christianity originates as a response to Jesus Christ. The first Christians have a love affair with Jesus, not so much the "Jesus of history"—that comes later—but the "Christ of faith," which the earliest Christians understand to be the same as the historical Jesus. Christians invent the idea of religious doctrine because their religion is fundamentally a "faith," which is to say, an understanding of Jesus—a trust relationship with Jesus that has to be taught and passed on. In this respect, we can speak of Christianity as an intellectual tradition. The word "tradition" means two things: the "handing down" of specific wisdom, and critical thinking about that wisdom. In that sense, the major world religions are all intellectual traditions, for they pass on wisdom (both practical and theoretical) from one generation to the next. Science and religion, like cultural norms and values, are traditions in this sense.

Christian theology, then, starts with Jesus Christ, and it involves both the "handing down" of teaching about Jesus—who he is and what he accomplishes—and critical reasoning about Jesus Christ and life in him. In Christian theology even the central theme of Jesus' teaching, namely, the Kingdom of God, is subordinated to teaching about who Jesus is— the Christ, which means the king in the Kingdom of God. Similarly, for Christian theology, all other questions, including issues such as the doctrines of the Trinity or of sin and salvation, creation or the end of history and the afterlife, are all subordinate to the question, "Who is Jesus?" For Christianity, what is parallel to the Torah in Judaism or to the Qur'an in Islam, is not the Bible but Jesus Christ (of whom the Bible functions as a witness). Hence, for early Christians, the Old Testament scriptures are not read for their historical, liturgical, theological, or spiritual value, but as witnesses to Jesus Christ.

The four Gospels of the New Testament, which narrate the life, death, and resurrection of Jesus, are our main sources for the life of Jesus. Three of them, called the Synoptic Gospels, tell the story in roughly the same order. They have a high point in the middle when Jesus asks his disciples, "Who do you say that I am?" That, of course, is the central question of the early Gospels. The Gospels are written, not simply to answer that question, but to confront each reader and listener with that question, which they are to answer for themselves. Peter's answer, found at the center of each Synoptic Gospel, is clear: Jesus is the Christ, God's Messiah (see Matt. 16:16; Mark 8:29; Luke 9:20). It is not coincidental that Peter's confession is followed by an episode called the Transfiguration, an event that reveals Jesus in glory and his identity as God's chosen and beloved Son.

The Fourth Gospel tells the story of Jesus differently from the Synoptics. Nevertheless, it too focuses at length on Jesus' identity. It begins with a prologue (John 1:1–18), which identifies Jesus as the preexistent word of God made flesh. A central feature of John's Gospel is a series of seven "I am" sayings, statements in which Jesus declares his identity. All "I am" statements recall the name of the God of Israel, which means "I am" (Exod. 3:13–14).

Early Christian theology begin with a reflection on the practice of Christian worship, and what is distinctive about Christian worship is that it is directed at Jesus Christ. Some of the earliest material in the New Testament, going back to the earliest Jewish Christianity, are Christological hymn fragments found in the Pauline corpus (Phil. 2:6–11; Col. 1:15–20; 1 Tim. 3:16), the Gospel of John (1:1–5, 9–14), and Hebrews (1:2–4). They demonstrate that the earliest thinking about Jesus grows out of worship practices that are modeled after the synagogue service, a pattern that consists of readings from scripture, singing, and prayer.

The earliest recorded Christian hymns, prayers, and sermons emphasize the resurrection of Jesus from the dead, including his exaltation to the throne of God. The first recorded Christian sermon, found in Acts 2:14–36, builds on this foundation. The resurrection and exaltation of Jesus helps to clarify the early church's most daunting problem, that its founder dies on a Roman cross as a criminal, is tried for sedition, and then crucified as an insurrectionist. The Christian proclamation of a crucified Messiah is difficult to substantiate in Roman times, as Paul indicates in 1 Corinthians 1:22–28. Justin Martyr, who composes his *Dialogue with Trypho* in the second century, grapples with Jewish objections to the idea of a crucified Messiah, quoting Trypho as saying that "this so-called Christ of yours was dishonorable and inglorious, so much that the last curse contained in the law of God fell on him, for he was crucified."[4] The Latin author Minucius Felix concludes that only "abandoned wretches" could possibly center their worship on "a man put to death for his crime and on the fatal wood of the cross."[5]

Against such objections, the early Christians seek to create a frame of reference that can disclose the transcendent significance of Jesus' death. Luke refers to the crucifixion early in Acts, putting into the mouth of Peter the core of his own theology: "this man, handed over to you according to the definite plan and foreknowledge of God, you crucified and killed by the hands of those outside the law" (Acts 2:23). He sees the ministry of Jesus from baptism to ascension as the working out of a drama of world redemption in which, though human beings are free to act on their own volition, the plot has been determined by God. Humans may reject the purpose of God, as the Pharisees and lawyers do when they ignore John's baptism (Luke 7:30), but the cross proves that God can turn even the ultimate rejection into victory.

The divine plan is both foretold and prefigured in the Hebrew scriptures. It is an integral part of the apostolic tradition that the life, death, and resurrection of Jesus has occurred "in accordance with the scriptures"

---

4. Justin, *Dialogue* 32.1.
5. Minucius Felix, *Octavius* 9.4.

(1 Cor. 15:3–4). From this starting point, the first Christians look back at the meaning of Jesus's earthly life, and even to his preexistence with the Father before his birth. And they look forward to his return in glory to consummate all things, raising the dead and establishing the kingdom of God on earth.

For early Christian orthodoxy, what is determinative for doctrine, that is, for faith in Jesus, is belief in his resurrection from the dead, his incarnation as the divine Son of God, and his promised return in glory. These beliefs are non-negotiable, essential to calling oneself "Christian"—a follower of Jesus Christ. The wisdom and message at the heart of Christianity, then, is not primarily a revelation about how to live but primarily the story of who Jesus is. Proper teaching about Jesus' identity later became the basis for the Christian life, a way of living that the apostle Paul calls dwelling "in Christ" (2 Cor. 5:17; Gal. 2:20), and the Fourth Gospel "abiding in Christ" (see John 15:4, a way of life patterned after Christ's death and resurrection; see Rom. 6:1–11; 8:10–25; Phil. 3:8–11).

Upon this foundation—the only one upon which believers can build, according to Paul (1 Cor. 3:11)—later Christians add theological scaffolding to establish orthodox unanimity on important concepts such as the nature of God (whether one or many), human beings (whether good, bad, or neutral), truth (whether objective or subjective), and the doctrines of creation, providence, sin, and salvation. To ensure sound doctrine and continuity, orthodox Christianity is shaped by episcopacy (governance by bishops), creedal formulations (short, concise summaries of what it means to be Christian), and a closed canon (an official and final collection of authoritative scriptures).

During the first several centuries of Christianity, Christian orthodoxy is debated, challenged, stretched, philosophized, misunderstood, and even ignored, but by the fourth century, Christianity develops consensus. As a result, those who disagree or keep questioning are declared "heretics," meaning unorthodox. Throughout Christian history, many who disagree are persecuted, tortured, ridiculed, or otherwise marginalized, but in retrospect, a large number of those thus vilified preserve their understanding of spirituality under duress, helping shape the views of Christian spirituality formulated during and since the Protestant Reformation.

The victors usually dictate history. Hence, what we know about the early centuries of Christianity—at least until the archaeological discoveries of the twentieth century—comes from the writings of orthodox theologians such as Justin Martyr and Irenaeus in the second century, who condemn the quest for higher *gnosis* (insight, wisdom or knowledge) and develop the idea of heresy to demonize and stigmatize it. Their efforts are discussed in the following segment, showing how they define and defend the developing Christian tradition and engage with sectarians and other opposing groups and views.

Another Christian response to early heterodox groups such as Valentinians, Marcionites, and Gnostics is to offer alternate orthodox paths to *gnosis*, by trying to appeal to the desire for higher insight and spirituality that attracts people to such groups. The important Christian theologians here are Clement and Origin, two influential intellectual leaders in Alexandria, Egypt. Their contributions to Christian *gnosis* are the subject of chapter 6.

Both strategies—the identification of heresy and the teaching of orthodox *gnosis*—contribute to the rich traditions that become Roman Catholicism and Eastern Orthodoxy, and by implication, that become orthodox Christianity. We remind readers that in its early centuries—prior to the conciliar period that leads to creedal orthodoxy and the establishment of Christendom in the fourth and fifth centuries—Christianity is astonishingly diverse, both in belief and practice. While groups such as the Gnostics, Valentinians, and Marcionites continue to evolve, they also help shape what becomes orthodox Christianity.

One of the principal concerns of the heterodox sectarians and apologists that help to shape orthodox Christianity is the continuity or discontinuity of Christianity with the earlier history of God's revelation in the world. While some Christian thinkers attempt to reconcile Christianity with the Greek philosophical tradition stemming from Plato and Aristotle, most focus on the church's descent from and fulfillment of the Jewish heritage, epitomized by the Old Testament, specifically by its accounts of the creation, the origin of evil, and its prophecies of the coming of the Christ.

Although some of the earliest versions of Christianity overemphasize their continuity with Judaism, the growth and expansion of Christianity into a chiefly Gentile phenomenon brings this continuity into question. The major sectarian movements of the first two or three centuries are those that stress radical, secret, or unheard-of aspects in the Christian message, over against continuity with the Old Testament or pagan and natural religion.

While already in the New Testament we hear that certain forms of Judaism are the origin of the earliest forms of Christian heresy (in Paul, for example, "to Judaize" is a term for "to teach false doctrine"), nevertheless, the most significant heresies of the second and third centuries are not Jewish but anti-Jewish. Thus, in the 140s a Christian teacher in Rome named Marcion proclaims the gospel of a God who, in granting salvation, is wholly other than the Creator of the Old Testament. Marcion disavows the Jewish Bible altogether, arguing that the God of the Old Testament is a lesser, inferior God from the Father of Jesus Christ. Marcion argues that the Old Testament should no longer be read as scripture by Christians. Instead, they should use only the letters of Paul and one Gospel about Jesus, that of Luke. Marcion tries to persuade other Christians in Rome to follow his vision, but they refuse. So Marcion cuts off his relation with such Christians and begins forming churches in cities other than Rome. Eventually a network of Christian churches devoted to Marcion's teachings and interpretations spreads throughout the Roman Empire and lasts for centuries.

The Idea of Heresy

Justin Martyr and Irenaeus, both called heresiologists, are concerned with identifying and rooting out Christian heretics. Initially, the word "heresy," which comes from the Greek word *hairesis*, has no negative connotation. It is a common word, meaning something like "school of thought," "faction," or "sect." Ancient teachers of medicine, for example, divide themselves into competing points of view or *hairesis*, schools of thought based on how they viewed sickness or disease. Likewise, the first-century Jewish historian Josephus uses the term *hairesis* to describe different sects within Judaism, such as the Pharisees, Sadducees, and Essenes.

Early Christians, worrying about dissensions and factions, emphasize unity and harmony. We see this ideal clearly in the New Testament, where believers are called the "body of Christ." In his first letter to the Corinthians, Paul laments that there are factions—*hairesis*—among the Christians at Corinth (see 1:10–11; 3:3), and the author of 2 Peter worries about false teachers "who will secretly bring in destructive *haireses*" (2:1), perhaps meaning "ways of thinking." The author of 1 Timothy attributes false Christian teachings to the devil (4:1), and he warns against "what is falsely called *gnosis*" (6:20). So already in the New Testament, Christian authors condemn the existence of factions or *haireses* and blame the devil for Christian teaching that they consider erroneous.

The first Christian credited with developing a full concept of heresy is Justin Martyr (c. 100–c. 165). He is called Justin Martyr because in 165 he suffers martyrdom for his Christian beliefs, executed under emperor Marcus Aurelius. A native of Palestine, Justin explores the major philosophical options of his day before turning to an investigation of Christianity. He wanders about the Mediterranean world as a Christian philosopher, finally settling in Rome, where he founds a Christian school. His two major writings that survive are both apologies, the first addressed to a Jewish rabbi (*Dialogue with Trypho*), and the other to Gentiles (*Apology*).

Justin takes the idea of *hairesis* or "school of thought" and makes it an entirely negative term. He argues that he and Christians like him are part of the one true church, but the Gnostics, Marcion, and the Valentinians are merely "schools of thought." No mere school of thought can be the source of truth. Truth comes only from the Word of God present in Jesus and in the church. Justin writes a book, now lost, against heresies, arguing that members of these groups are not really Christians, even if they claim to be. Having a dualistic (either/or) way of thinking, he argues that those outside of the church are but "godless and impious members of a school of thought," heretics, not true Christians. All heresies, according to Justin, are demonic, the product of demons opposed to God's Son.

At this point, Justin does not represent the official Christian church, since there is no such official organization. Not being a bishop or priest, he is simply a compelling Christian teacher and preacher like Marcion and Valentinus. All he can do is persuade people that he is teaching Christian truth, and that all rivals are teaching demonic heresy.

Irenaeus and Authentic Christian Orthodoxy

A major figure among the Christians of the late second century is Irenaeus (c. 120–200), who works to consolidate Christian orthodoxy. Born at Smyrna around the year 130, where he is a disciple of Polycarp,[6] he is ordained bishop of Lyons in Gaul in 178. Anxious to reconcile Christians in the eastern and western Roman worlds and to establish principles on which such unity might be affirmed and maintained, Irenaeus writes *Against Heresies*. This major work not only attacks false teaching, but it

---

6. Polycarp, Bishop of Smyrna, is said to have known John, the last of the disciples of Jesus. Polycarp becomes an early martyr, executed for his faith in 155.

also offers a full declaration of what Irenaeus considers the essence of authentic Christian faith. Like the philosophical insight of which Origen writes, faith has an intellectual content that can be defined with increasing clarity. Nevertheless, false teachers who deny aspects of the faith that Irenaeus identifies as orthodox are threatening this unity of faith. Included among these heterodox groups are Gnostics, who deny that creation is good or that the God of Jesus is the creator of the universe. To support their heretical views, Gnostics produce rival writings to the New Testament, including gospels, apocalypses, acts, and letters attributed to various apostles.

Irenaeus is highly influenced by the writings of Justin Martyr. At the center of Irenaeus's views of heresy and orthodoxy is an idea that comes to be known as "apostolic succession," namely, the idea of a succession of teachers and students. Irenaeus borrows the idea of succession from Valentinian teachers—who trace their academic lineage back to the apostles and Jesus[7]—and applies it both to groups he opposes and the Christians he supports. According to Irenaeus, Valentinus learns from the Gnostics, and rather than going back to Jesus, his spiritual lineage can be traced to Simon Magus, a character in the New Testament who offers the apostles money in exchange for the superior power of the Holy Spirit (Acts 8:9–13). Later Christians label Simon the first heretic and hence, like Satan, the father of all lies (John 8:44). As Irenaeus presents him, Simon is inspired by Satan to become the first teacher of false *gnosis*. All heretical teachers are intellectual descendants of him and his students.

Irenaeus also attacks the idea that Jesus teaches or reveals secret teachings to select individuals. The Valentinians, like the Gnostics and many Christian sectarians, seem to reserve certain teaching for advanced Christians—the spiritual ones (in this respect, see 1 Corinthians 2:6–8, 13–16). Irenaeus, however, denies that the apostles have secret teachings. If they do, they would surely share them with their successors, the bishops. For Irenaeus, all true apostolic teachings are clearly manifest and equally available to anyone truly Christian.

In his definition of orthodoxy, Irenaeus argues for a threefold approach to tradition: the canon of scripture, the rule of faith, and the authority of bishops. In countering heresy, Irenaeus affirms the necessity of a literary canon, a standard by which books could be used to define Christian teaching and practice. He refutes Marcionites, Gnostics, and

---

7. According to the Valentinians, Jesus teaches the apostles, including Paul. Then Paul has a student named Theudas, and Theudas teaches Valentinus.

other sectarian teachers with specific citations from the Old and New Testament, indicating which compositions he is using and thus showing which are truly authoritative and which are rejected. Using this method, Irenaeus represents an important stage toward the final formation of the New Testament canon. Unlike the heretics, who take only one Gospel as their norm, Irenaeus insists that there are four, just as there are four winds and four corners of the earth. The one gospel message rests on four pillars, "breathing immortality on every side and enkindling life anew in human beings." And unlike Marcion, who rejects most of the Gospels and the Old Testament altogether, Irenaeus promotes one of the first versions of what becomes a Christian canon of the Bible, comprised of the Old and New Testaments, the four Gospels, and most of the rest of what becomes the New Testament canon, a process finalized in the fourth century.

However, even Irenaeus's version of the Bible is not sufficient for opposing alleged heretics such as the Valentinians, because the Valentinians use the same scriptures as Irenaeus, only interpret them differently. To judge the truth or falsehood of competing interpretations of the Bible, Irenaeus relies on the "rule of faith," a creedal summary of Christian beliefs he claims the church receives from the apostles. The rule of faith states the basic doctrines of Christianity, and any teachings that violate the rule are clearly false.

Elements of a creed are already present in Judaism: "Hear, O Israel, the Lord your God is one God." Even the basic Christian claim, "Jesus is Lord," is a statement of belief. Various creedal statements also appear in the New Testament, such as in 1 Timothy 2:5-6 and in 1 Corinthians 8:5-6. Irenaeus's rule of faith, like the Apostles' Creed, presents an epitome of the scriptural story. As such, it also provides a guide to the reading of the scriptures.

The notion of the bishops as the successors of the apostles is already present in early second-century Christian thinking, but is argued more fully by Irenaeus, with specific attention to the bishops of Rome. Irenaeus's institutional argument directly opposes the Gnostic position concerning secret teachings, secret teachers, and secret books. For Irenaeus, the litmus test for true Christianity is clear, consisting of a public creed, an apostolic tradition, and a clear canon of scripture. The consensus of the patristic period, already visible by the end of the second century, is that the unity and truth of the church, represented by the orthodox tradition, is to be maintained by the apostolic witness, the succession of leadership from the apostles through the bishops, and fidelity to an accepted collection of scriptures. Such church standards develop more fully during the ensuing conciliar age (the declarations of the ecumenical church councils of the fourth through seventh centuries).

While Irenaeus disagrees with the Gnostics and Valentinians on the nature of *gnosis* and truth, he also promotes his own vision of Christianity, and in this respect, we find areas of agreement with the sectarians. For example, Irenaeus agrees that the ultimate God, whom he calls the Father, is unknowable. But instead of multiple intermediary beings between God and humanity, the Father has only two somewhat lower aspects of himself: the Son or Word of God and the Holy Spirit, who is also God's Wisdom. It is the Son who makes the Father known to humans, and through him, humans gain access to the Father. The Son is also the maker of the physical cosmos in which we live. Meanwhile, the Holy Spirit is in charge of the spiritual powers that serve God, and the Spirit is present among true Christians.

Irenaeus also develops a view of human salvation in response to Gnostics and Valentinians, who teach that Jesus saves people primarily by revealing true *gnosis* to them. In contrast, Irenaeus emphasizes the incarnation, that the Son of God becomes human in order to make human beings holy or sacred. And Jesus triumphs over all of the forces of evil—human and cosmic—in the resurrection. As Irenaeus sees it, human beings are morally and physically corrupt, and it is the purpose of God's incarnation to make us holy, thereby restoring God's original purpose for creation.

Irenaeus tries to do justice to the gnostic sense that humans are meant for a more spiritual existence than is possible on earth. But unlike the Gnostics, he believes that humans are destined to be united with God as spiritual *human* beings, which involves the body as well as the spirit. The Gnostics, Valentinians, and related groups consider their true selves to be only their spiritual selves, their bodies destined for destruction or annihilation. Irenaeus, in contrast, believes that our bodies are essential to who we are and need to become. The Son of God necessarily comes in a real body of flesh to make us holy, and the resurrection of the dead is a resurrection of the fleshly body we currently possess.

For Irenaeus, however, flesh cannot attain to union with God without passing through many stages. While humans are not created perfect, neither are they defective. Rather, they are made immature, and intrinsic to being human is that our perfection should be gradual. The tragedy of the fall into sin, according to Irenaeus, is that Adam and Eve are impatient, and in their attempt to speed up their spiritual maturity, they snarl the process of human growth. The role of Jesus is to unsnarl the process, and he does so by passing through every stage of human life—childhood, young adulthood, middle age, and old age—so that he can sanctify all human beings, from babies to the elderly. Irenaeus calls Jesus' accomplishment "recapitulation"; Jesus becomes what Adam and Eve are intended to be—humanity in the image and likeness of God. The incarnation and resurrection thereby restore the proper conjunction of flesh—in which the *image* of God resides—and the Spirit—who imparts *likeness* to God.

But sin is not a total disaster. By coming to know evil as well as good, human beings become more appreciative of the good and of the God from whom they come. The suffering that results from sin is educative, in that it trains human freedom. The final goal—the final perfection—is that humans should see God. However, this is a lengthy process. Humans must begin with a feeble life and an indirect vision, and only gradually become capable of the more intense life of eternity.

In this process, Christ plays a crucial part. In him the invisible God becomes visible, without losing his mysteriousness. In Christ, the union between flesh and Spirit, humanity and God, is effected. In him, the two parties become intertwined. This is why any denial of the humanity or the deity of Christ is disastrous. Unless God and humanity are united in Christ, humans have no hope. For Irenaeus, Christians are drawn into this union through baptism and the Eucharist.

Irenaeus stresses human freedom, insisting that sin is due to the wrong use of freedom. However, we cannot achieve perfection simply by the exercise of free will. Immortality is not ours by right. And it is futile to rush the process or to ignore its need and efficacy. If we think we are already a finished product, we shall remain stunted forever. It is foolish to want to be divine before we are even fully human. Our role is to place ourselves into God's hands—the clay yielding willingly to the potter. It is our part to "be made" by God. Yielding to the Creator is the proper exercise of one's freedom.

The resurrection of the flesh is necessary because the Kingdom of God is not spiritual or immaterial; it is a physical realm. In fact, for Irenaeus, the Kingdom will be in this world, miraculously transformed by God. Saved human beings, with real bodies, will live in this earthly Kingdom forever. They will grow in love for and in knowledge of God. They will see God in their bodies. Some special Christians, the holiest of all, will ascend to live in the heavens. But for eternity, most believers will dwell in a new City of God on earth (see Rev. 21:3: "See, the home of God is among mortals"). God will be present everywhere, to everyone.[8]

Irenaeus develops his teaching about God, Christ, the Holy Spirit, Adam and Eve in the Garden, the resurrection of the body, and life in an eternal kingdom here on earth, all in response to the "false *gnosis*" that he sees in the Gnostics and Valentinians. And all that he teaches, he claims, comes from the apostles. True *gnosis*, according to Irenaeus, consists of the teaching of the apostles; the ancient institution of the church; the succession of bishops, to whom the apostles entrust each local church; and the genuine preservation of the church's scriptures, its complete collection allowing for neither addition nor subtraction.

As valuable as this tradition is, Irenaeus's list sounds a lot like first-half-of-life spirituality. What about Christians who aspire to a more mystical and spiritual understanding of the faith? As we shall see, Valentinians appeal to Christians who seek a deeper, more philosophical understanding of Christian scriptures and teaching. Irenaeus does not have much to offer them, for he condemns the idea that there can be any higher Christian teachings reserved for more advanced Christians.

In the next chapter we examine the views of the Valentinian Christians and the Gnostics in depth, for such groups have much to teach us much about second-half-of-life spirituality. In chapter 6 we meet Christian teachers who join Irenaeus in condemning the Gnostics and Valentinians, but who teach their own versions of *gnosis*—a *gnosis* that is higher than that of Irenaeus and even secret, yet orthodox.

Questions for Discussion and Reflection

In addition to the questions listed at the end of the preface, answer the following questions, writing your answers in a journal. If you are in a group study, be prepared to share your answers with those in the group.

1. If Christianity could not have emerged apart from Judaism, what role or relationship should these faiths have for one another at the present time?

---

8. According to Revelation, the final book of the Bible, there is no "rapture" of the church from earth. Instead, it is God who is "raptured" to earth to live with us. At the end of Revelation, humans are not in heaven; there is no longer need for dualistic thinking, because God dwells on earth; and where God is, there is heaven.

Early Christian (Proto-Orthodox) Spirituality

2. If you consider yourself Christian, what role or authority does Christian orthodoxy have in your way of thinking and living?

3. In your estimation, is Christianity primarily a faith tradition or a way of life? Explain your answer.

4. In your estimation, how are dogma (doctrine) and spirituality related?

5. What role does Jesus play in your spirituality?

6. If diversity is a good thing, why are Justin Martyr and Irenaeus so focused on the concept of heresy, and why do they view it so negatively?

7. In your estimation, how important are the concepts of tradition and of episcopacy ("apostolic succession") to your understanding of Christianity?

8. In your estimation, how important are the concepts of canon and creed to your understanding of Christianity?

9. Briefly explain your understanding of Irenaeus's views on sin and salvation.

4

Gnostic Spirituality

MOST OF US HAVE heard of the Gnostics, how during the past 75 years, previously lost Gnostic writings have reappeared, from the Coptic codices found near Nag Hammadi in Egypt in 1945 to the *Gospel of Judas*, found in the 1970s in a cave near El Minya, Egypt. Although the texts in the Nag Hammadi codices are written in Coptic, which is the last phase of the ancient Egyptian language, these writings were originally composed in Greek. The manuscripts we have today are not original works, but translations copied around 350 to 400 CE, from Greek originals dating to the second century.

Perhaps you are wondering why this book on Christianity-based spirituality includes a chapter on Gnosticism. Aren't Gnostics heretics? And aren't their ideas based on myths, reconstructions of reality that appear far-fetched and irrelevant? As we shall see, Gnostic literature reveals beliefs and concepts that have much to teach us today, and the Gnostic mythological mindset can be instructive in revealing the true nature of Christianity, many of its doctrines and beliefs also mythological in nature. While the Gnostic texts provide insights into the diversity of Gnosticism, they also illumine the diversity of beliefs and practices of early Christianity. As we explore the myths, rituals, and teachings of the first Gnostics and of related groups, we come to understand their passion about knowing God and relating to God. In the early Christian centuries, Gnostics, Valentinians, Marcionites, Manicheans, and other related movements offer profound answers to the deep question of human existence, especially to the problem of evil. Orthodox Christianity develops partly in response to these groups.

While gnostic ideas possibly preexist the birth of Christianity, having appeared initially in Jewish and Hellenistic contexts, the so-called Gnostic school of thought flourish in the Roman Empire during the second and third centuries CE. In works such as the *Apocryphon* (The Secret Book) *of John* and the *Gospel of Judas*, we find Gnostics combining the book of Genesis with Jewish, Platonic, and Christian traditions to create a strange myth that explains how the universe came into being through an ignorant and malevolent god. Gnostics offer salvation from ignorance, fate, and the evil material world through knowledge of a higher God, who sends Jesus, and they claim that people can have mystical contact with God now.

The influential second-century Christian teacher Valentinus and his disciples revise the original Gnostic myth to make it even more Christ-centered, and they invite Christians to a deeper understanding of the Christian scriptures, sacraments, and doctrines. Valentinian forms of Christianity exist alongside of, and in competition with, orthodox Christianity for centuries.

The *Gospel of Thomas*, not a gospel in the traditional sense, is a "sayings source," containing 114 isolated sayings attributed to Jesus. Perhaps the most famous text from Nag Hammadi, *Thomas* does not share the Gnostic myth, but it does teach that to know one's self is to know God, that is, the Christ who is within you and who you are. Some scholars believe this document may incorporate traditions as old as or older than the Gospels of the New Testament, dating it to the first century. Most scholars, however, think that in addition to relying on first-century oral tradition about Jesus, the author of *Thomas* also uses the Gospels in the New Testament, meaning it probably comes from the early second century.

The original author seems to have borrowed from sources of varying origin and of different ages, composing a version that undergoes later revision. The best date for the earliest complete version of *Thomas* is around 140 CE, prior to the emergence of the full Gnostic myth as found in the *Apocryphon of John*, which dates closer to the middle or second half of the second century.

Gnostic forms of Christianity decline by the fourth century, beginning with the ascendance of Constantine to imperial power in 312, and end with the establishment of Christianity as the official religion of the empire by emperor Theodosius in 380. Gnosticism lives on in various forms, including in Manichaeism, a new worldwide religious founded by a Persian Christian named Mani (216–274), which enlists its followers in an ongoing war between the co-equal and eternal realms of Good and Evil, a religion that leaves its traces in one of orthodox Christianity's greatest heroes, Augustine, bishop of Hippo in North Africa.

Variants of Gnosticism also arise in Western Europe in the twelfth century, in a group called the Cathars or Albigensians, briefly successful in southern France and northern Italy until the Albigensian Crusade, a military movement instigated by Pope Innocent III, brings their alternative form of Christianity to an end. Around this same time, a Jewish form of esoteric religion known as Kabbalah appears in northern Spain. Like the Cathars, it, too, shows remarkable similarities to Gnosticism. Yet unlike the Cathars, Kabbalah continues to impact Judaism, particularly through Hasidic beliefs and practices. Many people today know about this form of Jewish mysticism through its central text, the *Zohar* (The Book of Splendor).

Said to have been the work of a second century Jewish rabbi named Simeon Ben Yohai, the *Zohar* is most likely written by the thirteenth-century Spanish mystic Moses de León. Arranged in the form of a commentary on the Torah, combining commentary with fiction and fantasy, this book continues to amaze modern readers. By the sixteenth century, the *Zohar* becomes the most widely read book in Judaism, ranking with the Bible and the Talmud as a sacred text.

The movements that scholars call Gnostic are labeled heretical by patristic and medieval Christian orthodoxy, but they are profound and compelling attempts to speak to the human condition, particularly regarding the origin and nature of evil and suffering, and they exert a strong influence on the history of Christianity and on other Western religions. By studying movements that are condemned as heretical and lost, we gain a new understanding of why orthodox Christianity develops as it does, and we encounter alternative religious paths to *gnosis* in the Western tradition.

Having introduced the term *gnosis*, which underlies Gnosticism, we need to define the concept. When the English word Gnosticism is invented in the seventeenth century, it is based on the Greek word *gnosis*, meaning personal, direct, and immediate knowledge. The adjective and noun "gnostic" comes from the Greek adjective *gnostikos*, invented by the Greek philosopher Plato to describe fields of study or parts of the human intellect having to do with higher knowledge, that is, knowledge that can make us wiser or more virtuous, as opposed to practical knowledge used to accomplish projects or trades such as carpentry or baking. *Gnostikos* becomes a technical term, used by philosophers, scholars, and mystics, but not necessarily by ordinary people.

However, around 180 CE, Irenaeus reveals that certain Christians are using the term *gnostikos* to refer to themselves. This is the first time in history that we know of people being called gnostic. These are the Gnostics, and they form groups called Gnostic schools of thought. Numerous individuals and groups claim to offer *gnosis* of God—including Irenaeus—but these folks make *gnosis* the defining feature of their religious identity.

When Gnostics speak of *gnosis*, they are not only speaking of revealed yet hidden knowledge of God. *Gnosis* also means knowing the truth about the physical world, that all materiality, including earth and heavens, planets and stars, is an evil prison for human souls or spirits, which originates outside the Pleroma,[1] the spiritual world beyond space and time, to which all spirits must return. For Gnostics, salvation involves knowing the distinction between spiritual and material reality, including the makeup, origin, and destiny of human beings.

While Gnostic sources are post-Christian, some scholars claim that Gnostic beliefs predate Christianity and may have influenced Christianity, since Gnosticism flourishes during the second century CE. Some Pauline scholars suggest that the central problem Paul deals with after the Apostolic Council stems from Gnosticism. There is no question that some of the scandals that arise in Paul's Corinthian churches point to Gnostic-like behavior and belief.[2] There is little question that incipient Gnosticism is present in first-century churches, but full-blown Gnosticism does not appear until the second and third century, borrowing from Christianity while distorting it.

The Gnostic worldview, as it affects Christianity, revolves around four factors:

1. *Cosmological element.* Most Gnostic systems begin with a philosophy of strict dualism. The cosmos is represented by two realms that oppose one another: the divine realm of light (the Pleroma) and the demonic realm of darkness. According to some Gnostics, the physical

---

1. For Gnostics, the word "*pleroma*," often translated as "fullness," has a similar meaning in the Deutero-Pauline writings of Ephesians and Colossians. In this regard, see particularly Colossians 1:19 and 2:9.

2. A partial list from 1 Corinthians includes (a) the presence of the "Christ-party" (see 1:12), (b) esteem of *gnosis* (1:17), (c) devaluing the earthly Jesus (12:3), (d) emphasizing glossolalia (speaking in tongues) over other gifts (13:1; 14:1–5), and (e) denying the resurrection of the body (15:12–19).

world originates from a disruption in the Pleroma, when Sophia or Wisdom, the lowest deity (*aeon*) in the Pleroma, chooses to create a material copy or image from the spiritual prototype, acting autonomously. That disruption in the Pleroma results in a qualitative difference between matter (viewed as evil) and spirit (viewed as good). Thus, life and death, truth and falsehood, salvation and the ruin of human life, are anchored in the cosmos. The world and all things visible in the universe are characterized as darkness and are under the control of evil spirits (often called rulers or *archons*). The *archons* are planetary deities (see Eph. 2:2), evil powers in the heavens whose task is to block the soul's escape from this world after death.

2. *Theological element.* Gnostics have many deities, some good (called *aeons*) and others evil (the *archons*). The primary God, who dwells in the abode of light and is Light, is unknown. A lesser craftsman or demiurge, created by Sophia's indiscretion, fashions this world, trapping particles of light in the darkness of matter.

3. *Anthropological element.* Humans consist of body (flesh) and soul (soul and spirit are sometimes further distinguished), two elements in conflict with one another. Within (some) humans is a spark or particle of light, placed into humanity during the primeval period by the demiurge. Apart from enlightenment, humans remain ignorant of their true (godlike) inner nature. Once redeemed, the spark must escape back to its source, the unknown God.

4. *Christological element.* Christ, an *aeon* sent into this world to bring saving knowledge of the world above—the Pleroma—is understood to be a divine messenger (actually God, for all beings of light are emanations [hence begotten] of God, hence God). Jesus is a redeemer (Savior) who provides knowledge (*gnosis*) about the unknown God and the divine element to those who by origin are divine. Because matter is evil, Christ is never really embodied. Either he dwells in the man Jesus temporarily or else his body is an illusion. In Jesus, Christ only appears human in order to deceive the forces of evil and to penetrate the realm of darkness with secret insight and knowledge.[3]

---

3. This view, which denies the humanity of Jesus Christ and argues that Christ only "appeared" to be human, is held by some of the dissidents in the Johannine churches. Called docetism, this view is condemned as "the spirit of antichrist" in 1 John 4:1–6 (see also 1 Cor. 12:3; 2 John 7; Col. 1:22).

Gnosticism's disdain for the physical world has been linked to a profound rejection of Judaism. The God of the Jews is the creator God, maker and ruler of this physical world, which means he is ignorant, malevolent, and evil. He forbids humans to eat from the Tree of Knowledge (*gnosis*) because he wants them to stay ignorant and under his power. He is described as an arrogant *archon* because he boasts of being the only God, thereby demonstrating ignorance of the Pleroma—the divine realm above.

Another area in which Christians and Gnostics disagree is the role of ethics. Although most Gnostics live according to high ethical standards, stressing asceticism and living like hermits in order not to be contaminated by the world's pollution and deception, a minority may have lived like libertines (see I Cor. 5:1–13), considering ethics superfluous. It is representatives of this latter group that cause Paul difficulties in Asia Minor and Greece, and are clearly his antagonists in 1 and 2 Corinthians. Whereas orthodox Christians see evil embodied in immoral practices, Gnosticism sees evil within human nature, primarily in spiritual ignorance. Hence the solution involves gaining insight and ignoring (or even overindulging) the flesh.

The movements that we label Gnostic tend to communicate their ideas in elaborate myths—sacred stories that tell who God is, how the universe comes to be, what the original human beings are like, and what happens in the future. These myths draw upon a variety of religious and philosophical traditions. The Jewish Bible, especially Genesis, is the major source for the themes and characters in Gnostic myth, although the Gnostics also look to the works of Plato and sometimes even to pagan mythology for their ideas.

These myths usually strike modern readers as strange and complicated, which they are. They include characters that may be familiar from the Bible and Christianity, such as Adam and Eve, their son Seth, Noah, Jesus, and even God's Wisdom. However, they also include divine beings that are unique to Gnostic mythology. Some of these have abstract philosophical names, like Forethought or the Divine Self-Originate, but others have obscure proper names like Ialdabaoth, Barbelo, and Eleleth. There are even some new human characters, like Norea, the sister of Seth.

For centuries, scholars interested in the Gnostics or Valentinians rely on Irenaeus. In the late 170s he becomes the leader of a small group of Christians in Lyons, a major city in the Roman province of Gaul (modern-day France), where most educated people speak and write Latin. However, Irenaeus speaks Greek, having immigrated to Lyons from his home in Smyrna (modern-day Turkey), then a part of Greece. Most of the Christians in Lyons are Greek-speaking immigrants from the Eastern part of the Roman Empire, and they are distrusted by the majority population. When Irenaeus becomes their bishop, they had just endured a horrible persecution. The most active and faithful members of the small group had been executed after prolonged torture. Others compromised and agreed to worship the Roman gods. Thus, when Irenaeus succeeds their elderly bishop Pothinus, who died during the persecution, he has a lot of work ahead, not only for his beleaguered congregation, but to attract new followers.

In his new task, he discovers he is not the only Christian leader in Lyons. Other teachers of Christianity offer people messages of salvation through Jesus Christ, messages that conflict with what Irenaeus teaches. While they share many terms and concepts, such as God the Father, Jesus his Son, sin and salvation, Greek and Hebrew scriptures, and the resurrection of the dead, their meaning is not what Irenaeus believes to be Christian. Irenaeus claims that these other Christian teachers teach false knowledge and should not be called Christians (followers of Christ) but Valentinians (followers of Valentinus). Irenaeus identifies these false Christians as Gnostics, and as noted in chapter 3, is the first to utilize the term "heretic," labeling all Gnostics "heretics."

Irenaeus takes it upon himself not only to stop Christians in Lyons from following this movement, which he characterizes as false teaching, but also to help other Christian leaders around the world combat them as well. He writes a massive work known as *Against the Heresies*, in which he describes false versions of Christianity to enable his readers to recognize these false teachings when they encounter them. In his view, only the Christianity that he and his bishops teach is the true Christianity, that is, true *gnosis* or knowledge of God. All the others are distortions of this single true Christianity that Jesus and the apostles teach.

For a long time, historians follow Irenaeus in believing that a single unified Christianity is born in the first century, finding this single original Christianity in the writings of the New Testament. While not calling alternative views "heretical," historians considered them aberrations of basic Christianity, seeing groups such as the Valentinians, and the more exclusively Gnostic schools of thought as diverging from mainstream Christianity.

Nowadays, most historians disagree with this assessment. They consider Christianity diverse from its inception. There probably never was a golden age when all Christians agreed unanimously—certainly not in the first centuries of the Christian movement. Instead, people respond to the ministry of Jesus in a variety of ways, sometimes disagreeing widely on their views.

This diversity is present in the New Testament, evident in tensions within the Gospels, for example, particularly between the first three Gospels and John's Gospel. Our earliest Christian sources, the letters of Paul, dating from between twenty to thirty years after the death of Jesus, reveal that the earliest Christians disagree about many things, including basic ideas like what the resurrection of the dead means. Another divisive issue involves how Gentiles are included in salvation. Do male Gentiles need to undergo circumcision, and do Gentile believers need to observe the Jewish Law by keeping a kosher diet? Disagreement on these issues persist among Christians for decades, even centuries.

Disagreement continues in early Christianity in part because there is yet no litmus test for truth, no worldwide structure to ensure that everyone teaches and practices the same things. Hence, while we cannot trace groups such as the Gnostics back to the earliest years of Christianity, their distinctive views, like those of Marcion, have roots in the period of the apostles.

While previous generations rely on Irenaeus, disparaging the Valentinian and Gnostic teachers and followers as immoral and theologically ignorant, we can now compare his portrayal of their views with those found in texts from Nag Hammadi, such as the *Apocryphon of John*, and from texts such as the *Gospel of Judas*, finding similarity and disparity.

For example, Irenaeus tells us that the Gnostics teach a myth that explains who God is, how the world we live in comes into being, how sin and death enter the world, and how God acts to save humanity. According to Irenaeus, the Gnostic God is like a vast mind or intellect, similar to but much greater than our minds. This God, though ultimately unknowable, is called the Invisible Spirit or the Invisible Virgin Spirit. Like an intellect, God is full of thoughts (*aeons*), viewed as emanations from God, much like the rays from the sun. The myth also tells about the creation of the world by revising and restating the stories in the biblical book of Genesis. Finally, the Gnostics believe that Jesus comes into this world as a representative of the Invisible Spirit, as the third member of something like a nuclear family, viewed as father, mother, and son. The purpose of the son—also called the Divine Self-Originate (in Greek *Autogenes*) or

Christ—is to save select individuals and to gather the souls of the saved at the end of time.

The most striking feature of the Gnostic myth as Irenaeus tells it is that the God of Genesis is a divine being who is lower than the ultimate God (the Invisible Spirit). This inferior God is arrogant, ignorant, and evil. He is hostile to human beings because they possess a share of the divine spirit that belongs to the higher God. The real name of the god who creates the world is Ialdabaoth[4]—a spiritual being who runs this universe like a tyrant.

This idea—that the God of Genesis is actually a malevolent cosmic ruler—has important implications for how Gnostics understand the rest of the Genesis story. If this god is hostile to human beings, then when he commands Adam and Eve not to eat from the tree of knowledge of good and evil, he is preventing them from knowing spiritual truth. When Adam and Eve eat from the tree, however, they gain *gnosis*, knowledge of the true God. As human beings continue to seek true spiritual knowledge, Ialdabaoth grows jealous of their devotion to the higher God and causes a flood to wipe out humanity. Fortunately, the higher God saves Noah and his family from Ialdabaoth's evil plot. Eventually, human beings begin to lose the knowledge that Adam and Eve gain when they eat from the tree. However, the higher God sends Jesus to restore this lost *gnosis* and to rescue them from Ialdabaoth and his fellow rulers.

Obviously, the Gnostic myth is a direct challenge to how Irenaeus sees God and Jesus, but we can draw two conclusions from his report. First, the Gnostics are concerned about aspects of the God of Genesis that do not seem godlike, such as regretting having created humans and causing a flood to eradicate them. Second, it confirms that Christians disagree about the role the Jewish Bible plays in their religion. When Paul says that salvation is based on faith in Christ and not on following the Jewish Law, he opens the door to Christians like Marcion, who conclude that the Jewish Bible is no longer relevant to Christians. Gnostics, however, take a different approach: the Bible is relevant, but it is not accurate. It tells the story of salvation, but from the wrong god's point of view.

---

4. This name is probably a taunt on the biblical appellation Yahweh Sabaoth, translated into English as "Lord of hosts" or "Lord of all" (see Isa. 1:9; Rom. 9:29; Jas. 5:4). The name Ialdabaoth also demonstrates disdain for the physical world and its inferior, evil, creator god.

Gnostic Contribution to Second-Half-of-Life Spirituality

Having considered some of the more distinctive views of the Gnostics, we need to examine teachings beneficial to spirituality. In this regard, we explore eight interconnected categories, examining them synchronously rather than individually or sequentially:

1. An intuitive rationality, open to newness
2. An open canon
3. An androgynist rather than a dualist or misogynist orientation
4. A passion for God
5. A dialogical relationality or mode of communication
6. An individualist perspective, yet equally communitarian
7. A capacity for mystery, expressed creatively through mythology
8. A "moderate" dualism

Second-half-of-life practitioners embrace paradox, mystery, doubt, and uncertainty. The second half of life is transformative, producing people who are less critical, less dogmatic, and less racist and sexist. While Gnostic groups follow distinct beliefs and behavioral codes, across the movement there is less focus on these issues. For Gnostics, *gnosis* is experienced truth, related to insight and wisdom and less about factual or intellectual knowledge. Like modern scientists, Gnostics remain open to ongoing insight and revelation, and unlike most orthodox believers, they are less concerned with absolutes or unchanging truths. Revelation is fluid and ongoing, and their scriptures can be modified or expanded, valued so long as their advice is practical and relevant, yet subject to change or modification. Building on common ideas, their theology is progressive in nature. Though Gnostics have recognized scriptures, their canon is more open than closed, its purpose temporary rather than ultimate.

Gnostics (like Christians in general) consider human beings to be composed of flesh, soul, and spirit. The origin of these elements, like their makeup, is twofold: mundane (that is, earthly and material) and extra-mundane (spiritual and supernatural). For Gnostics, not only the body but also the soul is a product of cosmic powers, inferior yet divine beings that govern the planetary bodies and shape the human body in the image of the divine or Archetypal Man. In addition, they also animate it with their own psychical forces (these are the appetites and passions within human beings, each of which stems from and corresponds to one of the cosmic forces or planetary spheres; together, these natural drives constitute a human being's "psyche" or soul). Through their bodies and souls, humans are subject to universal Fate, the means by which the planetary gods (the *archons*) collectively rule the world. In this respect, each individual is a prisoner of cosmic fate, a rule that oversees cosmic or natural law. Enclosed in the human soul is the spirit or *pneuma* (sometimes called the "spark"), a portion of the divine substance trapped in the material realm. As the world (the macrocosm) is enclosed in the seven planetary spheres, seats of the *archons* or "rulers of this world," so the spirit (the human microcosm) is enclosed in the seven soul-vestments (seven vices or passions of the soul) originating from them.

The spirit, in its unredeemed state, thus immersed in soul and flesh, is unconscious (forgetful and unaware) of its divine origin and true nature; in brief, it is "ignorant." This, for Gnostics and Valentinian Christians, is the meaning of sin. If sin is "ignorance," then salvation, understood as the entrapped spirit's awakening and liberation, is "knowledge," akin to rebirth.

"But knowledge of what," we ask? The clearest direct answer now available comes from the *Gospel of Truth*, a text from Nag Hammadi. This text, believed to be a sermon by Valentinus, is the most complete extant statement of Valentinian spirituality. The sermon is an invitation to every Christian to experience the hope, joy, and security of knowing God the Father through Jesus Christ. The sermon defines sin—what separates us from God—as ignorance. Salvation—our return to God—is discovering the Father through the power of the Savior, Jesus Christ.[5]

According to this text, everything that exists is in God the Father, and all real beings are emanations from God. For all beings, joy and blessedness are to know and to be known by the Father. Jesus makes possible the *gnosis* that removes ignorance and brings joy. For Valentinus—and possibly for some Gnostics as well—the journey back to God commences with rituals such as worship and observance of the Eucharist, but these groups also add mystical rites such as the "bridal chamber," a ceremony

---

5. For Gnostics, the knowledge needed for salvation is secret, esoteric knowledge available only to those who are chosen. The knowledge needed is ultimately self-knowledge, knowledge of who one truly is, of where one comes from, and of how one can return. For Christian Gnostics, true knowledge (*gnosis*) cannot be acquired by natural means, but only from a divine emissary, namely, Christ, who comes from the divine realm to impart this knowledge to those who possess the divine sprit or spark.

whereby participants become consecrated ritually in a "spiritual marriage" in anticipation of the final union with the Pleroma (the fullness of God) at the end of time.

For Valentinians and other early sectarian Christians, heavenly perfection is envisioned symbolically in terms of the sacred union between a man and a woman.[6] Since the world and the fall of the spirit originates through the disruption of this original unity, the return of the spirit to its ideal prototype is the decisive event at the end of time. The Valentinian rite of the bridal chamber symbolizes the Pleroma ideal of the eventual unity of separated elements. According to Gnostic teaching, the Gnostics or "pneumatics" (those spiritual persons who possess the perfect knowledge of God and undergo the proper rituals) are said to become "brides of the angels," and their entrance into the world beyond is likened to a wedding feast, when the saved enter the bridal chamber within the Pleroma and attain to a vision of the Father, at which time they become spiritual *aeons*, united with Infinite Reality.

Having introduced intriguing notions such as "brides of angels" and "pneumatic" individuals, further explanation is required. According to Gnostics, elements in the physical realm such as matter, soul, and spirit exist proportionately in various beings and things. These qualities make living beings such as angels and humans more or less spiritual (hence closer to deities and other higher beings), or more or less material (and closer to animals and other lower beings). For Valentinians, just as the three elements of matter, soul, and spirit are the building blocks of the cosmos, so, too, they are present in differing amounts and proportions in human beings. On this basis, humans can be divided into three categories, based on which element predominates in them: the "spiritual" (the pneumatics), the "psychic," (the animates) and the "sarkic" (the fleshly, earthly, or material humans).

The highest element, spirit, predominates in spiritual people. Depending on the group or sect, these are the Valentinians, Gnostics, or Christians, who possess *gnosis* of God and of themselves. Obviously, these people will be saved and enter the Pleroma. The lowest element, matter, predominates in material people. These are non-Christians or

---

6. A similar rite, called celestial marriage (also called temple marriage or The Principle), is practiced by branches of the Mormon Church. While this ceremony takes place on earth, it is celestial in origin and nature, destined to last beyond the grave and into eternity. For Mormon traditionalists, such marriage is a requirement for entrance into the highest level of heaven.

non-Gnostics, including pagans, Jews, and anyone who does not believe in Jesus or worship Christ. Like the material element to which they are oriented, these people will perish at the end of the world. Animate people (who possess the soul element) have the freedom to turn toward God, live righteous lives, and receive salvation, or to turn away from God, live sinful lives, and perish with the material people. The sources disagree on the destiny that awaits animate people.

According to Irenaeus, the Valentinians teach that the three categories are three different kinds of human beings, descended or derived from the three sons of Adam and Eve. Cain is the father of the material people, Abel the father of the animate people, and Seth the father of the spiritual people. As Irenaeus presents it, the spiritual people will be saved no matter what, and the material people will be destroyed no matter what. The only people whose destiny is uncertain are the animate people. They can choose to live righteous lives and gain limited salvation, or they can live sinful lives and be condemned. Based on research, many modern scholars disagree with Irenaeus's depiction, finding in the sources that Valentinians may not have been so deterministic. Valentinus seem to have taught that every person consists of all three elements, and that it is up to each individual to choose how to live and which to follow. Over time, these choices determine which element predominates and, thus, whether a person is spiritual, animate, or material.

Gnostics in general, together with some Valentinians and other early Christian groups, believe that humans have their origin in the spiritual world of the highest God. If so, this means that our True Self is not our body or ego and possibly not even our soul, for these substances are said to come from the lower universe and hence are not eternal. Our True Self is our spirit (Gnostics might call this our "mind" or "intellect"), which originates in the spiritual realm and is destined to return there. In this respect, knowledge of the *gnosis* that Gnostics offer is knowledge of one's True Self.

One group of Nag Hammadi writings that focuses on the issue of self-knowledge and self-realization grants unique authority to the apostle Thomas (Didymus Judas Thomas, also known as Jude, possible the namesake of the epistle thus named in the New Testament), credited in Christian tradition with bringing Christianity to Mesopotamia and India. The centerpiece of this group of writing is the famous *Gospel of Thomas*. This collection of traditional sayings, prophecies, proverbs, and parables of Jesus, composed as early as the second half of the first century, is attributed to Judas "the Twin" (Didymus means "twin" in Greek), who was honored by Syrian Christians as the apostle and twin brother of Jesus (a view rejected by modern scholarship).[7]

According to the *Gospel of Thomas*, the origin of the soul is divine, and, having fallen from perfection into the body and the material world, the soul's ability to return to its origin is through reunion with its True Self: "When you come to know yourselves, then you will be known" (Logion 3). Basic to *Thomas* is the idea that our bodies are not who we are. Our true selves are completely spiritual, not material, and the destiny of the Self is to return to the spiritual realm of light, from when it came. For example, in the *Gospel of Thomas* Jesus says, "For where the beginning is, there will the end be" (Logion 18), or "Blessed are the solitary and elect, for you will find the Kingdom. For you are from it, and to it you will return" (Logion 49). In *Thomas*, the terms "single" and "solitary" refer to a person who overcomes the divisions and multiplicity of life in this world and has become unified. In response to a question from the disciples, Jesus explains that salvation comes from combining opposites: "When you make the two one and when you make the inside like the outside and the outside like the inside, and the above like the below, and when you make the male and the female one and the same... and a likeness in place of a likeness, then you will enter the Kingdom" (Logion 22).

The idea here seems to be that before human beings are saved, they don't really know their true selves, and for this reason, they are divided. Humans focus on the temporal self, the one that lives in this world, having a family and perhaps a job, and this self believes that such things constitute life. However, this is the perspective of the false self. There is another self that does not belong to this world, but is spirit and light. When people achieve *gnosis*, the two selves become one.

Another possibility regarding these texts from *Thomas* is that when believers come to know their True Self, they also come to know Jesus, and the difference between the self and Jesus begins to fade. This idea may be symbolized by the name of the supposed author of the gospel, Didymus Judas Thomas. Both the named Didymus (Greek) and Thomas (Aramaic) could mean "double" or "twin" in their respective languages. Thus, the

---

7. In addition to the *Gospel of Thomas*, the Thomas corpus also includes the *Book of Thomas the Contender*, a writing also found at Nag Hammadi. A third volume, the apocryphal third-century *Acts of Thomas*, is well known because it is the first account of the familiar legend that the apostle Thomas becomes a missionary and spreads the gospel of Christ to India.

twinship of Thomas and Jesus becomes a metaphor for the relationship between the believer's soul and Jesus. As we note in *Thomas*, *gnosis* of self is *gnosis* of God; our True Self is divine, just as Jesus is divine. When we come to know ourselves as true light, we recognize our essential unity with Jesus, for like Thomas and Jesus, our true selves and Jesus are twins.

Having examined the meaning of the term "pneumatics," we need to consider the Gnostic and Valentinian concept of the wedding feast common to the saved, when pneumatics become "brides of the angels." Explaining this concept clarifies gender roles in Gnostic spirituality. When scholars first read the texts from Nag Hammadi in the 1960s and 1970s, they were astonished to find how regularly these books depict God and other divine beings as female. This strong female element suggests that the Gnostics have an inclusive, less patriarchal notion of the divine than do orthodox Jews and Christians, and possibly a more egalitarian practice in communal life. Since the 1970s, however, scholars have become more guarded about the roles of women in Gnostic circles.

In her groundbreaking book, *The Gnostic Gospels*, the scholar of early Christianity Elaine Pagels argues that the Gnostic writings challenge the emerging patriarchal theology of the Christian church. She suggests that, because Gnostics worship a God who is both Father and Mother, and because their myth features primal female deities, Gnostic communities are more open to female leadership than other groups. Pagels finds support for her argument in the writings of ancient Gnostic detractors, who accuse the Gnostics of allowing women to lead men, and of mixing women and men too easily. Of course, early Christian leaders such as Paul allow and even encourage such egalitarianism (see, for example, Gal. 3:28; 1 Cor. 11:11; and Phil. 4:2–3), but this does not necessarily lead to greater roles in the emerging Catholic Church. Before the year 200, women apparently have a significant voice and role in orthodox Christian circles, functioning as prophets, teachers, evangelists, healers, and possibly as priests and even bishops. However, there is no evidence that this continues after 200. By this time the majority of Christian churches oppose the move toward equality, endorsing as canonical 1 Timothy, a letter attributed to Paul but that contradicts the pro-feminist element in his undisputed letters, declaring that women should have no authority over men (2:12). Orthodox Christians also accept as Pauline the letters to the Colossians and to the Ephesians, which require women to be subject in all things to their husbands (Eph. 5:14; Col. 3:18). Such a view appears also in the apparent interpolation in Corinthians 14:34–36.

Gnostic Spirituality

What about Valentinian Christians and Gnostics? Are they more egalitarian in the second and third centuries than are orthodox Christians? Surely they are, but the evidence is not as clear as once thought. This ambivalence reflects Gnostic theology more than sociological practice. One of the core convictions of the Gnostics is that the ultimate God, called the Invisible Spirit, is unknowable and hence, beyond any human conception. This might make us think that God transcends any concept of gender. However, the Invisible Spirit is also called a Virgin Spirit. Of course, "virgin" can be either male or female, but the concept of virginity implies gender or sexuality. Apparently, the Gnostics cannot escape thinking that a living being must have gendered qualities.

In the Gnostic myth, things become more complex with the emanation of the first *aeon* from the Invisible Spirit, called *Pronoia* (Forethought) or simply Barbelo, who is described both in female terms (she is the universal "womb") but also in male terms (she is called "thrice male," meaning, "supremely" or "very" male). The *Apocryphon of John* describes the Barbelo as the "mother-father" and therefore as androgynous. In our conception, androgynous implies equal male and female qualities, but this is not necessarily what it means for Gnostics, who are influenced by a peculiar literary understanding of the creation of humanity in the first two chapters of Genesis.

When early Christians and Gnostics read Genesis, they read it literally, meaning that they find in Genesis, not two different accounts of the creation of human beings, but two consecutive accounts of their creation. When read in this manner, Adam (humanity) is created twice. In chapter 1, God makes human beings according to God's image: "male and female he created them" (1:27). In the original Hebrew text, it is not clear whether God makes multiple human beings who are either male or female, or whether God makes a single androgynous human being. In chapter 2, creation seems to start over again, and that is probably how most ancient people read these stories—as one continuous account. Hence, God makes the male Adam and places him in a garden, for God can find no suitable partner for Adam from among the animals. Thus, God constructs a female mate for Adam from Adam's rib. If in Genesis 1 God creates an androgynous human being, who is both male and female, then in chapter 2 God separates the human being into male and female. God does so by removing the female (the rib) from the male. This process does not emphasize equality, however, for the female appears to be less than the male. This explains why most ancient people do not think of male and female as equal partners, for the Genesis account presents the female as a derivative aspect of the male, and therefore as not fully male. Predictably, this inequality continues to this day among traditionalist Christians.

Given this context for understanding gender in biblical and early Christian times, it makes the use of the feminine in the Gnostic myth even more astounding. At some point Barbelo conceives the *Autogenes* (the "Self-Originate" or Christ), prompted by the gaze of the Invisible Spirit. The Spirit's gaze—an act suggestive of sexual intercourse—generates in the Barbelo a luminous spark, which begets the *Autogenes*, who is also called the "anointed one" or the Christ. Thus, the Christ comes into being in a manner different from the other *aeons*. It appears that the Gnostics think of the Invisible Spirit, the Barbelo, and the Christ as something like a nuclear family—as father, mother, and son. This triad lies at the heart of the Gnostic idea of God.

The Barbelo, the first aeon that comes forth from the Invisible Spirit, is the highest level of God that can possibly be known. It represents the Invisible Spirit's thought about itself, namely, God's first thought. If the Invisible Spirit were all there is to know, humans could never know God. The Gnostics seem to believe that human beings, like God's thoughts, ultimately come from the Forethought (the Barbelo) and will return to Forethought. In this life, human beings may experience fleeting moments in which they gain *gnosis* of Forethought.

When the Gnostics think of God as a collection of *aeons* or eternal beings, they call God "Pleroma," that is, the totality of spiritual reality. In the Pleroma, the divine emanations of God, called *aeons*, exist in pairs. Thus, the Gnostics think of the Pleroma as stable and serene because each *aeon* has another *aeon* that completes it. They compare this pairing of *aeons* to the complementary nature of male and female in humanity.

As the appearance of the Barbelo results in the emanation of *aeons*, each *aeon* existing in a male-female pair, so, too, the begetting of the *Autogenes* or Christ results in the emanation of more *aeons*. The material world is said to have come into being when Wisdom (Sophia), the female aspect of the lowest *aeon*, desires to think her own thought, apart from the will of the Invisible Spirit, and apart from the consent of her male consort. Hence, the divine being she produces, Ialdabaoth, is imperfect and tyrannical. Ialdabaoth, in turn, creates a multitude of *archons*, evil angelic beings, and then the universe from formless matter, which exist apart from the Pleroma and hence are an error of creation, a poor copy of the spiritual world.

Given human entrapment by Ialdabaoth in the prison-house of a material universe, how can humans be saved, that is, be brought back into the Pleroma and into harmony with God? Wisdom (Sophia), clearly a feminine figure for Gnostics, works tirelessly with the Barbelo to help humanity. It is Sophia who enlightens human beings about their true origin in the Pleroma and teaches them saving knowledge (*gnosis*).

Gnostics are famous not only for having female divinities but also for giving human females important roles. For example, the biblical Eve is given a large role in their salvation myth, and Gnostics include a new biblical character, Norea, sister of Seth, who defies male beings like Noah as well as evil rulers. In contrast to other Gnostic texts, the *Hypostasis of the Archons* regards Gnostics as descendants of Norea, rather than of her brother Seth.

One of the most remarkable Gnostic texts from Nag Hammadi is *Thunder, Perfect Mind* (or Intellect). It consists entirely of a revelation monologue spoken by a female divine revealer. In one passage, she describes herself in paradoxes, such as "I am the first and the last"; "I am the whore and the holy one"; "I am the bride and the bridegroom, and it is my husband who begot me." What do such paradoxes mean for ancient Gnostics? One persuasive hypothesis is that these statements form a riddle that reveals the identity of the speaker. What female is first and last and has a husband who gives birth to her? Quite possibly, the female revealer is the biblical Eve, here seen as the embodiment of the female divine, whether Sophia or the Barbelo.

This revelation monologue resembles at least two other personifications of the feminine mystique—the Jewish figure of wisdom in Proverbs 7 and 8 and a famous pagan text called *Isis Aretology*, a discourse on virtue by the Egyptian goddess Isis, whose devotees spread widely across the ancient Mediterranean world. In these texts, wisdom is powerful—and feminine. In the *Thunder*, Gnostics seem to be saying, "If you are looking for the true Wisdom of God, you will find her in Gnostic spirituality."

The *Gospel of Thomas*, while lacking many of the distinctive teachings and practices common to the Gnostic literature, uses its unique teaching to show how Jesus can lead people to spiritual *gnosis*. As we learned earlier, *The Gospel of Thomas* shares with the Gnostics the belief that salvation comes through *gnosis*, the special knowledge of God that Jesus brings. For *Thomas*, *gnosis* is knowledge of our true selves. The shortest saying in *Thomas*, "Be passers-by" (Logion 42), sums up what this gospel thinks about how humans should live in this world. Humans don't belong in this world of flesh and darkness. Rather, they belong to the Pleroma, the realm of spirit and light.

The final saying in the *Gospel of Thomas* is one of the most perplexing in all Gnostic-influenced literature: "Simon Peter said to [the other disciples], 'Let Mary leave us, for women are not worthy of Life.' Jesus said, 'I myself shall lead her, in order to make her male, so that she too may become a living spirit resembling you males. For every woman who will make herself male will enter the Kingdom of Heaven'" (Logion 114). While the meaning of this passage is much debated, it seems to be saying that for human beings to be saved, they must gain a state in which female is not separated from male. While this sounds misogynist, it may not be. In Valentinian and Gnostic teaching about salvation—including rites such as baptism, the Eucharist, and the bridal chamber, and what we find in the *Gospel of Thomas*—Peter and Mary are symbolic of male and female human elements. To be saved, both Peter and Mary must recover a state in which female is not separated from male. The two must become one, fully integrated and beyond division of any kind. That is the reality of the Pleroma (the kingdom of heaven).

The Mary mentioned in Thomas is of course, Mary Magdalene, a devoted follower of Jesus but never numbered in the New Testament Gospels among the twelve apostles. Mary appears frequently in many Valentinian and Gnostic-influenced texts. For example, the *Gospel of Philip*, an apocryphal gospel found, like *Thomas*, at Nag Hammadi, states that "There were three who always walked with the Lord: Mary, his mother and his sister and Magdalene, the one who was called his companion." In another passage, the apostles wonder why Jesus loves Mary more than he does them: "[But Christ loved] her more than [all] he disciples [and used to] kiss her [often] on her [mouth]." There is also an ancient Christian text called the *Gospel of Mary*, in which Jesus gives Mary Magdalene a special revelation. The secret teaching that Jesus reveals to Mary includes information concerning how the human soul, in its ascent through the natural realm, encounters seven hostile powers, including Darkness, Desire, and Ignorance. These powers try to prevent the soul from ascending to its true home, but when the knowledgeable soul tells them about its true nature, it can pass them by.

While the *gnosis* disclosed by Gnostics to their followers is a "knowledge of God," that is, of God as found in the Gnostic myth, on the practical side it is more particularly "knowledge of the way," namely, of the soul's way out of the world. The journey involves the sacramental and magical preparations for its future ascent, plus knowledge of the passwords that enable passage through each material (planetary) sphere. Equipped with this *gnosis*, the soul after death travels upward, leaving behind at each sphere the psychical "vestment" added to it. Thus the spirit, stripped of all foreign accretion, reaches the God beyond the world and becomes reunited with the divine substance. On the scale of the total divine drama, this process is part of the restoration of the Pleroma's own wholeness, which in pre-cosmic times is impaired by the loss of portions of the divine substance. Gnostic salvation, then, represents the restoration of balance and cosmic wholeness.

In the *Gospel of Mary*, Peter asks Mary to reveal any secret teachings that Jesus gives her that he and the other disciples do not know. When Mary tells her revelation, Andrew and Peter charge that she is lying, because these teachings are strange, and they are sure that Jesus would not have revealed such things to a woman in private. However, the apostle Levi comes to Mary's defense. He accuses Peter of being prone to anger and agrees that Jesus did love Mary more than he loved the male disciples. With other Gnostic gospels, the *Gospel of Mary* condemns emerging power structure in Christianity that restricts authority to male priests. Mary Magdalene, the first person to see the empty tomb, according to the canonical Gospels of Matthew and John, becomes a rallying point for this protest, just as Peter, the first person to see the risen Jesus (according to Paul in 1 Cor. 15:5), becomes a symbol for the emerging church structure of bishops and priests. In the end, of course, Peter wins this contest with Mary.

The *Gospel of Mary* reveals a division among early Christians over the role of women in the church, and over the nature of religious authority in general. In this gospel, Peter represents the orthodox Christian tradition, with its ensuing hierarchical male leadership, and Mary becomes a symbol, not of female leadership specifically, which this gospel does not oppose, nor of females generally, but rather a symbol for the female in relationship to God. The unique twist here, however, is that all human beings are female in their relationship to Christ, God, and to their higher angelic selves.[8] In Valentinian teaching, humans are spiritually female,

---

8. When speaking of "angel" in a Greek context, readers must bear in mind that in Greek, "angel" (i.e. messenger) has a masculine gender. Hence all pneumatic humans must attain again to angelic and indirectly, to masculine status in order to become part of the Pleroma and attain unity with God, that is, union with the original heavenly image of God (Forethought or the Barbelo), commonly depicted as female.

and they exist in a kind of alienation from their higher masculine selves, the angels. Humans are like the divine *aeon* pairs, only currently, like Sophia, all are female *aeons* separated from their male consorts.

This, then, is the meaning of the cryptic statement in Logion 114 of the *Gospel of Thomas*, when Jesus tells Mary Magdalene, "for every woman who will make herself male will enter the Kingdom of Heaven." And this is the meaning of Levi's unusual reply to Peter in the Gospel of Mary, "But if the Savior made [Mary] worthy, who are you indeed to reject her? Surely the Savior knows her very well. This is why he loved her more than us. Rather, let us be ashamed and put on the Perfect Man."[9] This passage presents Jesus and Mary as having a special relationship, but not one that symbolizes male and female divine principles. Rather, it symbolizes the relationship between our female human selves and our angelic male selves. Who, then, is Mary? We are all Mary Magdalene; all of us are called to have a special relationship with our higher angelic self, represented by Jesus. The name, Mary, serves as a symbol for the female in relationship to God. We are all female in our relationship to the Lord and to our higher angelic selves. For the author and these communities, in this knowledge lies our salvation.

In Gnosticism, all pneumatic humans must regain angelic status in order to become part of the Pleroma and attain unity with God, that is, union with the original heavenly image of God (Forethought or the Barbelo), often depicted as female. However, before this final union, the spirits or sparks of deceased pneumatic believers must ascend to reunion with Mother Sophia, awaiting with her the consummation of the world. According to Valentinian teaching, Sophia's own final salvation takes place when all the pneumatic elements in the world are saved by knowledge and perfected. Then the spirits, stripped of their souls, with their Mother enter the Pleroma, now transformed into the bridal chamber in which takes place the marriage of Sophia with Jesus and that of the spirits with their bridegrooms, the angels around Jesus. With this, the Pleroma is restored, the original breach finally repaired, and the material world finally ceases to exist.

---

9. In his commentary on the *Gospel of Thomas*, Jean-Yves Leloup suggests that the phrase "put on the Perfect Man" from Levi's response to Peter's rebuke of Mary in the *Gospel of Mary* be translated "become fully human," noting that the original Greek uses the term *Anthropos* (fully realized human being) rather than the more pedestrian "*Andros*," meaning male.

Gnostics and Valentinian Christians value the original unity between male and female, making essential deity equally male and female. There is almost an anti-hierarchicalism here, not yet equality between the sexes—something we have yet to achieve broadly in religion and society today—but these creative, intuitive individuals are well ahead of the curve, planting seeds that would sprout millennia later.

While Gnostics take evil seriously, they do not view it as co-equal or co-eternal with good. While dualists—dividing reality into opposing pairs such as the soul versus the body, good versus evil, light versus darkness, the Pleroma versus the material universe, even Gnostics versus non-Gnostics—Gnostics are not consistently dualist, since they posit one fundamental principle as the source of all reality, and one common destiny for all authentic spirituality. Unfortunately, the price paid for such unity is the dismissal of the body and all material things as temporal, shallow, and ultimately illusory. To this, the Judeo-Christian doctrine of creation replies with a resounding, Not So! The world, and all things material, including the body, are good, real, and of inherent value and worth. All human beings, creatures made in God's image, exist by the will of the loving and benevolent Creator of all reality, who pronounces all things "GOOD!" Evil is real—but only, as the Christian theologian Augustine argues, as a privation or absence of good. The human task—if we are up to the challenge—is to renounce evil and affirm the eternal goodness across the entire created realm.

In her perceptive book, *The Gnostic Dialogue*, Gnostic and New Testament scholar Pheme Perkins notes a feature common to the Gnostic-influenced writings, that Gnostics thrive on dialogue. Their very existence demands appropriating the insights of other traditions, and many of their writings adopt the dialogue as part of their literary form. Gnostic revelation dialogues, unlike most canonical Jewish and Christian revelations, prefer symbolism, paradox, and cryptic statements to set doctrines, philosophical posturing, or instructional discourses. Gnostic literature, like poetry, is meant to spark the imagination, its authors valuing creative response over uniformity or conformity. Gnostics are as diverse in their views as are early Christians, only they keep growing and thinking, while orthodox Christians prefer clarity, stasis, and finality.

Among the many modern admirers of Gnosticism—not for its symbols of alienation, revolt, or deficiency, but for its unifying transcendence, paradox, and depth of imagery—is the Swiss psychiatrist Carl Jung. Jung's particular interest in Gnosticism fits into his larger attempt to understand why traditional religious symbolism does not seem to meet the spiritual needs of modern people, and yet why his psychiatric patients continue calling up religious symbols and images to focus psychic growth and distress. Jung believes Gnostics have the ability to bring forth symbols crucial to psychic growth because they are in close touch with the instinctual dynamics of the unconscious. He is probably right in thinking that the Gnostic refusal to accept salvation based simply on faith but rather on self-awareness forces them to explore dimensions of the psyche often ignored by others.

However, unlike ancient Gnostics, modern people cannot accept a stance toward self and the world that rejects the created material order and its associated passions, the instinctual foundations of creativity itself. Jung believes one must rebel against constraining religious symbolism, insist upon human worth, and defend the right to search for oneself the meaning of religious symbolism.

Given what we humans have learned from history and through nature, we cannot expect God to transform the world from without; humanity must be transformed from within. As such, Jung argues that individual psychic transformation requires a shift in the psychic center from ego to Self. He notes that the Gnostic language about the unknown God (the Father) requires the necessary expansion of consciousness. The psychic symbols for this transcendental structure of consciousness take the form of what Jung calls "quaternity," the genuine wholeness of opposites: God *and* humanity, good *and* evil, male *and* female, consciousness *and* unconsciousness, the visible self *and* the shadow self, the material *and* the spiritual, first-half-of-life spirituality *and* second-half-of-life spirituality. This "coincidence of opposites" brings perceived polarities into a wholeness that can be effective not only in the religious or psychological realms, but also on the psychic level of cultures as a whole. In the past—whether in Gnosticism or orthodox Christianity—transcendence speaks from beyond, guaranteeing an order greater than humanity's psychic or intellectual apprehension of it. Today, transcendence speaks from within.

Questions for Discussion and Reflection

In addition to the questions listed at the end of the preface, answer the following questions, writing your answers in a journal. If you are in a group study, be prepared to share your answers with those in the group.

1. Assess the meaning of the author's comment that "the Gnostic mythological mindset can be instructive in revealing the true nature of Christianity."
2. In creating their mythology, why are Gnostics so reliant on accounts from the biblical book of Genesis?
3. In your estimation, are Valentinians Gnostics or simply heterodox Christians?
4. In your estimation, should Christians read the *Gospel of Thomas* as authoritative? Why is it not included with the four canonical Gospels?
5. Briefly explain your understanding of Gnostic views on sin and salvation.
6. In your estimation, what is the central message or idea underlying the Gnostic use of the word *gnosis*?
7. In your estimation, what is the most valuable contribution Gnostics provide to second-half-of-life spirituality?
8. Explain your understanding of the Gnostic concept that ultimate salvation involves the union of humans with angels.
9. What is the role of the biblical Eve in the Gnostic text *Thunder, Perfect Mind*?
10. In your estimation, why is Mary Magdalene featured so prominently in Gnostic and Gnostic-inspired literature?

5

Ancient Wisdom Spirituality

FROM THE EARLIEST DAYS of Christianity, the attraction and interaction of Christian theologians with pagan philosophy is pervasive. On the one hand, Gentile Christian theologians recognize their deep indebtedness to their Jewish heritage, with its historical and this-worldly emphasis. On the other hand, they are profoundly attracted to what we might call a higher spirituality—the soul's desire for higher things—one found in the Hellenistic philosophical tradition, with its allegorical and vertical concerns.

However, if one has nothing but pure allegory and a vertical spirituality, one is a Gnostic, concerned with rejecting material things and becoming entirely spiritual. Such a stance implies rejection of the Jewish roots of Christianity. Thus, early intellectual Christians attempt to hold together both dimensions—the horizontal and the vertical—but to do so requires a non-literal or allegorical reading of scripture.

When we explore the roots of ancient Gentile Christian spirituality, we turn to philosophy, for ancient philosophy is a form of spirituality, by nature religious rather than anti-religious. While ancient philosophers are skeptical of religious mythology, they are very much interested in the deeper truths believed to underlie mythology. Hence, pagan philosophers criticize Christianity, not for its religious nature, but because they believe they offer a better or higher spirituality. They blame Christians for being too Jewish, meaning overly materialistic, too invested in natural and earthly pursuits.

In antiquity, educated Christians view philosophy as essential to a good education, much as we view the study of science today. Hence, Christian scholars and theologians are attracted to philosophy, and cannot avoid interacting with it. The central themes of ancient philosophy are wisdom and happiness, stemming from the overarching philosophical question, "what is happiness?" To be clear, the Greek word we translate as "happiness" does not mean joy or pleasure, as we think today. Rather, happiness means something like "true success or true fulfillment in life," closer to what today we call "the meaning of life." So the question, "what is happiness?" can't be answered by assuming that happiness is what makes us feel good, or even what makes us feel healthy, because such qualities are seen as means to an end, rather than ends in themselves. If feeling good or being healthy are the goals of life, it might be better not to be born at all, for good feelings or good health are at best temporary—and in the end, ephemeral.

While there are certainly hedonists in ancient times, such philosophies are not attractive to ancient Christians. Rather, learned Christians pursue the most widely accepted view of happiness among ancient philosophers, shared by Stoics, Platonist, and Aristotelians, namely, that happiness consists in a life of wisdom. In their estimation, wisdom is valuable for its own sake. Wisdom is the goal of all other values in life, whether money, power, or health; for ancient philosophers, pagan and Christian alike, all cultural values are secondary to wisdom.

To become a person of wisdom requires both knowledge and understanding. The majority of ancient Christians, particularly those rooted in early Christian orthodoxy, give biblical answers to philosophical questions. To the question, "What is happiness?" such Christians answer, "everlasting life," which in the Bible is not confined to life after death, but rather something realized in the present as well as in the afterlife. According to the Gospel of John, "everlasting life" is to know God and Jesus Christ (17:3).

Thus, for early Christian philosophers, happiness is the goal of life, and happiness consists of a certain kind of wisdom, viewed as "the wisdom of God in Jesus Christ." To possess this wisdom is to possess everlasting life, and in order to possess happiness, Jesus Christ is the wisdom Christians seek. In 1 Corinthians, Paul calls Jesus "the power of God and the wisdom of God" (1:24). Early Christians note that the Old Testament book of Proverbs speaks of wisdom as being in the beginning with God (8:22–31), and they find the same teaching in the Gospel of John, where Jesus is called the Word with God in the beginning (1:1–5). Based on such correlation, early Christians naturally associate Jesus with God's eternal wisdom. For them, to know Christ is to know the wisdom of God, and to have happiness is to know Jesus Christ, the wisdom and power of God.

In this chapter we examine five philosophical movements in the Greek world, all influenced by traditions stemming from Plato and Aristotle, who live in the fifth and fourth centuries BCE. Four of these—Platonism, Stoicism, Hermeticism, and Neoplatonism—are pagan or secular in nature, and the other—the exegetical contributions of Philo—represents a Hellenized form of Judaism. All influence Christian thinkers, contributing to the development of early Christian orthodoxy.

Platonism

Human beings are fascinated with the universe, including their place in the order of things. Over time, they devise models of reality to help explain their experience and to guide their conduct. The ancient Greek philosophers are deeply interested in this endeavor, developing cosmological models to explain their understanding of reality. In the fifth century BCE, two pre-Socratics, Parmenides and Heraclitus, set the stage for later thinkers, arriving at diametrical conclusions about the universe. Parmenides, a monist, argues for the unity, permanence, and eternity of reality, declaring that all things in the universe are made of one thing, which he calls Being. A rationalist, he arrives at his model of the universe through reason, rather than through the senses, which he distrusts. Heraclitus, an empiricist, focuses on change and diversity in the universe. His observations lead him to conclude that there is no permanence, for everything changes. As he puts it, "no one steps into the same river twice." Unlike Parmenides, whose focus is on Being, Heraclitus is concerned with Becoming.

Two successors, Plato (427–347 BCE) and Aristotle (384–322), champion their concerns, developing comprehensive views of reality. Plato's model, the first grand synthesis, explains permanence and change dualistically. Plato posits two realms to reality, the Physical World, consisting of "particulars" (temporary things such as trees, horses, chairs, and triangles), which are always in flux, and the Ideal World, consisting of "universals" (ideals, essences, or "forms" such as treeness, horseness, chairness, and triangularity), which are eternal and unchanging. Concerned with permanence (Being), Plato views objects in the Physical World as copies of forms in the Ideal World.

In Plato's Ideal World, forms are related hierarchically, meaning there are lesser forms (such as treeness and triangularity), intermediate forms (such as beauty and justice), and a supreme form or highest ideal, which Plato calls The Good. Using a mathematical model for reality, Plato ingeniously combines the views of Parmenides (Being) and Heraclitus (Becoming), creating a model that demonstrated the superiority of permanence over change.

For Plato, there are two kinds of being, nonmaterial and material. Nonmaterial reality, consisting of forms or essences in the Ideal World, he calls "intelligible being," and he contrasts these with "sensible being." Both are perceptible, although not in the same manner. Some things are perceived by the senses, and some perceived only by the intellect. Intelligible things are absolutes or unchanging things, ranging from such things as mathematical truths to principles of virtue and ethics. They are perceptible only by the intellect. Sensible things, however, being material, are perceptible only through the senses. To visualize a thing perceived by the intellect, imagine yourself in math class, learning about the Pythagorean theorem. Initially you don't understand it, until finally you say, "Aha, now I get it, now I see it!" What you are seeing Plato calls "intellectual vision," seeing not with the bodily eye but with the intellect. What you are seeing, we might say, is an eternal nonmaterial truth, something called spiritual or divine truth. Such truths are not physical, yet physical things can be understood as made in the image of the intelligible form, such as a horse made in the image of "horseness," or a chair in the image of "chairness." If all horses or chairs were to disappear from earth, their ideal prototypes would still exist, for all such "forms" or "ideas" remain eternally in the Ideal World.

As Plato understands them, the intelligible forms are not simply abstraction. Rather, they are more real than the sensible images we see with our physical eyes. Sensible things come and go—mere imitations, shadows, or reflections of their forms, which are unchanging and eternal and therefore truly real. For Plato, the eternal world is the real world, and it is nonmaterial. In this respect, Platonists give Christians a nonmaterial way of thinking of the soul and of God. For Plato, the soul (the intellect), originating in the eternal world, has intellectual vision, which is the highest form of reason. The soul is not like the body, material or sensible. Though the soul takes up no space and cannot be seen, nevertheless it is more real than the body, which is changing,

Plato, at one with his teacher Socrates, rejects the intellectual skepticism and moral relativism of his day, which is based on the teachings of Sophists, then the reigning school of Greek epistemology (way of knowing). Led by Protagoras, Gorgias, and Thrasymachus, Sophists travel across Greece, questioning everything. Believing that humans cannot know anything with certainty, they nevertheless view humans as the standard-bearers for truth, alone determining the standards for knowledge. Plato paints a rather unflattering picture of Sophists as having no genuine interest in discovering truth, trained only to win debates and make a point. Our word "sophistry," which describes the skill of using plausible but deceptive arguments, stems from Plato's critique. Protagoras appears to have limited knowledge to sense experience, which is relative and subjective because everyone's perceptions are different. Plato's harsh judgment reflects his disdain for Protagoras's famous dictum, "Man is the measure of all things." Gorgias rejects Protagoras's view that truth is relative and declares that truth does not exist. Thrasymachus takes this radical skepticism to its conclusion, teaching that truth is opinion, and that individuals should seek their own self-interests by continually asserting their own wishes. It remains for Socrates, Plato, and Aristotle to probe the deeper questions of knowledge.

For these thinkers, humans can know certain things with certainty. Socrates and Plato argue that there are absolutes (norms, ideas, and ideals), and that they are knowable—not by experience or by opinion—but through reason. Truth refers to things that are knowable, discovered through reasoning, using what we call "the Socratic method," a process of dialogue and discussion that asks careful questions and proposes reasoned answers to discover truth. In Plato's estimation, the resultant truth is said to be certain because it is based on his theory of "recollection," that is, on the principle that eternal knowledge is originally within each soul, but is lost when it goes through the "River of Forgetfulness" prior to birth. Reason, these philosophers posit, is the function of the soul, itself a divine spark trapped in a material body.

A human being, in Plato's view, is a dualism of mind and body. The mind or soul is eternal, while the body exists merely as a temporary vehicle for the soul. When a person is born, according to this view, the soul, fallen from the eternal realm, is united for a lifetime to a body. However, at death the soul flees from its physical prison as a bird from its cage. The soul's true desire is to return to its heavenly abode, but before it can return, it is judged according to its moral conduct on earth and then experiences rebirth until it arrives at ultimate release, whence it makes its final ascent to the eternal realm from which it originates.

In his *Republic*, Plato uses a famous image to describe the upward journey of the soul to the light of the sun by means of a gradual emancipation from the land of shadows in which we habitually dwell. He considers human beings to languish as prisoners in a cave, where they ignorantly suppose that reality consists of the shadows cast by the light of the fire on to the back wall of the cave. The soul has to be gradually turned around and led up into the light of the sun, to whose brilliant rays it is gradually accustomed. The sun in the allegory stands for the supreme idea, the idea of the Good, the source of reality and value to the rest of the universe.

In some of Plato's writings, such as the *Phaedrus* and the *Symposium*, the supreme form is that of beauty and not of goodness. The ascent to beauty is less a matter of being led upwards from shadows to reality, than of following the natural attraction each of us has for beauty and sublimating it, so that we pass from the love of beautiful physical objects, to love of beautiful actions, and thence to love of absolute beauty. For Plato, the contemplation of absolute beauty is the highest human ideal. It is impossible to exaggerate the influence of such language on the development of Christian thought and on the ensuing Christian mystical tradition.

Plato's approach to epistemology leads him to conclude that the possibility of knowledge, and therefore of morality, is the preexistence of the soul, from which he infers its immortality. These twin beliefs in the existence of "ideas" (universals, forms, or ideals) and the immortality of the soul are the basis of Plato's spirituality.

Aristotle, Plato's pupil, seeking unity *in* the universe, disagrees with Plato's dualistic approach, using a biological model to explain how things can change, yet remain the same. Aristotle claims there is only one reality—the physical—arguing that the form (essence) of a particular thing is within the object. Using analogies from nature such as how acorns become oak trees, he explains that what changes is the matter, but not the form of an object. Building on Heraclitus's principle of Becoming, Aristotle postulates that all things change, going from potentiality to actuality, and that all motion or change originates with a Prime Mover or a First Cause, which he calls the Unmoved Mover. For Aristotle, this first cause of motion is itself unmoved, unchanged, and unalterable. Aristotle's "God," though eternal and perfectly fulfilled, is impersonal and therefore indifferent to the world, a "do-nothing God" occupied solely in self-contemplation.

Aristotle's interest spans many disciplines (logic, biology, psychology, ethics, metaphysics, politics, and art), and while he contributes to each of these, perhaps his single most important achievement is his contribution to epistemology. By dividing human knowledge into several broad fields, he lays the foundation for much of Western philosophical and scientific study. Unlike the Sophists, Aristotle declares that knowledge consists of facts and the meaning of facts. Knowledge includes observation and theory, fact and interpretation. Everything in the universe is a combination of matter and form, potentiality and actuality. The closer things are to pure actuality, the more form they contain.

For Aristotle, at birth the mind begins as an empty tablet, but it contains the abilities of sensation and of thought. Reason, therefore, has the potential to obtain knowledge of reality, but it must do so thoroughly, probing and analyzing until it reaches its conclusions. Thus, by using reason, unaided by any higher power, humans can attain conclusions that are reliable and true.

Stoicism

The word "stoic" derives from the Greek word "*stoa*" or porch, the location in the Athenian *agora* (marketplace) where Zeno (c. 336–264) conducts his school. Unlike Plato, who in his distinction of sense and intellect is a dualist, Zeno and his followers are all materialist monists. For ancient philosophers, "materialism" means that everything is composed of one or more of the four elements of life: earth, water, air, and fire—all physical things. Light, for example, is said to be made from fire—a material thing. If God is light, which many Stoics believe, then God is a material being. At death, the human soul, conceived as a "fiery breath," returns to God, its source.

The most perfect substance, permeating all things, is perfect reason, which is, in effect, God. The Stoics tolerate worship of popular Greek gods, although later Stoics allegorize the mythological, anthropomorphic Homeric deities. Stoics view the world as God's body, and they believe that God inhabits the universe as its soul, conceived as the Logos or divine principle of rationality. Viewing God as the soul of nature, they encourage people to live in harmony with nature and one another. Unlike Platonists, Stoics believe the human soul to be corporeal, the noblest and purest form of matter. Because all humans possess reason—a spark of the divine—they are equal. After death, all souls, as all reality, return to God, as waves return to the sea.

However, it is by their ethical teaching rather than their metaphysics that the Stoics exert influence. They are the most influential moral philosophers of the ancient world. For them the end of life is happiness, and this is achieved by "life according to nature." This entails acceptance of whatever happens and a severe restriction of desire to what lies within our power, namely, our moral choice. They are non-hedonists, believing that the road to wisdom is a life of virtue free from passion. Mastery of all disordered feelings and passions—*apatheia*—becomes for Stoics the necessary means for gaining true happiness. They emphasize the natural virtues, such as kindness, patience, courage, and honesty, recognizing that the virtue lay not in knowing how to act, but rather in living according to these ideas. A life of virtue is a life of excellence. One who lives in this manner is wise. A person of wisdom is not driven by passion (by emotion), but rather by reason, by the responsible will. To live this way is to be free. For later Alexandrian philosophers like the Jewish Philo and the Christian Clement, *apatheia* becomes a necessary stage in the acquisition of contemplation, the ultimate end of life.

To modern people, passion is generally viewed as a good thing, for it is what makes us human and not machines. Ancient people do not have machines, so their greatest fear is to lose control of their behavior, and therefore to act inhumanely, like a beast. In the ancient world, a good person lives according to reason, not passion—freely, not compulsively or obsessively.

Philo of Alexandria

According to ancient records, the Jewish community in Egypt is both sizeable and influential, numbering about one million in the first century CE, a large percentage living in Alexandria, Egypt's great northern port city. For several centuries, the Alexandrian Jews enjoy a great degree of political independence. Egypt's Ptolemaic rulers (332–30 BCE) assigned two of the city's five districts to the Jews, thereby allowing them to live according to their religious laws and cultural customs. Many of these are descendants of Jewish exiles forced to flee from their Jewish homeland as their small but strategic territory midway between Egypt and Mesopotamia comes under the military control of successive empires ruled by Assyrians, Babylonians, Greeks, and Romans. Philo of Alexandria (c. 20 BCE–c. 50 CE) stands at the apex of the cultural activity of the Jewish-Alexandrian community, his literary work climaxing a long chain of Jewish-Hellenistic writings whose aim is to establish the validity and integrity of Jewish religious thought in the face of the counterclaims of the intellectually powerful Greek tradition. Educated primarily in a Hellenic environment, the son of a wealthy, aristocratic Jewish family, in his mature years Philo gains a profound interest in his Jewish heritage. His aim is to demonstrate that the truth discovered by Plato and other Greek philosophers is a development from the God-given teaching of Moses, and thus that it is the same truth revealed in scripture.

Other than heading the Jewish delegation to the Roman Emperor Caligula in 39–40, following a violent pogrom against Jews in 38, little is known about Philo, aside from his voluminous writings, cast in the form of a commentary on the Pentateuch (the first five books of the Old Testament). He could have fashioned his synthesis of Judaism and Hellenism in the form of philosophical essays dealing with the major themes of biblical thought, but chooses instead to pursue an exegetical approach, combining reverence for the text with the greatest possible freedom in interpreting it. This he achieves by the method of allegory, a method he learns from the translators of the Septuagint, the Greek version of the Hebrew scriptures, but more importantly from the Greek allegorical tradition associated with the writings of Homer. In order to justify Homer against the detractors of his theology, this exegetical tradition attempts to demythologize the Homeric gods, employing ethical allegory to explain the Homeric epics as discussions of virtue and justice. Philosophical groups such as the Stoics later view the gods as personifications of natural substances useful to human life: bread becoming Demeter, wine Dionysus, water Poseidon, and fire Hephaestus.

Choosing the dramatic form of the philosophical dialogue, a form associated with Plato and characteristic of Middle Platonism (that is, a highly Stoicized form of Platonism accompanied by Neopythagorean concerns), Philo becomes convinced that it is possible to reconcile Judaism and Hellenism. He does so following a Neopythagorean ploy of "one-upmanship," which views Plato as a mere pupil of Pythagoras. This is a game in which Philo joins eagerly, putting forward Moses as the greatest authority of all, as being the teacher of Pythagoras and indeed of all Greek philosophers and lawgivers. Armed with Greek allegorical exegesis, which seeks out the hidden meaning that lies beneath the surface of any particular text, and given the Middle Platonist and Neopythagorean penchant to read back new doctrines into the works of a venerable figure of the past, Philo is fully prepared to do battle for his ancestral tradition. Unfamiliar with the Hebrew language, he relies exclusively on the Septuagint translation, which he considers inspired.

Philo seems to have anticipated the Gnostics by depicting God as consisting of multiple powers and by teaching that a lower, second God created this universe. Philo points out that in the book of Exodus, when Moses encounters God in a burning bush, God identifies himself as "I am." Philo concludes that the names of God in the Greek Bible, such as "God" and "Lord," refer not to the ultimate God but to powers or aspects of God. The name "God" (*Elohim*), Philo says, refers to God's creative power, and "Lord" (*Adonai*) refers to his ruling power. According to Philo, "God" and "Lord" are not the only powers of God, just the most senior ones. In Genesis, God creates the world by speaking, so Philo takes the name for speech—the Logos or Word of God—to be God's chief messenger, a "second God."

In the second century, when Christian bishops and teachers criticize Gnostics and Valentinians as "heretics," rabbis (Jewish teachers) complain about Jewish sectarians and heretics who claim there are at least two powers in heaven—not one God but multiple Gods. Such references could include Philo, though a later Jewish text, the Targum Pseudo-Jonathan,[1] which retells stories from Genesis, presents God as having a lower manifestation or aspect called God's *Memra* or Word. It is the Word, according to this targum, who walks in the Garden of Eden and causes the Flood.

This idea is not particularly strange to philosophically influenced Greeks. In fact, it is similar to ideas found in other philosophical works that are indebted to Plato. Though Plato lives some 350 years before Philo, many philosophers of the early Christian centuries, including Jews and Christians as well as pagans, look to Plato for inspiration.

In one of his most popular works, the *Timaeus*, Plato describes how a god named the Demiurge or Craftsman creates the universe by making

---

1. The targums are revised versions of the books of the Bible, written in Aramaic during the early centuries of the Common Era, when most Jews in Palestine do not read or speak Hebrew. The targums do not simply translate the biblical stories; rather, they revise them as they tell them. In so doing, they show us what Jews of the time believe or think about as they read the biblical accounts. Though the Targum Pseudo-Jonathan dates in its final form to perhaps the eighth century CE, it contains traditions and concepts that go back much earlier, to the first and second centuries CE.

it as a material copy of an ideal spiritual world made up of eternal ideas. Does Plato think there is a god higher than the Demiurge? Plato is not very clear on this point, but later readers of Plato agree that there is such a higher god. For one thing, the craftsman god in Plato's *Timaeus* makes our material world as a copy of the spiritual world. If that is true, who makes the spiritual world? Platonist philosophers conclude that some higher God has done so. In another work, Plato speaks of a God he calls The One, who is beyond description and even beyond normal existence. The craftsman god does not seem much like The One, so again, most people suppose that Plato teaches the existence of an ultimate God, higher than the craftsman god, whom humans cannot know.

Philo believes something similar. Assuming that Plato and the Jewish Bible are saying the same thing, Philo believes that the ultimate God does not create the world directly. Rather, God does so through a lower aspect of deity or a mediating principle, which Philo calls Logos or Word of God. The Word creates this world, just as Plato says, as a copy of a spiritual world in the mind of God. Philo also teaches that God has other powers as well, such as Wisdom.

The Gospel of John in the New Testament implies similar ideas. It starts out saying that the Word (*Logos*) is there in the beginning. Though the Word is with God, the Word is also God. Through the Word, or Logos, all things are created. Furthermore, it is this Word of God, not the ultimate God (God the Father), that becomes human in Jesus. Thus, both Philo and the Christian Gospel of John can be said to agree that it is too simple to say that there is only one God. Rather, there is an ultimate God—the Father—who has divine powers, including Wisdom and Word, and it is the latter power who actually creates the universe in which we live.

The sources that inspire Jews like Philo and others who divide God into multiple beings are twofold—Greek philosophy and scripture. According to Plato, the most perfect God is highly spiritual and remote from humanity, and therefore a lower god—the Demiurge—creates this world. Philo assumes that Moses teaches the same thing in Genesis. The Jewish Bible also provides material for thinking in this way, in passages such as Genesis 18, where the biblical author depicts God's appearance to Abraham in the form of three persons. Reading this passage, Philo concludes that it represents the ultimate God and two of his divine powers, the creative and ruling powers.

The influence of Philo is considerable, including upon later Gnostics and the Christian Platonists of Alexandria, Clement and Origen. The so-called Alexandrian school of exegesis, therefore, can look upon Philo as its founder. Indeed, in later years Philo is disowned by orthodox Judaism and is sometimes thought of as a Christian bishop. The preservation of much of the Philonic corpus by Christianity is due to the support of the fourth-century church historian Eusebius, who mentions a tradition to the effect that Philo meets Peter on his journey to Rome during the reign of Claudius, and Eusebius regards Philo as teaching the doctrine of the Trinity. Jerome, the translator of the Bible into the Latin Vulgate, even includes Philo in his list of Church Fathers. Left to Jewish tradition, Philo's work would undoubtedly have perished.

The spiritual ideal that Philo outlines in his writings represents an amalgam of Stoicism and Platonism, a fusion of the active or virtuous life and the contemplative life of study and prayer. This combination represents for him a life controlled by the moral quality of *apatheia*, mastery over the tyranny of the passions—above all, anger, desire, fear, and pleasure.

Passionately devoted to a mystical form of Platonism, Philo is convinced that the goal of human life and the attainment of ultimate happiness lie in the knowledge or vision of God. Indeed, the mere quest is sufficient to give a foretaste of happiness. The soul has a natural longing and love for God and is drawn to God as one is drawn to beauty. The first step toward God is the recognition of one's own nothingness, which induces us to let go of our self-obsession. Released from devotion to self, seekers are then asked to attach themselves completely to God. This attachment to God involves the realization that it is God alone who acts, and as long as the human mind supposes itself to be the actor, it remains lost.

For Philo, the mystic vision of God is a timeless experience that carries the human soul to the uttermost bounds of the universe, enabling the soul to gaze, not on God, who is unknowable, but on the divine Logos. For Philo, this mystic state produces tranquility and stability. Unlike later mystics, who understand ecstasy as raising one's natural faculties to their most exalted and truest state, for Philo, ecstasy seems to mean that for its duration one's natural faculties recede before God and are replaced by God. In the exceptional case of Moses, Philo abandons the usual restraints and ascribes to him not only unity with God, but also as having been "divinized" by ascending to God.

Hermeticism

Hermeticism refers to a body of literature associated with the divine revealer named Hermes—the Greek messenger god who transmitted communications among the gods and between the gods and human beings—and the Egyptian god Thoth, the scribe of the gods. The basic features of the Hermetic view are remarkably similar to the views of the Gnostics and the Valentinians. According to the Hermetists, our true self is our soul or intellect, which is a fragment of the divine. Our true existence is immaterial and unchanging. Nonetheless, we are imprisoned in this world of material change, dwelling in bodies that impede our knowledge of God and matters of eternal truth. Because we are divine in our true selves, God wants us to know him, much as God wants to know us. However, this communion between God and human beings cannot take place as long as we live in ignorance—thinking that the material world is our true home and that our bodies are our true selves.

The first step in overcoming ignorance is philosophical study. At some point, a Hermetic initiate must have an experience of enlightenment (a rebirth)—a vision of or contact with God. Through this rebirth, the Hermetist becomes divine and gains immortality. Obviously, he or she is still a composite of body and soul, still tied to this changing world of matter, but the initiate has become a god by achieving *gnosis* of God and of the true divine self within.

Neoplatonism

The doctrine of the incomprehensibility of God, shared by Christians and pagans, is not a uniquely religious notion. Rather, it has a philosophical component, one developed by the great third century Neoplatonist philosopher Plotinus (205–270), an important thinker for Christian theologians of the fourth and fifth century who are defining the Christian doctrine of God.

Neoplatonism, an adaptation of the ideas of the Greek philosopher Plato, is formulated by Plotinus and his biographer Porphyry (c. 234–c. 305), and further developed by philosophers such as Iamblichus (c. 250–320) and Proclus (412–485). Like the Gnostics, Plotinus seeks to achieve *gnosis* of the ultimate God, but unlike the Gnostics, this new approach emphasizes humanity's essential connection to God rather than its state of alienation from God. Like the Gnostics, Plotinus believes in a remote

Ancient Wisdom Spirituality

and indefinable source of all that is, which he calls The One. The One thinks, and his thinking produces the first emanation from him—Mind or Spirit. In turn, Mind generates Soul, the principle that gives life to all, so that all human souls participate in this divine Soul.

Thus, when Plotinus thinks of God, he thinks in terms of threes. While not speaking of God as personal, he conceives of God as three "hypostases" (a hypostasis is a complete individual being, entity, or divine principle),[2] using a term that profoundly influences later Trinitarian Christians. The three hypostases represent a hierarchical or descending arrangement, remaining eternally distinct from each other. Yet despite this distinctness, reality is also a continuum, and for Plotinus there are no sharp lines drawn across the map of the universe. The clearest illustration of this conundrum is the doctrine that the soul is never totally fallen, but always remains in the realm of Mind above it.

In his *Timaeus*, Plato asserts the existence of three primal principles, but he establishes no relation among them. Plotinus organizes them in a descending triad; from this divine triad, all of reality emanates. For Neoplatonism, it is not quite right to say that The One exists, for the One is Being itself. From The One, all being emanates through Mind and Soul, creating new levels of reality that are both lower than and contained in The One. Everything that exists is thus an emanation from or a level of reality within The One. Everything derives from The One, and everything is intended to return to The One. Plotinus agrees with the Gnostics that the material world is not true being, but he does not believe that there is a clear separation between spiritual reality and the material world. Rather, everything exists on a continuum.

Plotinus's idea of the divine Mine—his middle hypostasis—influences Christianity directly. It is a Platonic element, related to intelligibility. As we note earlier, intelligibility is what gives us "aha" moments, moments of awareness, recognition, or deep insight. These occurrences are said to be evidence of the divine Mind, which, according to Platonist philosophy, is full of "ideas." Prior to the use of "methodical doubt" by René Descartes in the seventeenth century, Western thinkers do not imagine themselves having autonomous ideas. All such thinkers think Platonically, assuming that "ideas" are of divine origination. Prior to

---

2. The later Latin tradition substitutes the word "*persona*," meaning person or mask, for the Greek hypostasis. A hypostasis can be a person, but also a cat, a tree, or anything that is complete in itself. A hand, however, is not a hypostasis, because it is a part of something greater, and not a complete individual entity.

Descartes, the only being said to have "ideas" is the divine Mind or God. Ideas, for Plato, are eternally intelligible forms, essences, or truths such as beauty, justice, or goodness. For Plato and his intellectual descendants, to know these ideas is not to figure them out or arrive at them autonomously, but an intuitive "aha," an intelligible way of seeing. When you "get it," you are experiencing intelligible truth, when time touches eternity. To think this way, to see intuitively, is to experience the divine Mind, which is all-seeing and all-knowing—pure intelligence perceiving intelligible truth.

This way of seeing, however, is not the highest level, for the highest way of seeing belongs only to The One. Our minds have many ideas, but The One, being singular, has no parts and thus, no manyness. Think of this way of seeing as a geometric point—an abstract point without space or time, having no dimensions of depth, height, or width—yet all of geometry is driven by this simple, divisionless point. This is a metaphor, but it is how the concept of The One works in Neoplatonism. The One has no parts or division and yet is the source of all the manyness of life, including all of science, mathematics, and ethics—all things are said to be generated by The One.

According to Neoplatonism, the divine Mind is "eternally generated" by The One—and this is precisely the same vocabulary used by the bishops at the Council of Nicaea to speak of the Son, who is said to be eternally generated by the Father, begotten not once but eternally so. Hence, the begetting of the Son occurs outside of time, meaning that though he comes into being, there was "never a time when he was not." For church theologians, the concept of eternal generation is incomprehensible—necessarily so. For Nicene theologians, because the Father is incomprehensible, so is the Son, the Father's equal in every respect.

Christianity differs from Neoplatonism at this crucial point, because for Plotinus, when The One generates or begets divine Mind, it begets a lesser entity, less than itself. Platonists think hierarchically—what is generated is lower than its source. That is precisely what the Nicene doctrine of the Trinity denies. Though the Son's source is the Father, the Son is equal with the Father. Thus, while there is a hierarchy in the Neoplatonic triad, there is no hierarchy in the Christian Trinitarian doctrine of God. However, like the Neoplatonist One, the Christian God is incomprehensible because God is not intelligible, having no structure or parts to understand. In Christianity, God is understood as the geometric point that gives all things definition, yet is itself singular and therefore incomprehensible.

Though Plotinus views the body as distinct from the true self, he does not set the soul and the body in opposition. Instead, the unity and beauty of the body manifest the presence of the soul, which animates the body. Like the body, the material world is not a flawed imitation of the spiritual world but the visible manifestation of that world. The cosmos gets its unity and beauty from the divine Soul, which gives it life. As the body is not the true self but a manifestation of the true self, so, too, the true self is not separated from its source. Rather, the self consists of layers of being, and the deepest or most central layer remains in The One. Presently, humans exist both in heaven and on earth, both in The One and apart from it. Describing the One as Being, Plotinus also depicts the One as The Beautiful and The Good. Because everything that exists has its being from The One, this means that all things are also good because they participate in The One's Goodness and receive goodness from The One. They are more or less good depending on how close they are to The One or how deeply they participate in The One. Thus, evil does not really exist; it is simply a deficit or privation of goodness.[3]

Because everything derives from the One, everything is intended to return to The One. Of course, humans are seldom conscious of their connection to The One. Rather than attending to their higher selves, they are distracted by lower, less real concerns. Instead, they should cultivate awareness of the true being at the center of their selves. Aware of this ignorance and distraction at the center of human existence, Plotinus focuses on a program of return or ascent in five stages, not sharply distinct from each other. In practical terms, seekers should study philosophy and live disciplined lives that are not focused on material needs and concerns. They should practice contemplation and try to heighten their awareness of the connection to The One. This practice of consciousness and purification, which for Plotinus is the same as acquiring moral and spiritual virtues, leads to fleeting experiences of true *gnosis*, times in which individuals see Beauty itself and stand fully within the divine. As in Hermeticism, humans do not need to wait for some future moment to return to The One—they can do so now. According to his biographer Porphyry, Plotinus achieves this unitive state four times in his life.

For centuries, Neoplatonism influences the thought and behavior of educated Christians such as Augustine, helping mold the ensuing Christian mystic tradition, in the East through Pseudo-Dionysius (Denys

---

3. The doctrine of evil as a privation of goodness becomes central to Augustine's doctrine of creation.

the Areopagite) and Maximus the Confessor, and in the West through Eriugena, the St. Victor School, the Rhineland Mystics, and finally John of the Cross.[4]

Questions for Discussion and Reflection

In addition to the questions listed at the end of the preface, answer the following questions, writing your answers in a journal. If you are in a group study, be prepared to share your answers with those in the group.

1. Assess the influence of pagan philosophy on early Gentile Christianity.
2. What role does allegory play in how philosophically trained Gentile proto-orthodox Christians interpreted scripture, especially Old Testament views of God and the requirements of Jewish Torah?
3. Briefly define the Greek concept of happiness and its relation to living wisely.
4. Explain and assess the early Christian connection between wisdom and everlasting life.
5. In your estimation, how does Platonism influence the beliefs of Gentile proto-orthodox Christians?
6. In your estimation, why are early Christians more attracted to Platonism than to Aristotelianism?
7. In what ways are proto-orthodox Christians influenced by Stoicism?
8. In your estimation, how might the Jewish philosopher Philo have influenced proto-orthodox Christians?
9. In your estimation, how does Plotinus influence the development of the Christian doctrine of the Trinity?

---

4. We examine the Eastern Christian mystical tradition in chapter 8.

6

Christian Gnostic Spirituality

PEOPLE DIFFER IN MANY ways, psychologically, sociologically, spiritually, and emotionally. While some people are primarily legalists, communalists, or traditionalists, others are primarily charismatic, individualist, and progressive by nature. During the second and third centuries, the search for *gnosis* of a remote and perfect God becomes popular among educated, spiritually inclined people in the Roman Empire. Gnosticism and proto-orthodox Christianity articulate different kinds of human experience, appealing to different types of people. Gnostics and Valentinians appeal to this desire for *gnosis*, as does the *Gospel of Thomas* and influential Christian teachers in Alexandria, Egypt such as Clement and Origen. Non-Christians are part of this trend as well, including proponents of Hermeticism and Neoplatonism.

As we note in chapter 3, early Christian teachers and leaders such as Justin Martyr and Irenaeus oppose rival forms of Christianity by inventing the concepts of heresy and orthodoxy. Irenaeus questions the idea that Jesus and the apostles reserve special teaching only for advanced believers, affirming that "true *gnosis*" is publicly available in the preaching and teaching of bishops who practice true apostolic succession. This discussion takes quite a different course with two younger contemporaries of Irenaeus, the great Alexandrian theologians Clement and Origin. Though these scholars are anti-Gnostic, they recognize the appeal of a more advanced understanding of the Christian faith, affirming Christian alternative paths to *gnosis*.

As we have seen, the most significant heresies in the early church are those grouped under the name "Gnostic." The name itself, of course, is the creation of modern historical scholarship. Early Christian writers usually refer to an individual Gnostic group by the name of its founder or master, and the word "Gnostic" seems a perfectly respectable name for a Christian who has access to the knowledge (*gnosis*) revealed by Christ. This understanding continues centuries later, as apparent in the title *The Gnostic*, a book about the ideal monk written by the orthodox Christian teacher, Evagrius of Pontus.

Clement of Alexandria

Ironically, the first early Christian who claims in his own writings to be Gnostic is not Gnostic. He is Clement of Alexandria (150–c. 211), who teaches small groups in the instructional (catechetical) school in Alexandria, Egypt. At this time, Alexandria is one of the leading centers of intellectual life in the ancient world. Two important institutions—the museum and the library—support serious scholarship in the city. These institutions are a kind of think-tank, where scholars carry out research, lead seminars, and give lectures. People come to Alexandria from across the Roman Empire to study with well-known scholars, some of whom are Jewish or Christian. One of these is Philo, a contemporary of Jesus and Paul and the most famous Jewish philosopher of his era.

Some modern scholars argue that an early source for the biblical Gospel of John, the so-called "Signs Gospel" or "Signs Source," is written in Alexandria around the middle of the first century, predating the first version of John, itself possibly written in Alexandria. We know that Alexandrian Christians have a high regard for the Gospel of John. In fact, the first commentary written on this Gospel is produced in Alexandria early in the second century by a Gnostic Christian named Heracleon, suggesting that John may have revised the so-called Signs Gospel in Alexandria.

Most historians believe that Valentinus spends his early years in Alexandria before moving to Rome around 140. It seems likely that the Gnostic school of thought originates in Alexandria as well. All of these teachers and groups use Greek wisdom, including philosophy, mathematics, and astronomy, to deepen their understanding of the Bible. And Christians like Valentinus believe that their teachings about Jesus continue this great tradition of Greek learning.

This is the environment in which Clement works. Unlike Irenaeus, Clement does not have any ordained position in a church. Rather, he is an independent teacher, as Justin Martyr had been in Rome. Christians with the intellectual talents and financial resources for advanced study of philosophy meet with Clement. He guides them in reading sacred texts and works of philosophy and helps them improve their ethical lives. In this respect, Clement is like a Christian spiritual guide, who helps students become as wise and virtuous as they can be.

Clement accepts the basic reality that not all Christians can attain the same level of ethical perfection and intellectual understanding of the faith. However, unlike the Valentinians, who divide Christians into animate and spiritual people, Clement believes that Christians are at different points on a single path leading from ignorance and sin to *gnosis* and salvation. Every person has the possibility of making this journey, although only a few reach the final stage and become, as Clement put it, true Gnostics.

In Clement's time, of course, very few people are born and raised Christian; everyone starts in a state of ignorance and sin. According to Clement, God's Logos or Word leads people to Christianity in two ways, through the Bible and Jewish tradition and through Greek philosophy. God's Word speaks through both of these, but the Logos is fully present only in Jesus Christ.

When people become Christian, they begin a process of growth. In this respect, Clement envisages theological life as beginning with faith and ending with knowledge, the intervening stage consisting of growth in moral excellence, which comprises two elements, *apatheia* and charity (unconditional love for God and neighbor). As we see in chapter 5, *apatheia* is a Stoic term, meaning mastery over all disordered feelings and passions. For Clement, Christians are to be Stoic heroes like Christ, free not only from anger, fear, or lust, but practically passionless, pursuing a life of self-mastery yet also given to the Christian virtue of charity (seen more as purity of heart than as altruistic love for one's neighbor, particularly when this love is motivated by duty or emotion). Such altruistic love has no place in Stoicism or Platonism, or in Clement's Christianity.

In Clement we encounter a principle commonly associated with the Western theologians Augustine and Anselm, "I believe in order to understand." The Christian life begins with faith, seen as the basis and origin of all knowledge. By "faith" Clement has in mind "the conviction of things not seen" of Hebrews 11:1, though he also believes, like Irenaeus, that Jesus and the apostles establishes a kind of rule for what Christians should believe, which Clement calls "the ecclesiastical norm."

However, unlike Irenaeus, Clement does not think that Christians should be satisfied with simple faith in the basic teachings of the church. He expresses frustration with Christians who "are called orthodox" but are content only with "bare faith." Instead, Clement encourages Christians to move beyond mere faith to true *gnosis*—a deeper understanding of the mysteries of Christianity. For Clement, this true *gnosis* consists mainly of a more spiritual understanding of the scriptures. People who have "bare faith" understand the Bible literally and simply, but people who have *gnosis* learn to read the Bible symbolically and find in it multiple meanings.

When speaking of *gnosis*, Clement focuses on prayer as a way of life, lived in fellowship with God. Acknowledging that weaker Christians might need to focus on verbal and liturgical prayer, for Clement the goal of prayer is not absolution or petition but rather thanksgiving and recollection. There is little in Clement's conception of perfect prayer to distinguish it from the private intellectual contemplation found in the writings of Plato and Aristotle. The principle thing in his spirituality is not liturgical or sacramental piety, but rather intelligible *gnosis*.

Clement presents himself as uniquely qualified to lead interested Christians from simple faith to advanced *gnosis*. He does so by claiming to have received through apostolic succession secret teachings not found in the scriptures but taught by Jesus to his apostles. The apostles, in turn, teach this unwritten knowledge to their students, and Clement receives it from them. But unlike the secret teachings offered by the Gnostics and Valentinians, Clement claims that the *gnosis* he offers does not violate the church's ecclesiastical norm. It is orthodox *gnosis*.

Origen of Alexandria

A persecution of Christians breaks out in Alexandria shortly after the year 200. During that turmoil, Clement leaves the city and resettles in Palestine. His successor in Alexandria is a teenager named Origen (c. 185–c. 254), who ends up becoming one of the most original and brilliant theologians in the history of Christianity. When Origen is ten years old, his father is martyred during the persecution of the church by Emperor Severus (193–211), the same persecution that drives Clement from Alexandria. According to one story, the young Origen wishes to follow his father in martyrdom, but his mother keeps him safe in the house by hiding his clothes.

Trained in both secular and Christian learning, Origen quickly excels, developing special competence in the languages and contents of the Jewish and Christian scriptures, so that at the age of eighteen he begins to preside over the Christian school in his native city, Alexandria. By means of allegorical and figurative interpretation of the scriptures, Origen is able to show the correlation, as he sees it, between Greek philosophy and the Bible. In 232 he moves to Caesarea, where his program of teaching and writing is so colossal that he has stenographers on hand during his lectures to record his discourses. He is among those tortured during the persecution of the church under Decius (249–251), and dies from those injuries in 254.

As a teenager, Origen is a charismatic teacher, and he successfully attracts students who want to study Christianity with him. Valentinian Christianity is very popular among educated and wealthy Christians in Alexandria, and Origen becomes known for his opposition to their views. Upper-class Christians begin throwing dinner parties, followed by after-dinner entertainment, often featuring a debate between Origen and a Valentinian teacher. One prominent Valentinian Christian whom Origen persuades to give up Valentinianism is named Ambrose. Ambrose is so taken with Origen's intelligence and highly moral life[1] that he financially supports him for decades. Ambrose even pays for a team of scribes to record Origen's theological works as he dictates them.

The majority of his voluminous literary output is devoted to the exposition of the Bible, either by homily or commentary, including commenting on most of its books. For the benefit of discussions with the Jews, he compiles his *Hexapla*, a six-column edition of the Old Testament, setting Greek versions in parallel with the Hebrew. Origen also produces an extended apologetic response, *Contra Celsum*, to an earlier attack on Christianity by Celsus, a Roman philosopher of the second century, and the first Christian systematic theological treatise entitled *De Principiis* (On First Principles), in which he provides a philosophical foundation for Christian belief, the so-called "rule of faith."

Origen's theology is controversial, but it sets the agenda for Christian thought for centuries to come. He develops his theological vision in

---

1. Origen leads a highly ascetic life, remaining celibate until his death, and he eats, drinks, and sleeps very little. It is reported that he has himself castrated, so that no one can suspect him of impropriety when he teaches women.

part to create an alternative to Gnostic and Valentinian myth. Although Origen defends orthodox Christianity against Gnostics, Valentinians, and other "heretics," he eventually comes into conflict with Demetrius, the bishop of Alexandria, who resents his growing popularity. At this time, Origen is traveling to places like Arabia, Palestine, and Athens to preach and teach at the request of other bishops. When Demetrius hears that a bishop in Palestine has ordained Origen a priest without his permission, he has Origen expelled from the Alexandrian church. The basis for his expulsion is the charge that Origen has said that even Satan would eventually repent and be saved, a charge that may be accurate.

Origen's life reveals a complicated relationship with the organized church. On the one hand he is, like Irenaeus, faithful to the church, an opponent of heretics, and a member of the clergy. On the other hand, he is also like Clement and even Valentinus, dedicated to advanced learning, highly creative, eager to help people advance to higher *gnosis*, and always questioning, unwilling to settle for easy or customary answers.

Origen appeals to Christians who want a more intellectual, less close-minded approach to Christian truth. However, he understands that some people find the myths of the Gnostics and Valentinians attractive. The stories they tell explain the nature of God, how and why this world comes to be, and where human beings come from and are going. The Gnostic myth is a compelling response to human suffering, oppression, and death, and it offers hope for serenity and equality in this life and in eternity. Thus, Origen realizes that orthodox Christianity needs a better myth than that of the Gnostics and Valentinians—a more complete story of creation, fall, and salvation than offered by a literal reading of the Bible. In his sermons, commentaries, and theological writings, Origen lays out his comprehensive vision of Christian truth, refining and elaborating on that vision for the many students and listeners that attend his services and lectures, some of them pagans.

Origen's mythological account of salvation resembles that of the Gnostics in that it is a story of a fall from a blessed existence in another world into life in this world, and then a return to union with God. However, Origen's story emphasizes God's love for humanity and the freedom of human beings. God wants everyone to be saved, that is, to return to the original blissful existence, and it seems that this will happen. Origen's story does not make this universe a mistake, nor does an inferior or hostile God rule over it. Instead, this universe is a good creation, made by God to help us return to him.

Like other religious and philosophical views then current in Alexandria, Origen believes that God is both one and multiple. There is only one God, but the unknowable, inaccessible Father makes himself known through his Word or Son, who exists with him eternally. Likewise, there is God's Holy Spirit, which is God's immediate presence among Christians. Origen insists that the Son and the Spirit are not emanations, like the Gnostic *aeons*. Instead, they are integral aspects of God and have eternally existed with God.

Long before this universe comes into existence, God creates and rules over a multitude of rational beings. These are pure intellects, who contemplate God through the Word. Their very reason to exist is to be educated by God's Son. Yet these rational beings have free will, and can choose to turn away from God, which they do. Like students in a classroom who get distracted and stop paying attention, they neglect contemplation of God, and this becomes the origin of sin, the fall of rational beings from *gnosis* of God.

Because God loves all rational beings, he wants to bring them back to contemplation of himself. For this reason, the Father creates the physical universe, doing so through the Word. God then places the fallen intellects in material bodies, each body appropriate to their condition and need. While the rational beings all fall from their original communion with God, they do so to varying degrees—some very little, some a great deal, and some in between. Hence, they need to be healed and educated in different ways. So God assigns each fallen intellect to the body and place in the universe that is best for its rehabilitation. The intellects who fall away the least become the archangels, angels, and other good spirits; they do not need much re-education, and so they have the least difficult bodies to manage. The rational beings that fall away the farthest become Satan and his demons. Between the angels and the demons are human beings. They fall away from God less than the demons, but more than the angels and heavenly beings. God assigns each human being to be born in the appropriate body and at the appropriate time and place, so that they can begin the process of improving themselves morally and learning about God intellectually.

Thus, Origin agrees with the Gnostics and Valentinians that our physical bodies are secondary parts of who we are. However, our bodies are not prisons from which we need to be liberated, nor are they the means by which evil cosmic rulers enslave us. Instead, they are gifts from

God, like training wheels for the bicycle of the soul. If we can master our bodies, then we can educate our souls as well.

In Origin's account, one intellect does not fall away from contemplating God through his Logos or Word. In fact, this one intellect loves and studies the Word so intensely that it is filled or fused with God's Word, just as iron placed in a fire becomes infused with the fire's heat. This intellect becomes the soul of Jesus. United with this created but unfallen intellect, the Word of God enters a human body and lives and dies as Jesus. By his life and in his death, the Son of God lives and dies for all fallen beings, showing human beings how to live a moral life and how to relate to the Father. In this way, the Son makes it possible for the fallen beings to reform their lives and regain *gnosis* of God.

Origen is aware that in his day few people actually become Christian and start their return to God. And he knows that, during their lifetimes, very few Christians reach the level of contemplation of God that they experienced long ago when they were purely intellects. This is due to free will, for people can choose whether to live righteously and pursue *gnosis*. However, God loves all rational beings and will not give up on them. Like an effective teacher, God ultimately leads all people to love and know him, though not through coercion. Thus, Origen argues that after this universe comes to an end, there will be future worlds, ages to come, in which fallen intellects continue their journey back to God. Unlike reincarnation, where individuals are reborn in this universe, Origen has in mind something akin to continuing education, like going on to graduate studies after finishing college. People who regress morally in this world will have bad experiences we call hell, and those who improve will have pleasant experiences we call heaven. However, neither of these experiences—heaven or hell—are eternal. Because God does not compel love or *gnosis*, it may take ages to bring all rational beings back, but ultimately, all things will be restored. The grand finale to Origen's redemption account is the Apocatastasis (the salvation or Restoration of all).

Though Origen's doctrine of Apocatastasis is not acknowledged by Christianity as orthodox doctrine, this does not imply that it is incorrect, particularly if it is anchored to eschatology (meaning *hope* for the salvation of all) and not to soteriology (meaning that universal salvation is *assured* dogma). While Christians may hope all are saved, there is no guarantee this will happen.

Despite the stage setting, much of it based on philosophical and cosmological speculation, it becomes clear that if one looks at Origen's salvation story as a whole, it is the same story—though somewhat dressed up—told by orthodox scholars such as Irenaeus or Gregory of Nyssa. The fundamental pattern is a movement from innocence to experience. The creative purpose of God extends from the Beginning to the End, and is only achieved when the process encompassing fall and incarnation is completed. Undergirding Origen's story is the authentic vision of the early church. That vision unites all of human history in a single movement from the childhood of our first creation to the perfect humanity of the new creation revealed in Christ and consummated at the End of time.

Origen's vision is a beautiful and awesome story of a fall from God and a return to God. It explains why humans suffer and why this material world exists—all this is for our long-term benefit. And it reassures us that God loves us and desires our love. It preserves human free will and God's sovereign love for all creation.

One of the most hotly disputed questions concerning Origen is the respective influence of his two main sources of inspiration, the Bible and Plato. There can be no doubt that both control his thought. He is a great biblicist, and his work is infused with biblical imagery and quotation. On the other hand, it is impossible to ignore that his doctrine of preexistence and fall has more in common with Plato's myth in the *Phaedrus* than with the book of Genesis, or that his stress on the intellectual, unchanging nature of God, has more in common with Middle Platonism than with the God of the biblical patriarchs. Additionally, his view of God as supremely beautiful and his disembodied view of the origin and end of humanity is more akin to Plato's *Symposium* and *Phaedo* than to teachings in Paul's letters or in the Gospels.

Though Origen's doctrine of God is deeply influenced by Platonic and Neoplatonic notions, we must keep in mind that he writes centuries before Christianity formulates its doctrine of the Trinity. In order to retain monotheism, Origen insists upon the unity of God. At the same time, he needs to preserve the uniqueness of the Word (or Son) of God. The clearest way to describe Origen's conception of the Son's relation to the Father is to say that their relationship is like that between a thought and its thinker. In relation to himself, the Son (or Word or Logos) is a distinct being. He can be equated with Plato's Demiurge, but also with the Model or archetypal Form by which the Demiurge fashions the visible universe. As mediator, the Word also informs and guides rational beings (see 1 Tim. 2:5). Hence, the Word of God occupies a distinct and crucial position for Origen, identical both with God and yet also with the rational souls who participate in God through him. Origen is less concerned with the ontological implications of his view and more with its mediatorial implications, for the Word binds God and the creation together in unity. In this respect, the Word represent humanity to God and God to humanity. Thus, the Father is archetype with respect to the Word, while the Word is archetype with respect to rational beings.

Nevertheless, the return of the soul to its former state is described as a journey, and for it Origen utilizes the biblical journey of the children of Israel from Egypt to the Promised Land. Origen is not the first to do this—Philo precedes him in his *Life of Moses*—nor is he the last—Gregory of Nyssa does the same in his work of the same name. With them he shares the conviction that it is by devout meditation on the text of scripture that understanding of God and God's purposes is revealed. That is important, because, though it appears at times as if Origen replaces a Christian understanding of prayer with Platonic contemplation, overall, his exegesis of scripture is Christocentric. For him the Bible is not a cryptogram by means of which certain physical and moral truths are conveyed, as it is for Philo, but rather a way of entering deeply into the mind of Christ, in whom the entire Bible finds its meaning.

In addition to the metaphor of the journey, Origen uses another metaphor to describe the pilgrim's progress toward its destiny—the growth to maturity. Using Genesis and passages from the apostle Paul, Origin distinguishes in each human being between the "inner" and "outer" nature (2 Cor. 4:16). The inner nature is the soul or mind made after God's image, while the outer nature is the corporeal person of dust. For each "nature," Origen finds that there is spiritual food corresponding to the stage of development of one's inner nature. Using 1 Corinthians 3:2–3, Hebrews 5:12–14, and Romans 14:2–4, Origen arranges this food in a hierarchical order: "milk" for "infants in Christ," "vegetables" for the weak, and "solid food" for the mature. In principle, the soul is meant to grow from childhood to maturity, and all souls are destined to receive the solid food. The different foods are to be equated with the Word of God, who accommodates his nourishing revelation to the condition of the one receiving it. As revelation descends through a series of stages, human response ascends through the same series. This is how we humans receive our "daily" bread, which strengthens us and enables us to grow to maturity. Likewise, the Word of God nourishes us through the scriptures, and different passages and books are thought to correspond to the different foods.

A third metaphor Origen uses to describe the Christian life is that of warfare. Just as the martyrs led in procession to execution are really celebrating the triumph of their victory against the forces of wickedness and evil, so the pilgrim soul on its journey encounters war and must be ready for it. Shifting the metaphor slightly, Origen thinks of the warfare as an athletic contest. On the one hand, it is a moral struggle that aims to assert the control of the mind over the body and its passions. There is, as well, a dimension of the struggle that goes beyond morality. Origen believes the world to be filled with spiritual forces of evil. These hosts of wickedness war against Christians, tempting them and seeking to destabilize their faith. This idea includes not only what we call temptation—the attempt to make us sin—but also the idea of testing or affliction. In both senses, temptation is meant to test our true character.

Using Paul's metaphor from 1 Corinthians 3:12–15, Origen thinks of temptation as a testing of gold in the fire. However, temptation not only tests what we are, it is also a providential process by which we are fashioned into what we should be. What Origen has in mind is that growth is a painful process, and that temptation and struggle never leave us until we have attained the maturity of perfection. The struggle with temptation is not only against sin and evil in our outer life; it is also intellectual in character. In particular, it is a struggle with the scriptures, where intellectual and spiritual temptations abound.

The journey, the growth to maturity, and the warfare or contest are all dependent upon the freedom of the Christian. But they are also placed within the context of God's providence, which continually trains our freedom. Christ accompanies Christians on their journey, feeding them with true bread, and assisting them in their struggle. In addition to Christ's presence, God's providence also includes the moral example of the saints in scripture and the power and protection mediated through God's guardian angels. If our warfare is against Satan and his hosts, we have spiritual powers for good on our side, so that the conflict is not unequal. For Origen, Christian progress is placed within the cosmic struggle between good and evil.

In his *Commentary on the Song of Songs*, Origen relates the three biblical books attributed to Solomon to the traditional divisions of Greek philosophy: moral life (Proverbs), natural life (Ecclesiastes), and contemplative life (Song of Solomon). In this regard, Origen's association influences a long and fruitful development in the history of Christian spirituality. It defines the Christian life as comprising three stages:

purgative, contemplative, and unitive. We must not, however, lock Origen into a fully systematic approach to spirituality. While he does regard the three stages as progressive, in that believers pass from ethics (the purgative stage) to physics (the contemplation of the natural order) to the contemplation and love of God, the three are interrelated, and there is a sense in which the higher stages include the lower ones. It is probably better to speak of the three as different aspects of the Christian life arranged in hierarchical order. The preliminary aspect is the moral life, by which the Christian prepares for growth in faith (Proverbs). The next aspect involves the intellectual contemplation of the created order and the realization of its "vanity" apart from the Creator (Ecclesiastes). The highest aspect, the contemplation of God, is represented by Song of Solomon.

Not only must we not suppose that Origen is speaking of definite and separated stages, we must also beware of relating his idea too systematically to ways of thinking about human nature, such as body, soul, and spirit. Anthropology, like spirituality, has an underlying unity, one we must preserve when thinking about the growth to spiritual maturity. While the pattern may be seen as progressive, there is a cyclical aspect that allows for setbacks, repetition, and failure. Nevertheless, the idea of three aspects of Christian spirituality helps clarify Origen's understanding. While moral preparation is necessary for spiritual growth, at some point we progress to contemplation of the natural order, learning to distinguish what is temporal from what is eternal. Discernment is key here. Wisdom requires a new way of seeing, learning to look beyond corporeal and visible things to the Creator. If sometimes Origen expresses his ideas as a rejection of the world, we must remember that it is the Gnostic notion of the world as a fallen order and as a place of torment for the soul that he rejects. In Origen's view, the body and the material world are not evil, but essential to the education of the soul.

To those who might view Origen's final, unitive stage of the Christian life far-fetched, impractical, or overly mystical for ordinary believers engaged fully in their everyday lives and concerns, the following four points may make it seem more relevant and accessible. First, Origen believes that in the highest aspect of Christian spirituality, knowing or seeing God is best understood as a metaphor for union in love. Second, this destiny represents the completion of human nature and not something realizable in mid journey. Humans are created after God's image, meaning they possess the capacity for fellowship with God. Third, our natural destiny is merely potential until God awakens our hearts and minds and empowers them to become what in principle they have been all along. Fourth, for Origen the goal of life is not fulfilled or consummated by the third aspect of spirituality, because contemplation of God is an endless and dynamic process. Origen's emphasis is never upon the face-to-face vision that marks human destiny, but rather upon the inexhaustible character of the quest for wisdom and the inability of thinking ever to find a final resting point.

The endlessness of the quest for truth and wisdom is, of course, a Platonic theme and is integral to the spirit not only of Christianity, but also of Plato and Neoplatonism. Origen's description of the highest aspect of the Christian life borrows additional themes from Plato, such as the goal of life as *theosis* (divinization), a theme we find particularly in Eastern Orthodoxy. While "being made divine" represents the end of the human journey, as indicated by the Apocatastasis, we must beware of supposing that this means that Origen gives priority to the contemplative over the active life. For Origen, contemplation bestows upon the soul the vision that enables it to act. Like Plato's philosopher, the soul that glimpses God returns to the cave and to work. A circular pattern is thereby established, and the Christian life is not thought of as exclusively spiritual or contemplative. In this respect Origen is followed by the fourth-century Cappadocian Fathers, Basil the Great (c. 330–379), his brother Gregory of Nyssa (c. 335–c.395), and their close friend Gregory of Nazianzus (329–389). It is only in the fifth century, with Evagrius of Pontus and Pseudo-Dionysius, that the notion arises that the contemplative life is higher than the active. Like Plato, Origen wishes to show how our Heraclitean experience is informed and made meaningful by its participation in the Parmenidean world of ultimate reality. Moreover, as a Christian, Origen is persuaded that our human destiny has been revealed in Christ.

In the end, we come closer to understanding Origen if we allow him two basic premises. The first is his conviction that there need be no contradiction between Greek philosophical and biblical thought. Like Philo, Origen argues that the truth discovered by Plato and other philosophers is the same truth revealed in scripture. To be sure, philosophers err, and the truth of the scripture is the treasure hidden in the field. However, if one searches wisely and carefully, one begins to find the place where contradictions are resolved and obscurities disappear. Following the rules of Greek literary analysis, Origen argues that read literally, the narratives of scripture are filled with impossibilities and incongruities. These obstacles mean that the letter of the text cannot be followed and that deeper meaning must be sought.

A second premise is his assumption of the fundamental unity of mind, will, and spirit. For Origen, it is the mind that wills and preserves the spiritual kinship between the individual and God. This is a unity modern people no longer assume. Today, we think of "will" as a separate and different faculty from the intellect. As a result, we tend to confine words like "knowledge," "understanding," "mind," and "reason" to the intellect. However, for Origen, "mind" includes not only people's intellectual faculties, but also their moral and spiritual faculties. For Origen, these three aspects of the Christian life are not separate but function as a unity.

While we may call Origen a "Christian Platonist," the form of Platonism reflected in his writings is better called Neoplatonism. Origen is believed to have studied under the Platonist teacher Ammonias Saccas, who also teaches Plotinus, though some twenty years later. While Plotinus is widely regarded as having founded Neoplatonism, Origen must also receive some of the credit, for he shares with Plotinus a concern to move beyond skeptical and dualistic forms of Platonism. However, Origen is committed to the church and to Christian religion, whereas Plotinus is not.

Despite his christocentrism, Origen believes that the treasures of scripture could be unlocked primarily through the intellect, and in *De Principiis* Origen discusses the three main senses of scripture: literal, moral, and spiritual. Origen's fundamental distinction here is between the letter (the literal) and the spirit (the deeper theological meaning toward which a text points), although at times the deeper meaning is subdivided into the "soul" and the "spirit" of scripture. At one level, this theological meaning involves the fulfillment of the Old Testament by the New, often through typological relationships, where the shadow (type) of the Old yields to the image of the New. In some cases, images in the New Testament serve as the shadow for Origen's vision of the universal destiny of humanity in eternity. In this case, Origen's approach to scripture seems nothing more than his theological presupposition.

We are left in a circle, where one's presuppositions yields one's hermeneutical conclusion. There is no question that Origen approaches scripture with preconceptions that are partly determined by his philosophical training and intellectual inclinations. However, it can be argued that all interpreters approach scripture with presuppositions. While one's presuppositions determine the questions one asks of the text, they need not determine the results, so long as the interpreter respects the autonomy of the text and follows acknowledged exegetical principles. Nevertheless, one's conclusions invariably influence one's presuppositions.

Admittedly, one of Origen's main concerns is to defend the use of the Old Testament against Marcion and his followers, who maintain that because the picture of God offered by the Hebrew scriptures is unworthy of the true God, it is the work of an inferior deity and hence should be rejected as scripture. Origen's defense of the Old Testament as scripture is directly linked with his use of the allegorical method. However, he also uses allegory to deepen and enlarge the mind's activity in the study of scripture. It is the mind that makes us like God, and by the action of the mind that we become once again fully godlike.

Origen, one of the towering intellects of the Western world—and one of the most creative—is unjustly condemned as a heretic in 543, at the instigation of Byzantine Emperor Justinian. His indictment is accompanied by the destruction of most of his writings, consisting of some two thousand books. For that reason, the vast bulk of his surviving writings are in Latin. The translations come largely from the hand of Rufinus, who modifies some of Origen's more daring speculations in the direction of orthodoxy. The charges against Origen boil down to the accusation that his theology is corrupted by his philosophy, but this is not how he sees himself. He believes he is a seeker of Christian truth, his primary source being the Gospels and the writings of Paul, for the Christian scriptures have not yet been canonized.

Origen's spirituality is centered on three loves—an absolute love for the Word of God (the Logos or Christ), a deep commitment to the Christian scriptures, and a lasting devotion to the Christian church. The central feature is his passionate love for the Logos, which takes on humanity in Jesus. Origin finds this Logos everywhere in scripture, arguing that the entire Old Testament speaks of him only. The Logos is available to humanity in a threefold incarnation: in a historical body (in Jesus), in an ecclesiastical body (in the universal church), and in scripture (whose meaning is animated by God's Spirit). For Origen, these three forms of incarnation constitute a vast and all-encompassing sacrament, God's Spirit dwelling in each fully.

Conclusion

Together, Clement and Origen provide an orthodox *gnosis*, including a version of the cosmic myth that can compete with what the Gnostics and Valentinians teach. In the process, they make major contributions to the theology and spirituality of what becomes orthodox Christianity. Yet both remain controversial. Neither is an official saint of the Roman Catholic Church, although Clement becomes recognized a saint in the East. Though Origen is tragically and unjustly declared a heretic by a church council in the sixth century, long after his death, his theology sets the agenda for Christian thought for the next several centuries.

Origen's vision of God's transformation of humanity through free will remains at the heart of Eastern Orthodox Christianity. Origen's influence is considerable, above all on the fourth-century Cappadocian Fathers, who make an anthology of his surviving writings, the *Philokalia*, for the benefit of those who wish to see how faith and philosophy might be harmonized. His influence is also discernible in the work of Evagrius of Pontus (c. 345–399), through whom Origen's contribution passes in the East to Maximus the Confessor and in the West through John Cassian to the monastic movement.

Questions for Discussion and Reflection

In addition to the questions listed at the end of the preface, answer the following questions, writing your answers in a journal. If you are in a group study, be prepared to share your answers with those in the group.

1. In your estimation, what is Clement of Alexandria's greatest contribution to second-half-of-life spirituality?

2. In your estimation, how does Origen of Alexandria's theology "set the agenda for Christian thought for centuries to come"?

3. Assess the meaning of the concept of "Christian *gnosis*."

4. What is Origen's purpose in creating a counter-Gnostic myth of sin and salvation? Compare and contrast his salvation story to that of proto-orthodox theologians such as Irenaeus and Justin Martyr.

5. Assess the advantages and disadvantages of developing a theology like Origen's, equally influenced by biblical and nonbiblical points of view.

6. In light of the finality of Christian doctrinal views attained through its ecumenical councils, to what extent should Christians be open to non-Christian or heterodox concepts and worldviews?

7. Which of Origen's three metaphors for the return of the soul to God do you find most compelling? Explain your answer.

8. Explain the value and benefit of Origen's three stages or states of the Christian life. In your estimation, is it better to understand these as progressive stages or simply as three different ways of living and thinking?

7

Augustinian Spirituality

IN THIS CHAPTER WE consider the concept of grace, and its relationship to two other essential elements of spirituality, faith and love. In our thinking of these topics, we focus on the contributions of Augustine (354–430), the single-most influential Christian thinker outside of the Bible, although his influence is more in the Western Church—Catholicism and Protestantism—than in the Eastern Church—Eastern Orthodoxy.

Whenever a conversation arises concerning Christian doctrine, invariably Augustine is cited. Everyone has heard of Augustine, often in connection with his *Confessions* or his *City of God*, two monumental works that break new ground in the areas of Christian autobiography and church history. Additionally, people credit Augustine for his contribution to the doctrine of the Trinity, particularly for his perceptive use of psychological analogies to affirm both the unity and the plurality of the Godhead. Nevertheless, when speaking of Augustine, people invariably think negatively of his contributions to theology, focusing on his doctrines of predestination and original sin. You may be pleased to note that these themes will not receive much attention in this chapter.

As we notice, throughout much of Christian history, certainly from the fourth through the fifteenth centuries, prominent Christian theologians attempt to combine or synthesize biblical and Greek ideas, particularly ideas associated with Plato and Aristotle. For them, all truth is God's truth, independent of origin. Prior to 1250, Platonic ideas exert the primary influence on church theologians, while after that period, beginning with Thomas Aquinas's *Summa Theologica*, Aristotle's influence becomes predominant.

Whereas first-century Christians, including authors of the New Testament documents, tend to perceive a sharp contrast between emerging Christian theology and Greek philosophy, in the second and third centuries, Christian apologists and other educated thinkers come to believe that great insights from other cultures or pagan philosophers can be used to support and advance biblical ideas. Of course, some of this methodology is already evident in the composition of the biblical documents themselves, as we see in Paul's quotation from pagan philosophers in his speech to the Athenian elders in Acts 17:22–29, his use of natural theology in Romans 1:19–20, and the borrowing of Logos ideology in John's prologue. Beginning already in the first century and continuing through the Middle Ages, the Renaissance, and into modern times, specific Christian thinkers seek to weave biblical and nonbiblical ideas together, manipulating competing traditions in a multitude of ways to render them more compatible.

Most important among Christian thinkers who significantly shape Western society and history are Aquinas, Luther, Calvin, and John Wesley. Their interpretations and commentaries on Judeo-Christian theology establish major patterns for Western thought and culture. In profound ways, all are impacted by Augustine, a colossal figure who gives Christian thought much of its formative character.

Biographical Considerations

An African by birth, Augustine is born and raised in Tagaste, Algeria. His father, a non-Christian, is unconcerned about morality and allows his son to do whatever he wishes. Augustine's mother, Monica, in contrast to her husband, is a devout Christian who dearly loves Augustine. At the age of twelve, the precocious youngster is sent to a school for intellectually gifted children. There he furthers his education by reading Virgil and other Greek and Roman poets. As a teenager, his sensuality takes over, and he indulges in sexual affairs. When he is sixteen years old, his father dies, at which time Augustine goes to Carthage, continuing his schooling at the expense of a wealthy benefactor.

Carthage, a seaport on the Mediterranean Sea, has an ethical reputation for being one of the most corrupt cities of the Roman Empire. Monica, Augustine's Christian mother, advises him against fornication, but unable to heed her advice, in Carthage he takes a mistress and fathers a son. Meanwhile, his intellectual growth continues. In his late teenage years he is influenced by Cicero, who argues that people find true happiness only in the pursuit of wisdom, that is, in philosophy. Augustine is inspired to seek true wisdom, but he runs into two problems. First, according to Monica, Christianity is the highest form of wisdom, but when Augustine turns to the Bible, he finds that it is not particularly well written and that many of its characters are clearly immoral. Second, though inspired by Cicero's claim that true happiness comes from philosophy, Augustine finds it difficult to give up material forms of happiness, such as sex and other sensual pleasures.

Disillusioned with Christianity and the Bible, during his twenties Augustine joins a sect called Manichaeism. It founder, Mani (216–274), raised an Elchasaite Christian in a village near Babylon, worships Jesus but places great emphasis on ritual purity. The recipient of visions and inspired revelations, he becomes convinced of his role as the seal of all prophecy and therefore as the one destined to unite all existing religions into one Truth.

Mani teaches a view of reality that is thoroughly dualistic, positing an eternal conflict between two antithetical kingdoms, a cosmic kingdom of light forever waging war against a cosmic kingdom of darkness. This conflict extends to human beings, themselves a combination of good and evil, fragments of light trapped in material, bodily, prison houses of darkness. Salvation comes from awareness, right thinking, and an ascetic rejection of physical appetites and desires. The Manichaean myth is quite complicated, but it has widespread appeal due to its clear explanation for the existence of evil and suffering, and for why people often feel torn between good and evil.

According to Mani, evil is real because it exists from the beginning. God does not create evil or even allow it to come into being. Instead, evil, in the form of a realm of darkness, always exists, and humans now find themselves trapped in that realm, particles of light, spiritual in essence, trapped in physical bodies, evil by nature. Manichaeism explains why humans are attracted to both good and evil. Evil impulses arise from our bodies, which are composed of darkness. While our bodies of darkness draw us to evil deeds and keep us in ignorance, our souls, composed of light, prompt us to want to do the good. As Paul indicates in Romans 7, there is a war within each of us, and for Mani, that war is also in the natural realm. For Manichaeans, salvation comes from awareness (right understanding) coupled with an ascetic rejection of physical appetites and desires.

Adherents of Manichaeism are divided into two classes: the few, called the Elect, lead celibate and mostly pure lives, while the many, designated the Hearers, lead normal married lives. Attracted to its emphasis on rational demonstration of wisdom, its rejection of the Old Testament, and its rigorous spirituality, Augustine remains a Hearer for ten years.

On one of his visits to his home, Augustine tells his mother of his interest in cosmic dualism and the Manichaean plan of salvation, but upset that this abstract system makes no room for Jesus' redemptive activity, Monica tearfully orders her son to leave her house. Restless and troubled, the thirty-year old Augustine decides to move from Carthage to Rome. Disenchanted with Manichaeism, he becomes a skeptic in search of a new faith. While in Rome, his search for a new faith leads him to Neoplatonism. A year later he moves to northern Italy to take a teaching position in rhetoric. Upon arriving in Milan with his mistress and son, he rents a villa, and when he is not teaching, he studies Neoplatonism. For a while he is fascinated by Neoplatonism, which had certain similarities with Manichaeism. But under the influence of Monica, who comes to live with him, he begins to attend church, where he listens to the sermons of Bishop Ambrose. These stir his heart and mind and interest him in Christianity. He learns he need not interpret the Bible literally, and this helps overcome many of his reservations with scripture.

When he is thirty-two years old, a friend challenges him to answer the question, "What am I doing on this earth?" After his friend leaves, Augustine goes out into his garden and hears the voice of a child playing nearby. When the child cries, "Take up and read," Augustine finds the nearest book, a Bible, and opens it at random to read Paul's words, "Not in reveling and drunkenness, not in debauchery and licentiousness, not in quarreling and jealousy. Instead, put on the Lord Jesus Christ, and make no provision for the flesh, to gratify its desires" (Rom. 13:13-14). Instantly he is converted. The following Easter he is baptized by Ambrose.

Shortly thereafter Augustine returns to Africa, and in response to a need in the town of Hippo, he goes to serve the Christians there. Four years later, amid great jubilation, Augustine is ordained a priest and a year later, bishop. For the next thirty-three years, until his death in 430, he remains in this small town, addressing the doctrinal questions of his time. After converting to Christianity, he continues synthesizing Greek and biblical thought, but as he grows in understanding, he differentiates more and more between its teachings and Greek ideas until his mature theological thought is more consistently biblical.

Augustine's Doctrine of Grace

The concept of grace is central to spirituality, a connection enhanced by Augustinian scholar Phillip Cary.[1] When we speak about grace, we are participating in a larger debate regarding the doctrine of salvation. Let us be clear, when we speak of salvation in *The Second Journey*, the emphasis is not on believing or doing certain things to assure entrance into heaven. That focus or concern is certainly important for first-half-of-life spirituality, but that concern, if it is present at all, is marginal to second-half-of-life thinking and living. For that reason, I am grateful to Dr. Cary for speaking of salvation in a nuanced way, as the fulfillment of the so-called Double-Love Command (coming to love God with all of one's heart, soul, mind, and strength, and one's neighbor as oneself; see Mark 12:30–31).

In this respect, we may think of grace as a transformative element, without which one cannot be saved. What grace accomplishes, then, is to transform human beings into children of God, for according to Christian teaching, human beings are not children of God by nature. Rather, humans are sons and daughters of God by adoption—by the grace of adoption (see Rom. 8:14–25). This adoption changes our status (we become, with Jesus, "heirs of God"), but it also changes our nature, because grace gives us the gift of everlasting life. In so doing, Christian grace transforms human nature from mortality to immortality, making us more like God, who never dies. Church theologians in the Eastern Roman Empire call this transformation *theosis* (deification), meaning not that humans are children of God by nature, for we are creatures who come into being, unlike God, who never came into being.

This idea of adoption into immortality is explained further in 2 Peter 1:4, where believers are said to "become participants of the divine nature," meaning they have a share in the divine nature by sharing in immortality—everlasting life. According to orthodox Christian teaching, this transformation occurs through Jesus Christ. Faith in Christ, according to Paul and other New Testament authors, unites us with Christ (2

---

1. I am grateful to Dr. Cary for his Great Courses lectures on Christian theology. The discussion on grace in this chapter is adapted from his lecture, "The Doctrine of Grace," Lecture Twelve in *History of Christian Theology*, 45–49.

Cor. 5:17; see Eph. 1:3–10). In Trinitarian terms, this union with Christ is also union with God, for Christ is God.

Augustine, however, shifts the current understanding of grace from the context of overcoming death to overcoming sin. In his thinking, all humans are sinners by nature, and humans cannot overcome this innate propensity to sin without the help of an inner gift of divine grace, which not only forgives past sin but also gives humans the power to love God and neighbor authentically and wholeheartedly. In his famous argument and ongoing debate with Pelagius, a British monk who comes to Rome and North Africa, Augustine argues that humans cannot be saved apart from the grace of God. In other words, they cannot become better people simply by trying harder, or even by believing in Jesus or in his teachings. Pelagius thinks that human effort is sufficient, and that if humans want to change morally, they can do so. Augustine disagrees, arguing for the necessity of divine grace, which alone can accomplish the inward change of the human heart.

Augustine's argument for the necessity of grace is based on three observations. The first of these is the practice of prayer. The basic premise of Christian prayer is clear; its purpose is to invoke God's help in changing our will so that we can have a deeper love for God and neighbor. Augustine is insightful on this point, for this is how Christians pray. They pray believing that God will grant their deepest desire to be more loving. This form of argument became widely used in the Western world, formulated in the famous Latin saying, *"lex orandi, lex credendi"* (the law of praying is the law of believing). At its best, Christian prayer is for greater love, and when we pray, we believe God will answer. This, of course, is how Christians are taught to pray in church, through the liturgy, and the belief is that God will grant their prayer. Such prayer is grace at work.

Augustine's second argument for the necessity of grace is based on the widespread practice of infant baptism. While this practice does not apply to all Christians today, it is universally practiced in Augustine's day. Augustine argues that since baptism bestows forgiveness for sins, there is an intuitive assumption of the part of Christian parents that infants must be guilty of sin, or else they would not need to be baptized. Since infants have not committed any "actual sin," they must be guilty of some inherited sin, which Augustine calls Adam's original sin. Augustine's doctrine of original sin means that every human being is somehow "in Adam" when Adam sins. Thus, according to Augustine, humans are born "in Adam," partakers of his sin. Not only are they born with a corrupted nature, but they are born guilty and deserving of damnation, Hence, when ancient Christians practice infant baptism they are doing so to save children from damnation, transferring them from death in Adam to life in Christ. This, then, becomes Augustine's second argument, that all humans are in need of grace, and that without grace they are damned.

Augustine's first two arguments are based on Christian practice. His third is more psychological. Dealing with the Pauline argument that the Jewish religious Law is no longer applicable for Gentile Christians, Augustine applies it to the summation of that Law, namely, that God's will is fulfilled when we love God with all our ability and others as ourselves. What happens when we hear that command? Do we obey it? Augustine argues that we cannot, that as a result of Adam's sin, the human will is "unable not to sin" (*non posse non peccare*). According to Augustine, when we hear the Law, we actually resent it. We would rather not have to keep it, and find that even if we want to fulfill its demands, we are unable to do so. However, out of fear of punishment, we try to love God fully, and fail, because fear cannot be a motivation for love.

How, then, does love work? How is God's law fulfilled? Such fulfillment requires an inward change in our will, which only occurs through grace. When we pray for grace, God provides it, thereby transforming our heart. As a result, we find we want to love God. The grace we need, which God provides, yields not only compliance, but becomes an inner gift of delight (see Rom. 5:5), increasing our longing for God and our love for others. If things are delightful, they are easy. Even hard work, if it is delightful, is easy (see Matt. 11:30).

Augustine works out the implications of grace in his treatise *On the Spirit and the Letter*, based on Paul's argument in 2 Cor. 3:6, "the letter (the Jewish Law and its commands) kills, but the spirit gives life." Building on Paul's contrast between the external and the internal, Augustine notes that the help we need is not additional outward legislation, but rather the inward grace of God's Spirit. The role of the Law is not to drive us to guilt or terror but to the grace of God, and that gift of grace—acquired through prayer, worship, and a life based on faith—transforms us so that we end up loving God for others' sake and others for God's sake, and that becomes our salvation.

For Augustine, salvation is like a journey to God. Faith gets us on the right road. Then there is this long road to travel, a road we travel by love—of God and others. For Jesus and Paul, this is the summation of the religious Law, which goes back to the Old Testament, and Augustine puts it at the heart of Christian ethics. Love is like gravity—a force of attraction—and it pull us upward, not downward. Love for God attracts us to God, pulling us upward, like sparks from a fire, ultimately uniting us with God.

In his attempt to know God and to understand God's will, Augustine begins with faith. For Augustine, faith is not some nebulous cognitive act by which one hopes God exists, but an activity requiring the whole of one's being—heart, mind, soul, and strength. In his commentary on the Gospel of John he writes, "Understanding is the reward of faith. Therefore, seek not to understand in order that you may believe, but believe in order that you might understand." Augustine shortens this to the motto: *credo ut intelligam*—"I believe in order that I might understand," taking this motto from Isaiah 7:9: "If you do not stand firm in faith, you shall not stand at all."[2] In other words, unless one begins by accepting certain truths, one will not understand later on. While modern versions of Isaiah 7:9 read somewhat differently, Augustine is working with Old Latin texts of the Old Testament, before Jerome (a contemporary of Augustine) produces the Vulgate, which becomes the standard Latin Bible in the medieval period and the basis of Catholic Bibles to this day.

Building on passages from the Gospels of John and Matthew, Augustine notes that Jesus first invites followers into a relationship with himself and through him, with the Father (see John 17:3), and it is on the basis of this relationship of knowing and trusting God that he says to his disciples in Matthew 7:7, "Search (seek), and you will find." Thus, people are to believe first what they later come to understand. Augustine is not asking believers to scrap or compromise reason—he is not asking for "blind" faith—but simply subordinating reason to revelation. For Augustine, divine revelation, as given in Christ, is the precondition for all religious knowledge. Once believers begin with God, then they are to seek to understand all truth in light of God. In our journey toward God, the task of reason is to seek deeper understanding of what we already believe by faith.

Truth, for Augustine, requires God's illumination of the mind. In this respect, religious truth is real, objective, and unchanging. It is truth because it is illumined to our minds by God. While truth is rational (capable of rational explanation), it is not rationalistic (not dependent on abstract human reason, which is prone to usurp divine revelation in

2. In his reading from Isaiah, Augustine is following a different version than the one upon which modern translations are based.

Christ; see John 1:9). For Augustine, both faith and reason are needed in the search for truth, not as cognitive processes, that is, as ways of requiring belief, but as affective processes involving our desires, our will, and our commitments. As Augustine makes clear, knowledge is not simply a means of knowing for its own sake, as a purely rational endeavor. He wonders whether such knowledge is even possible.

Augustine believes that everyone's search for truth begins with the acceptance of authority, not merely in religion, but in all areas of human life. Historical claims in particular must be accepted or rejected on the basis of authoritative testimony. Christianity involves such historical claims, and Augustine seeks to show that it is reasonable to accept the testimony upon which Christianity rests. Thus, we have three distinctives in Augustine's search for truth: (1) that all knowledge involves our affective side, meaning that to know and relate to God, our heart must be right; (2) that the purpose for seeking truth is that it lead to knowledge and love of God; and (3) that knowledge involves acceptance of authority. For Augustine, faith is indispensable, but it is only the start of the journey to God. The journey requires grace, which increases our love and brings us closer to God. Relying on authority is not, however, a substitute for reason. Augustine views authority as no more than a short cut: authority shows us what reason later discovers for itself.

For Augustine, grace increases human merit or worth. In speaking of merit, Augustine is following an argument central to Roman Catholicism, but not for Protestants, who, following Martin Luther, speak of faith alone, or grace alone. For Augustine, humans must cooperate with God, and when our wills cooperate with grace, the resulting works of love have merit. At this point, Augustine distinguishes between "operative grace"—the initial gift of grace that changes our hearts, turning our will toward God—and "cooperative grace," which works together with our good will to produce meritorious works of love. As the late medieval theologian Thomas Aquinas argues in the thirteenth century, following Augustine, "operative grace" is the divine help given to humans whereby "God is the sole mover," and "cooperative grace" is our response, whereby we become active participants in our salvation.

Although for Augustine grace and free will are seen as compatible, the human propensity is to sin—that is, to love in the wrong order (loving self more than others, or things more than God), seeking happiness in lesser things, when only God can make us truly happy. Grace enters our will and strengthens it to love the right things. For Augustine, the will's primary role is to love, and grace helps it to love the right things, in the right order. Operative grace is where God works in the human will apart from its cooperation. It is God's grace entering deep into one's heart, transferring it from selfishness (self-absorption) to selflessness (authentic, selfless love of God and others).

In the sixteenth century, Protestant Reformers such as Luther and Calvin deny Augustine's notion of cooperative grace, arguing that humans cannot merit God's grace or contribute in any way for their salvation.[3] They understand salvation more as a guarantee of eternal life with God in the afterlife than as a journey that begins in the present and continues into eternity. They certainly value Augustine's understanding of operative grace, which is what they mean by "grace alone." Such grace results in what later revivalist call "conversion," where the will is turned, not by coercion, but by sheer delight, as fulfillment of one's deepest longing and truest happiness.

When we are on the journey home toward God, our desire to love is strengthened by grace. Augustine calls this strengthening grace, "assisting grace." He also speaks of "healing grace," since humans are wounded by things less than God, things they pursue such as money, alcoholic drink, sex, and power—any impulse that distracts them from love of God and neighbor. Augustine views these distractions as a disease, and just as people addicted to things seek them in excess, so the diseased heart seeks things that are not for its good. God's grace, both operative and cooperative in nature, is necessary in our journey toward greater love of God and others, stimulating, healing, and strengthening our will to love.

This brings us to the question of free will, for apart from free will, we cannot truly love. If God turns our will apart from our cooperation, does that violate free will? For Augustine, it does not. Even in those moments when grace holds the initiative, grace and free will are compatible. It is not a matter of free will responding to grace, but of grace turning our will. However, grace turns our will freely, through the action of inner delight, without violating our free will.

From this assumptive point, Augustine speaks of predestination, one of the most controversial doctrines of orthodox Christianity. We

---

3. Of course, Roman Catholics do not believe they can "earn" salvation. For Catholics, sin continues throughout the believer's life, for which there is forgiveness. The important thing is to be on the journey, and on the right road. As Catholics believe, Christians don't get home to God until after death. However, life should be an ever-improving journey toward one's destination with God.

credit Augustine with the formulation of this doctrine and its corollary, operative grace, because no one prior to Augustine works out the implications so comprehensively. John Calvin, the Protestant Reformer who formulates an equally comprehensive and even more controversial understanding of predestination, bases his understanding of predestination on that of Augustine.

Augustine's argument derives from his doctrine of original sin. If all humans are born with a corrupted nature—a nature attracted to things that may be good in a secondary but not ultimate way because they are not God and thus not capable of yielding lasting happiness—what can turn us around? By way of answer, Augustine cites Paul's argument in Romans 9:6–33, where Paul uses the analogy of a potter and clay, fashioning from the same clay objects of elegance and others for ordinary use (9:21). For Augustine, all humans, born from Adam, are made of the same lump of clay, a mass having no eternal value or worth in itself. God, by virtue of being the Potter, chooses some vessels for grace—for salvation—and others for damnation. Of course, all deserve damnation (that is, eternity without God), but some are chosen for salvation (eternity with God). Thus, God chooses some, but not all.

Augustine never accuses God of being unjust, for on their own, all humans are at peril. Those who are chosen receive grace; justice condemns the rest. God is not condemned or accused of unfairness, but rather praised for justice and mercy. While the process may be unequal, it is not unjust. God has mercy on whomever he chooses, and shows compassion on whomever he chooses (Rom. 9:18; see Exod. 33:19). At this point we are dealing with a doctrine central to both biblical Testaments—the doctrine of election. As we note in chapter 2, God's election of some individuals or groups over others is not based on merit, but on God's initiative. For first-half-of-life spirituality, election is for salvation (broadly understood as rescued from damnation), and this is how orthodox Christianity understands the doctrine, following Augustine. For second-half-of-life spirituality, however, election is for service; election becomes the means by which God's blessing might be extended to all humanity.[4]

When we wonder why God chooses some over others (such as we find in Romans 9:13, where Paul, citing Deuteronomy 21:15, quotes God as saying he loves Jacob but hates Esau—twins by birth, yet one is chosen over the other even before birth), Augustine's answer comes from

---

4. The idea of election is revisited in chapter 11 below, in the thought of Karl Barth, the important twentieth-century Neo-orthodox theologian.

later in Romans: "O the depths of the riches and wisdom and knowledge of God! How unsearchable are his judgments, and how inscrutable his ways!" (Rom 11:33). In other words, Augustine, like Paul, has no idea as to the answer. While Augustine believes there is a reason, since God always chooses wisely, it is not a reason mortals can know. The reason appears arbitrary, for it is made before the beginning of time—and hence is truly predestined.

Conclusion

From Augustine's view of grace come several important implications, one of the most important being his view of evil. The presence of evil in the world, you might recall, perplexes Augustine before his conversion to Christianity—not only cosmic evil, but ethical evil, his double inability as a young adult, like Paul's in Romans 7:15–20, to enact the good he desires, or to prevent the evil thoughts or actions he opposes. Despite his pessimistic views, Augustine writes in his *Confessions* that "whatever is, is good." In saying this, he is not ignoring evil, but affirming that everything created by God is good. All that exists is God's creation, and God only creates good things. Such a concept, while clearly biblical, is nondualistic.

Evil, when it appears, only takes the form of privation. Like darkness, evil is the absence of light. In speaking of darkness, of course, we are not referring to blackness, which is a real color, for darkness does not exist ontologically but only as the absence of goodness. While, according to Augustine's definition, evil might appear unreal, as the absence of something, nevertheless it is real, as shadows and absences are real. The results of evil have effects on us, like stumbling in the dark. Despite having no substance or reality of its own, the presence of evil is like a vacuum, simultaneously real and unreal. The universe is good because God makes all things inherently good, including human nature. Even the devil—an agent of evil in orthodox Christianity—is good by nature, though evil by free will. Likewise, sinners have a good nature, and though they might reject God, they cannot escape the notion that they are God's good creatures.

Thus, in a deep philosophical sense, Augustine is an optimist, though he does leave a legacy of deep and sometimes terrifying thoughts in his doctrine of grace. Yet through them all come wonderfully winsome concepts, such as his concept of inner delight in God, this love for God that grace instills in human beings. Augustine's legacy deeply influences future Christian thinkers—not only in the medieval and Reformation periods but modern theologians as well.

Questions for Discussion and Reflection

In addition to the questions listed at the end of the preface, answer the following questions, writing your answers in a journal. If you are in a group study, be prepared to share your answers with those in the group.

1. Can you identify areas in your thinking and living where, like the Manicheans, you are dualistic? As we grow spiritually, should we attempt to eliminate all dualistic thinking?
2. If this world is created good by God, how do you explain the existence of evil?
3. How would you answer the question Augustine ponders concerning human purpose, namely, "What am I doing on this earth"?
4. In your estimation, why is the doctrine of salvation also called the doctrine of grace?
5. What do Christians mean when they state that people become children of God by adoption? Explain the results of adoption in the process of salvation.
6. If the role of religious law is central to first-half-of-life spirituality, what is its role for second-half-of-life spirituality? What is the role of grace in first-half-of-life spirituality?
7. Do you agree with Augustine that accepting external authority is central to one's quest for truth? If so, provide examples of reliance on authority in your spiritual journey.
8. Assess the merits of Augustine's doctrine of original sin. How does Augustine connect this doctrine with the doctrine of predestination?

8

Christian Mystical Spirituality

WHILE MOST CHRISTIANS CONSIDER themselves disciples of Jesus and try to follow his teachings, a smaller number focus on practical acts of service or solidarity. While these can be done in tandem, some Christians feel compelled to pursue the difficult mystic path. Throughout Christian history, many mystics follow the monastic path, pursuing spiritual perfection through self-denial, ascetic practices, and extreme devotion.

Unfortunately, the mystical path is often described in vague terms, making it appear unappealing or perhaps inaccessible to most. However, what if we define "mysticism" to mean "experiential knowledge of spiritual things," as opposed to head knowledge, book knowledge, church knowledge, or other forms of secondhand knowledge?

Much of organized religion, without meaning to, actually discourages us from taking the mystical path by telling us to trust outer authority exclusively—whether in the form of scripture, tradition, or reliance on specific religious experts—instead of encouraging and supporting the value of inner experience. This first-half-of-life approach—trusting the "containers" instead of the "contents"—blocks access to second-half-of-life spirituality (what we are calling the "second journey"). Discouraging or denying people's actual experience of God can create passivity and lead to the conclusion that either there is no God to be experienced or that such experience is not possible. This approach can result in distrusting our soul, and hence the Holy Spirit within us.

Contrast this with Jesus' common advice, "Go in peace. Your faith has made you well" (see Mark 5:34; also Luke 17:19). He says this to people who make no dogmatic affirmations, do not think he is "God," do not pass any moral checklist, and rarely belong to the "correct group." They are simply people who trustfully affirm, with open hearts, the grace of their hungry experience, and that, in that moment, God cares about it.

Admittedly, personal experiences are easy to misinterpret, and we cannot assume that our experience is always from God. We must develop filters to clear away our own agenda and ego. We need a solid grounding in theology, psychology, and sociology, along with good and wise counsel. We cannot forget Paul's reminder, which is meant to keep us humble, "For we know only in part, and we prophesy only in part" (1 Cor. 13:9).

The irony in all attempts to rely on externals is that people end up relying upon their own experience. Most of us—by necessity—see everything, mystical and otherwise, through the lens of our own temperament, early conditioning, brain function, role and place in society, education, personal needs, and cultural biases and assumptions.

Monastic Spirituality

The desire for an extreme existence among some Christians seems consistent with elements in the New Testament that exhort believers "not to be conformed to this age" (Rom. 12:2), and with images of the first believers as sharing possessions and having nothing they called their own (Acts 2:44–45; 4:32–35). Some precedents exist in Judaism—such as the Essenes, who live communally and on the margins of society—and in the Greek world, where philosophical schools often "live apart" in community. The Epicureans and the Pythagoreans have a long history of "life together" outside the bounds of ordinary society, in some cases even sharing possessions.

The first form of monasticism is the lonely hermit (the word "hermit" comes from the Greek word for desert, and is a reminder that the monastic life begins in Egypt, where a short journey either east or west from the narrow Nile River puts one in a rigorous desert). Antony (250–355), inspired by a sermon on Christ's words to the rich young ruler ("go, sell what you own, and give the money to the poor," Mark 10:21), takes this literally and departs into the desert, living the life of solitude in a tomb. Later legends recount his battles with temptation and wild beasts, but despite such stress, he lives a full life of 105 years. His example proves contagious, for he has hundreds of imitators.

Around the year 320, a former soldier named Pachomius institutes the first Christian monastery. Instead of permitting the monks to live singly or in groups of hermits, he establishes a regulated common life, in which the monks eat, labor, and worship according to a fixed plan. From these beginnings in Egypt, the ascetic movement spreads to Syria, to Asia Minor, and eventually throughout Western Europe. The monastic ideal in the East spreads through the influence of Basil the Great, who dies in 379, his *Rule of Discipline* guiding Greek Orthodox monasticism to this day.

The first to introduce monasticism to the West is Athanasius. The circulation of his *Life of Saint Antony* helps spread the monastic ideal. Augustine, bishop of Hippo, writes the first western monastic rule for his community of clerics. In 415 the monk John Cassian founds a monastery near Marseille and writes valuable books on meditation. The greatest contributor to Western monasticism, however, is Benedict of Nursia (480–550), whose *Rule* provides the constitution for Western monasticism and gives it its motto—*orare et laborare*—prayer and labor. Every Benedictine monastery includes a library, where monks copy and read the great works of antiquity. We are indebted to them for preserving the writings of the Latin church fathers and the masterpieces of Roman literature. Monasteries also become a great missionary force, rendering immense service in the spread and development of Christianity and of civilization during the darkest ages of European history.

Throughout the Middle Ages, the monastic life provides one of the few venues where women are allowed to participate in the religious life. Early praise for virginity plays a part, especially after the Virgin Mary becomes prominent in the church's liturgy and theology. Thus Hildegard of Bingen (1098–1179), an early example of female leadership in a monastic setting, becomes founder and first abbess of a Benedictine community on the Rhine River. A Renaissance woman, she is renowned not only for her mystical visions but also for a remarkable set of writings on scientific, theological, and musical subjects. In addition, she provides advice to kings, bishops, and leaders of other monastic institutions, as evidenced by a significant body of letters.

The rise of monasticism may well be one of the most beneficial institutional events in the history of Christianity. For over a millennium, in the period between the reign of Constantine and the Protestant Reformation, almost everything in the church that approaches the highest, noblest, and truest ideals of the gospel is done either by those who choose the monastic way or by those who are inspired in their Christian life by monks. Protestantism, we might recall, begins with the monastic experiences of Martin Luther. Luther and Calvin turn repeatedly to the work of Augustine, including his monastic order. In fact, Luther begins his adult life as an Augustinian monk. Throughout the ages, monasticism provides an alternative lifestyle that enables Christians to express discipleship in a more radical way. Monasteries become important centers for reform and in the early medieval period of the West, monks enhance education, copying manuscripts and preserving for other Christians a great body of teaching about the discipline necessary to be an authentic Christian.

The breadth and depth of monastic influence in the church is comprehensive. If we read scripture in our native language, we benefit from a tradition inspired by the monk Jerome (342–420). If we sing hymns, we follow the pattern established by the monks Gregory (540–604) and Bernard of Clairvaux (1090–1153). If we pursue theology, we find ourselves indebted to the monks Augustine and Thomas Aquinas (1225–1274). If we focus on Christian missionaries, we think of efforts pioneered by the monks Patrick (387–461), Boniface (680–754), Cyril (826–869), and his brother Methodius (815–885). If we are interested in the early record of Christianity in English-speaking areas of the world, we cultivate a concern begun by a monk known as the Venerable Bede (673–735). If we relish in nature and its goodness, we follow the friar Francis of Assisi (1181–1226). Monasticism may not be a perfect answer to the question of how to live the Christian life, but its impact is been sizeable.[1]

Because the monastic movement often challenges the church, it serves as a source of renewal. Following a period of striking ecclesiastical degeneration in the ninth and tenth centuries, the founding of a monastery at Cluny in 910 ushers in administrative and spiritual reforms that are felt over the next century and a half, even to the highest reaches of the Vatican. Over time, however, wealth and power has a corrupting effect on the rigor of monastic life. The entry of the nobility into the monastery and their inevitable ascent to power lead, in turn, to the election of abbots of Cluny as bishops, and even as popes. By the year 1100, more than one thousand Benedictine monasteries belong to the Cluniac order.

The emergence of the Dominicans and the Franciscans in the thirteenth century sparks another cycle of renewal in the life, thought, and service of the church. These orders become known as mendicant (the term comes from the Latin word for "beggars"), and the term "friar"

---

1. Noll, *Turning Points*, 79.

distinguishes them from monks because, unlike monks, they go forth to live and serve among the people. Just as monastic houses arise to minister in the countryside, so the mendicant friars focus on meeting the spiritual needs of townspeople.

The first approved mendicant order iss founded by Francis of Assisi (1182–1226) in 1209. Abandoning his wealth and status to serve Christ in poverty, the charismatic Francis leaves home in ragged clothes, wandering the countryside with followers he calls his "little brothers." Preaching the joys of poverty and paying attention to outcasts, they survive by depending on alms. A noblewoman named Clare, a friend of Francis from Assisi, establishes a corresponding order of women known as the Poor Clares. The early history of the Franciscans is complex, and over time it becomes difficult to maintain Francis's original, radical ideals. The order eventually commits to scholarship and gives rise to great theologians and mystical teachers such as Duns Scotus (1265–1308) and Giovanni di Fidanza, better known as St. Bonaventure (1217–1274).

The second order of mendicants, the Dominicans, is founded by the Spaniard Dominic de Guzmán (1170–1221). He studies arts and theology, and then sells his possessions during a famine to help the poor. He becomes enthralled with the ideal of preaching the gospel to pagans before founding an order of preachers, approved by Innocent III in 1216. The great learning and dedication of this order produces great theologians such as Thomas Aquinas and great mystics such as Meister Eckhart, John Tauler, and Henry Suso.

Because of their zeal to oppose heresy, both Dominicans and Franciscans are used by the papacy in the process of inquisition. Together, these mendicant orders not only serve as instruments of papal policy, but they energize evangelization and the care of the poor. Their commitment to the intellectual life also makes them leading movements in the development of medieval universities.

Mysticism, an expression of Christian faith, flourishes during the fourteenth and fifteen centuries. The fourteenth century experiences the Great Plague, or the Black Death, which begins in 1331 and extends to 1351. It decimates Europe as it does the rest of the inhabited world. The bubonic plague, spread by fleas carried by rats, kills half the population of China before spreading to the Middle East and Europe, were it yields similar results.

Mysticism is particularly evident in England in the fourteenth century. Among the most powerful and remarkably beautiful of the mystical works of this period is *The Cloud of Unknowing*, an anonymous guide to the contemplative life written for monastic readers. The book recognizes that between humans and God there is an impenetrable cloud, so that the point is not knowing God but loving God. Of the writings of the mystics of the late Middle Ages, one still widely read is *The Imitation of Christ*. Attributed to the fifteenth-century Thomas à Kempis, the book may be based in part on earlier works. It begins: "He that followeth Me walketh not in darkness, saith the Lord . . . Let therefore our chief endeavor be to meditate upon the life of Jesus Christ." For the author, as for Christians in general, the life of Christ exceeds all others.

Among the anchorites (those who live as hermits within the context of the cathedrals) are two English figures, Richard Rolle (1300–1349), known for his beautiful poems on the passion of Christ, and Julian of Norwich (1342–1416), who uses female attributions to the divine in her series of visions she calls "Showings." Her *Revelations of Divine Love*, written around 1395 and widely acknowledged as one of the classics of the spiritual life, is the first book in the English language known to have been written by a woman. The century that sees the Black Death ravage Europe also witnesses a rebirth of classical learning.

During the Reformation of the sixteenth century, Protestant thinkers begin questioning doctrines and practices established during the medieval period, including ecclesiastical hierarchicalism, the authority of the pope, the estrangement between laity and clergy, sacramentalism, monasticism, the veneration of relics and saints, the emphasis on good works as meritorious for salvation, and the sale of indulgences. In so doing, most Protestants are not rejecting church authority, but rather subordinating it to biblical constraints. While retaining the ancient creeds and the theological formulations of the great ecumenical councils of the fourth and fifth centuries, mainline Protestants reject those doctrines, practices, and ceremonies for which no clear warrant existed in the Bible, or which seem to contradict its letter and intent.

It takes the Church of Rome some time to respond fully to the Protestant challenge. At first the defiance is local and personal, but when Catholicism finally realizes the seriousness of the revolt, it responds comprehensively. Some historians interpret the response as a counterattack against Protestantism, while others describe it as a genuine revival of Catholic piety. The truth is the movement is both a Counter-Reformation and a Catholic Reformation. The mystical experience is a large part of Catholicism's recovery. The sixteenth century produces a remarkable variety of Catholic saints, including the English humanist Thomas More, the missionary Francis of Sales, the Spanish mystics Teresa of Ávila and John of the Cross, and the most influential of all, the Spanish soldier Ignatius Loyola.

The Incomprehensibility of God

In the history of Europe, the medieval period (the thousand-year period said to last from the fall of the Western Roman Empire in 476 to the fall of Constantinople in 1453), alters the Western and Middle Eastern worlds profoundly. However, the start of the fourth century, beginning with the Edict of Milan in 313, changes the fortunes of Christianity forever. With the conversion of Constantine to Christianity in 312, state persecution of Christians ceases, and Christianity is on its way to becoming the official religion of the Empire (an event made official by Emperor Theodosius in 380). This dramatic change of church-state relations, with Christianity no longer endangered but established, has a profound effect upon prayer and spirituality. On the one hand, it leads to an impressive display of liturgical worship. Spacious churches are built and richly decorated, where the Eucharist can be celebrated in formal splendor. At this time there is also a rapid development of pilgrimages, the cult of the saints, and devotion to the Virgin Mary. On the other hand, ascetic piety, present in Christianity from the start, assumes a more articulate form with the emergence of monasticism as an organized movement, distinct from the life of the parish. Both the "way of affirmation" and the "way of negation" become more sharply differentiated.

Yet the polarity between the city and the desert should not be exaggerated. Their interdependence is symbolized by the personal friendship existing, at the very start of monastic history, between Athanasius, Archbishop of Alexandria, and the hermit Antony. While monasticism could easily have developed along schismatic lines as an "alternative church," overall this did not happen. Bishops in the fourth and fifth centuries, some high-ranking functionaries within the civil structure of the Christianized Eastern Roman empire, are also in many cases monks. The monks, on their side, also contribute to the elaboration of liturgical worship, and in the eighth century play a leading role in the defense of icons. The two "ways" of affirmation and negation exist within a single, all-embracing framework of church life, each presupposing the other.

The division of Christianity between East and West, based on the geographical and linguistic distinction between the Western and Eastern Mediterranean world, one Greek-speaking and the other Latin-speaking, one Roman and the other Byzantine, comes to mean two different ways of doing theology. The Eastern half of the Roman Empire, including such modern countries as Greece, Turkey, Syria, Palestine, and Egypt in Northern Africa, becomes the theological homeland for Eastern Orthodoxy (primarily Greek and Russian Orthodox churches), and the Western half, including Italy, France, Spain, and Algeria and Tunisia in Northern Africa becomes the theological homeland of Catholicism and Protestantism. Many of the early church councils take place in the East, their proceedings and creeds formulated in the Greek language.

In chapter 5, when thinking about Neoplatonism, we speak of the Christian doctrine of the incomprehensibility of God—a mystery beyond human understanding. That doctrine, as it develops historically, comes to be understood in two ways, one in the Eastern and the other in the Western half of Christendom. While there are numerous correspondences and interactions between these two great halves of Christianity, there are important differences. The Western Church becomes deeply influenced by Augustine, the Eastern Church far less so. One of the most important issues in Christian theology is the doctrine of God. While both sides agree on the doctrine of the Trinity, they disagree on the incomprehensibility of God. The Eastern theological tradition clearly identifies the incomprehensible God of the Trinity with the incomprehensible god of Neoplatonism named The One, whereas the West, acknowledging Augustine's conception of grace, views God as potentially intelligible to the human soul.

When Athanasius sums up the message of salvation in his famous dictum, "God became human, that humans might become gods," he pens perhaps the most comprehensive mystical statement ever devised: The word "god" in reference to humans should not come as a surprise, since the word "*theos*" or god in the Greek world refers to beings who are immortal. Therefore, if humans receive immortality or everlasting life, a gift Christians claims to have received through Christ, they become "gods," that is, immortal. Even in the Old Testament we occasionally find texts that speak of angels as gods. These are not gods the people worship, but they are believed to be immortal.

The Eastern Christian tradition seeks to give full emphasis to both parts of Athanasius's statement. The implications of the first part, "God became human," (the doctrine of the incarnation) are explored by Eastern theologians from the fourth to the seventh centuries, unpacking what it means to affirm that Jesus Christ is fully God and fully human, yet a single undivided person. It is in response to this three-sided question that the first six ecumenical councils, from Nicaea I (325) to Constantinople III (680), develop the classic expression of Trinitarian theology and Christology. This period marks the contribution of Eastern theologian such as Gregory of Nyssa, Evagrius of Pontus (c. 345–399), and Pseudo-Dionysius (the late fifth-century theologian known in the West as Denys the Areopagite).

What the Council of Nicaea means for Athanasius is a clear recognition of the absolute ontological gulf between God and humanity. Nevertheless, through the incarnation, Christ offers humans participation in his own blessed life. Emphasis on the gulf between divinity and humanity calls in question traditional Hellenistic ideas of human kinship with God, such as reflected in Paul's statement to the Athenian elders in Acts 17:28, whereby humans might attempt to ascend to God—ideas also found in Clement and Origen. For Athanasius, deification no longer means restoration of a natural human state; the emphasis is on God's condescension to humans rather than on our ascent to God.

In the centuries that follow, the main focus of attention in the Eastern or Greek tradition shifts from the first to the second part of Athanasius's dictum, "that humans might become god." What are the effects of the divine incarnation in the life of the Christian? What is signified by *theosis* (deification)? How is it possible for humans, without ceasing to be authentically human, to enjoy direct and transforming union with God? These become the master themes of later Byzantine theology and spirituality. Two writers in this period stand out with particular promise, Symeon the New Theologian (949–1022) and Gregory Palamas (1296–1359). Each is rooted in the past, yet both are at the same time explorers, developing the earlier tradition in fresh ways.

As we learn in earlier chapters, a key feature of the Greek world is *gnosis*, the quest to experience first-hand acquaintance with God. Some Gnostic texts describe practices of contemplation that can lead to mystic knowledge of the Barbelo *aeon*. In the *Gospel of Truth*, Valentinus invites Christians to experience intimate knowledge of the Father through communion with the Son. This quest for *gnosis* continues in the Christian tradition, apart from groups that became known as heretics. Already in the second century, Clement of Alexandria teaches that Christians should aspire to transcend mere faith in the doctrines of Christianity and achieve *gnosis* with God. The ideal Christian, Clement says, is the true Gnostic.

One of Clement's greatest future admirers is Evagrius of Pontus, who comes, as his name implies, from Pontus, a city in modern-day Turkey. He is a younger contemporary of the Cappadocians, having known Basil and Gregory of Nazianzus, whose disciple he claims to be. A promising church career is cut short by an ill-advised love affair, and he flees to Jerusalem, eventually becoming a monk in Egypt. There he attracts many followers, becoming the greatest teacher of spirituality in early monasticism.

An early letter written from Constantinople, prior to his becoming a monk, contains hints of his later teaching, and shows him to be a man of daring intellect, more unreservedly Origenist than the Cappadocians. Like Origen, he sees the Christian journey to God as requiring three stages of ascent, which he names *praktike* (cultivating the virtues), *physike* (contemplating the created order), and *theologike* (becoming acquainted with God). One of the shrewdest psychologists of antiquity, Evagrius orients spirituality toward the restoration of knowledge of God and unity. Unlike Augustine, his younger contemporary, he finds the seeds of good remaining in fallen creatures; though humans are capable of evil, they are not evil by nature. Recovery begins with faith, which is present even in those who do not believe. Faith, when activated, promotes reverence of God, which leads to self-discipline and the desire to practice the virtues. Full practice of the virtues leads to *apatheia* (overcoming the passions), resulting in charity, which is the "door to *gnosis*."

Apatheia, for Evagrius, is not a goal in itself, nor is it a condition to which we can attain permanently, for temptation continues throughout our lives. Evagrius names four deterrents to *gnosis*: material possessions, thoughts (*logismoi*), passions, and demonic spirits. Demons, being fallen creatures,[2] orchestrate warfare against humans, using many wiles, which Evagrius illustrates. However, they cannot penetrate our minds, though they observe our reactions. Unable to lead us to sin, their power over us depends on ourselves (in this respect, see Matt. 13:36–43; also Eph. 4:27; 1 Tim. 3:7; Jas. 4:7; 1 Pet. 4:8–9). The essential enemy is passions (by definition disordered affection), and the most effective remedy is not through direct action—trying to subdue them through force of will—but rather indirectly, by desiring virtue.

---

2. Evagrius fully accepts Origen's explanation of the fall of pure intellects, demons having fallen the farthest from their original contemplative state with God.

Our natural passions are obviously stirred by material possessions and by specific people, so withdrawing from persons and individuals that might tempt us is a useful start. However, for the introverted seeker, the essential struggle is with thoughts (*logismoi*), because ultimately it is they that stir our passions. As Evagrius notes, all harmful thoughts spring from self-love (what we today call the ego or false self), and result in false notions of God. Evagrius identifies eight types of *logismoi*: thoughts of gluttony, lust, love of money, depression, anger, sloth, vanity, and pride. His analysis is taken over by his disciple John Cassian (c. 360–c.432), and later adapted to produce the familiar seven deadly sins.

For Evagrius, prayer is the highest and most proper activity of the mind (see 1 Thess. 5:17), but, paradoxically, prayer, at its purest, means "the putting away of thoughts," or, as Zen Buddhists put it, taking as thought "the thought of no-thought." Because God is said to have neither shape, form, or complexity, the mind, in order to be united with God, must also shed shapes, forms, and desires. Demons may try to make us accept or settle for visionary forms of God, but this is vanity. In pure prayer, the mind is illumined only by the light of the Holy Trinity, which excludes all knowledge or sensible vision. In the highest prayer, God is not in any ordinary sense an object of knowledge, for in this state there is no more consciousness of ourselves than there is when we are asleep. Hence, the realization of the mystic: "You were here all along, God, and I never knew!" (see Gen. 28:16).[3]

In mystical spirituality, God is not bound by any definition, localization, or particularization, so our knowledge of God might best be described as "unbounded ignorance." For the Christian gnostic, pure prayer is wordless and imageless; all that is left to the formless mind is an intense yearning for God. For Evagrius, the goal of spirituality is a vision of God beyond images or pictures, for though these might be good, ultimately they distract us from God, who is beyond anything we can say or imagine. To achieve this goal requires emptying our mind of all things, in order that God might fill it.

After his death, Evagrius's teaching becomes an object of controversy, and he is condemned at the Council of Constantinople in 553. As a result, much of his recorded legacy is lost, at least in the original Greek, preserved only in Syriac translation. Some material circulated anonymously, and some is attributed to other writers.

---

3. See Kushner, *God Was in This Place*.

Another central figure in the history of Christian mystical spirituality is the mysterious Pseudo-Dionysius (known in the West as Denys the Areopagite), a Greek-speaking Christian living in Syria who, early in the sixth century, publishes a set of works about God and other theological topics. The author writes pseudonymously, claiming to be Dionysius, a resident of Athens whom the apostle Paul converts to Christianity in Acts 17:34. In other words, the author claims to be a disciple of Paul and to be writing in the first century. The pseudonymous character of his writing reflects a time when writers try to appropriate the prestige of an eminent authority for their own work. In addition, the author probably writes pseudonymously on account of orthodox Christianity's displeasure with theologians such as Origen and Evagrius, soon to be officially condemned, as well as to disguise extensive borrowing from Proclus, an influential fifth-century Neoplatonist philosopher.

While Greek apophatic theology[4] flourishes in the East as early as the fifth and sixth centuries, due in part to the writings of Evagrius and Pseudo-Dionysius, the West does not develop a full-fledged apophatic spirituality until the ninth century, when the writings of an unknown Greek author are translated into Latin and achieve near-canonical status in Europe. The author uses the name Denys the Areopagite. For centuries, Christians believe him to be Paul's first Athenian convert. However, in the modern period, scholars reveal that the author borrows liberally from Proclus, meaning that the pseudonymous author lives toward the end of the fifth and the beginning of the sixth century. For this reason, scholars now call the author Pseudo-Dionysius, though the name Denys remains in the West, and it is this name we use in future references. During the medieval period, Denys has a profound influence on nearly every major Western theologian.

Combining the Bible with Neoplatonist philosophy and monastic theology, Denys asks, "How do we know God?" Building on the metaphysics of Neoplatonism, which understands God as "beyond being" while attributing categories to God such as Being, Mind, and Soul, Denys also borrows from Proclus the idea of the soul's threefold movement to God, from rest in God, out in procession, and back in return. Using

---

4. The term "apophatic" refers to ways of knowing God that are direct and not mediated. Apophatics reflect an intuitive form of spirituality, which views God as ineffable and indescribable. Apophatics are comfortable with ambiguity and, when speaking of God, they prefer terms such as Mystery or Spirit. They prefer to worship God in silence or by striving for justice and peace in the world.

the word "theology" to explain *theosis* (deification) or union with God, Denys introduces his own triad: symbolic, kataphatic, [5] and apophatic to explain the traditional pattern of purgation, illumination, and perfection or union, a pattern borrowed from Origen and eventually to become standard in the language of mysticism. According to Denys, *all* engagement with God has this threefold character. The three "theologies" are the three ways in which union with God is furthered, a goal not understood primarily as gaining knowledge of God through communion but rather as "knowing by being known." The three theologies may be regarded as corresponding to the metaphysical Neoplatonist triad as follows:

- symbolic theology—the spirituality of procession
- kataphatic theology—the spirituality of return
- apophatic theology—the spirituality of rest

For Denys, human beings know God in three ways. First, through the created order, because God pours himself into the creation. Symbolic theology corresponds to seeing God in material things, and by seeing how material things bear God, either through a natural likeness, by their inspired use in scripture, or by their use in the Christian sacraments. Symbolic theology thus yields a vision of the natural world as full of God and as bearing God to us. Thus, nature is said to possess a sacramental quality, which conveys grace as well as discloses deeper reality. For Denys, symbolic theology—like a steeple—points beyond itself to the Creator.

If symbolic theology is the spirituality of procession, kataphatic theology is the spirituality of return. In kataphatic spirituality we celebrate the nature of God that is revealed through creation and redemption. Thus, this approach to God is concerned with perfecting our praise of God. In his treatise on the *Divine Names*, after discussing the terms we use to praise the majesty of the Triune God, Denys considers the attributes of God, names we use of God such as Good, Just, Life, Wisdom, Power, and so forth. Kataphatic spirituality focuses on the terms we use in worship, on the affirmations we make in our praise of God. However, as Denys reminds us, using such language doesn't limit God, but rather

---

5. The term "kataphatic" refers to ways of knowing God that are indirect and mediated. Kataphatics reflect a sensate form of spirituality, which prefers concrete images of God. Kataphatics are often divided into two groups: those who prefer to worship verbally and sacramentally and those who prefer to worship spontaneously and wholeheartedly, with the senses and the emotions.

is a way of affirming God as the source of all things, as above them, yet as their origin. Using language that goes back to Plato, Denys reminds us that God is not only beyond intelligibility but also beyond essence and being and therefore, as "hyper—or super-essential." In this regard, God is the Good beyond Goodness; the Wisdom beyond knowledge; the Being beyond understanding. Like the sun that diffuses light, God is the Good that diffuses goodness, making all things good, because for Denys, creation is full of God's outflowing goodness.

Throughout the *Divine Names*, Denys reminds us that all affirmations fall short of God, that no human concepts can describe what is unknowable, and this leads to apophatic theology, with its realization that "the most divine knowledge of God" is that known through "unknowing." Both symbolic and kataphatic theology point beyond themselves to a state where symbols and concepts are transcended and where God is known by unknowing. This is apophatic spirituality—the term in Greek means "negation" or "denial"—the theology of rest. The West picks up some of this way of thinking, speaking of the *via negativa*, saying what God is not, such as immutable (not changing), immortal (not mortal), and incomprehensible (above human understanding). In this respect, the fourteenth-century English work known as *The Cloud of Unknowing*, written in the apophatic tradition, is a masterpiece of negative mystical theology.

Denys identifies the Trinity as simple, meaning God has no parts and therefore is above intelligibility. Intelligibility of God is a manner of understanding unavailable to humans beings because it is likened to looking directly at the brightness of the sun, something human sight is not designed to view. Looking at God is therefore not like trying to see in the darkness, something human beings can achieve to a limited extent, but rather more like looking at a darkness that is so bright—like looking directly at the sun—which darkens our eyesight through brilliance. There is a divine darkness, says Denys, which is like the dazzling brightness of the sun. It is above intelligibility, above light, above understanding, because, like the sun, God is a brightness too visible to see, too dazzling to understand.

The Christian mystic engages in both kataphatic and apophatic ways of knowing God, fluctuating between affirming things about God and then denying those very things, even to the point of negating one's negations about God. Such theology creates space within the mystic, a place of "unknowing," which God's divine energy can fill. In this form of *gnosis*, we negate our mind and even our egoic self so that God can take over. In apophatic spirituality, the seeker gains *gnosis* of God through a-gnosis—knowledge through non-knowledge. This activity of negation is partly something we do—Denys uses the analogy of a sculptor cutting away in order to reveal hidden beauty—but more deeply, in the darkness of unknowing, something God does. By submitting to God, the soul experiences an ecstasy of love, surrounded by God's own ecstatic love of his creation. It is reassuring that even when talking of darkness, Denys relies on the Christian definition of God as love.

Ultimately, there are not three "theologies," three ways to experience communion and union with God, potentially in conflict with one another, for all spirituality is rooted in Denys's conviction that God, who creates *ex nihilo* (out of nothing),[6] is a totally different order of reality from creation and thus unknowable. Moreover, since God is unknowable, God is "known in all things, and also apart from all things . . . Therefore, everything may be ascribed to [God] at one and the same time, and yet [God] is none of these things" (*Divine Names* VII.3.872A).

Such is Dionysian spirituality, destined to have a profound influence in both Eastern and Western Christianity. While in the East the balance between knowing and "unknowing" God is better preserved, in the West that dichotomy is a constant source of fresh imagination.

In his *Mystical Theology*, Denys draws on the apophatic tradition already developed by Philo, the first-century Jewish Platonist, and by the fourth-century Cappadocian theologian Gregory of Nyssa. In his *Contemplative Life*, Philo notes the limitations of language and of the intellect in speaking of God. In Philo's spirituality, communion with God results in a state of spiritual exaltation akin to ecstasy, whereby one's natural faculties recede before God and become replaced by God. Gregory of Nyssa, in his *Life of Moses*, utilizes Origen's three stages of the soul's ascent to God, only for him they become a movement from light to darkness, unlike Origen, who understands them as a movement from darkness to light. In speaking of the three stages of spiritual ascent, Gregory compares them with three stages in the life of Moses: the revelation at the burning bush and Moses' two ascents of Mt. Sinai, the first into the cloud (Exod. 24:15–18), and the second into the darkness, where he asks to see God face to face (Exod. 33:17–23; see also 20:21). In his journey toward God, Moses moves from the revelation of light (Exod. 3:1–15), to the darkness of the cloud, and beyond that to the thick darkness "where God dwells."

---

6. Denys's view of creation differs from that of Plotinus and Neoplatonism, where all things are said to emanate from God.

The reason for Gregory's reversal of Origen is clear. For Origen, the soul's ascent to God is its restoration to its original state, a movement from the darkness and confusion of its fallen state. For Gregory, the soul's ascent to God is its drawing ever closer to the One who is utterly different from it, One who is utterly incomprehensible because there is no natural kinship between God and humanity. In his writings, Gregory depicts vividly the bewilderment, despair, and longing that possess the one who seeks God. In the dark, humans can form no clear or certain conception of what is there; this experience is interpreted by Gregory in terms of an endless longing for God, continually satisfied yet always yearning for more.

Such language reminds us of the sixteenth-century Spanish mystics Teresa of Ávila and John of the Cross, perhaps the pre-eminent mystical authorities of Western Catholicism. Both emphasize that the relationship of God requires emotional detachment from those things on which we rely for our comfort, self-esteem, and personal security in this world. In this lies the clue to John's much-misunderstood phrase "the dark night of the soul," which speaks less of privation than of union with God. John's doctrine of "*nada, nada, nada*" (nothing, nothing, nothing) is not a doctrine of *nirvana*, understood as the extinction of human personality, but rather of *nirvana* understood as divine fullness. The experience serves to purify the intention, stripping the will of all unworthy motives for praying and leaving only the desire of God for God's own sake.

While the dark night is often felt as an inability to pray, the inability is only apparent. The spiritual darkness is really a light, which the soul that is not enlightened or properly purged is unable to recognize, since this "night" darkens natural intelligence. Filled with wise and sympathetic guidance for safe passage through the nights of ambiguity, anguish, and uncertainty, John's "dark night" has in view the highest positive human goal of all, true self-fulfillment in accordance with the all-loving purpose of the Creator.

The contemplative dimensions characteristic of John's "night" have nothing in common, except at the most superficial level, with the kinds of devotional prayer of meditative techniques commonly associated with biblical images such as envisaged, for example, in the *Spiritual Exercises* of Ignatius Loyola. The distinction here is crucial. Entry into the passive "night" of the thought and senses necessitates radical change in common Christian conceptions of prayer, associated with liturgical, devotional, or other Christianized forms of piety. Simply put, John's (and Gregory's) obscure sense of presence, of possession (or rather of being possessed), is best understood as the soul's understanding of being the object of God's love, a love that awakens within the seeker a passionate response of love as that person senses the beauty of God that transcends comprehension. The mysticism of divine darkness, whereby the soul is united with the unknowable God, is the summit of mystical spirituality, a spirituality that helps shape Christianity's dogmatic theology. During the medieval period, apophatic spirituality becomes ingrained in Western Christian consciousness, and it is this way of the heart to God that religion should take if it is to have a central and hopeful role to play in twenty-first-century spirituality.

While Denys the Areopagite is influential in the East, Augustine is even more so in the West. Like Denys, Augustine conceives of God as incomprehensible, but he interprets the concept differently from Denys. For Augustine, the human mind is like an eye, made to see the light of divine Truth. However, due to human sin, no one can see God naturally; as a result, our human soul—including our will, intellect, and understanding—is corrupted. However, if our mind's eye is healed by grace, and we are guided on our way to God by divine love, we will—by the nature of our intellect—be able to see God. That is what our intellect was made for—to see the truth. It is natural for humans, you might say, to seek God. This is the path we humans have been on our whole lives—the path of love—and when we receive God's grace, we finally find the truth we have been searching for. This is the happiness we desire; it is joy in the truth, says Augustine. In this respect, when human beings receive God's grace, God is intelligible, and it becomes possible for humans to look directly at the "sun" and not be dazzled.

This notion is unique to Augustine. The rest of the Christian tradition, in both East and West, says it is not natural for humans to see God—like the natural eye is not made to look at the sun. However, at its best, this way of seeing is partial and transitory, Augustine admits, enabling only a glimpse of God. Just because the physical eye can see an object, this does not mean it can comprehend it. While the eye might see an object such as a cup, it can only see one side at a time. Thus, the eye can see a cup, yet not comprehend it. The same holds true for God. We may be able to see God by our intellect, but we cannot comprehend God.

Following Augustine, the West faces a problem that has to be solved. The Western tradition believes that human happiness depends on seeing God. Yet the West also inherits the view of Denys, whose work is translated into Latin and becomes influential. The resolution between these traditions comes in the thirteenth century, in the theology of Thomas

Aquinas, a brilliant thinker viewed by Roman Catholicism as the supreme medieval theologian.

Aquinas agrees with Augustine that happiness consists in seeing God with the mind's eye, and that this is the ultimate goal of life. On the other hand, he agrees with Denys that no created being can see the divine essence. This raises the million-dollar question: "How can humans have happiness, if with their natural mind's eye they try to gaze on an incomprehensible God?" Eventually disagreeing with Augustine, Aquinas declares that it is not possible naturally for humans to have a "beatific vision" of God (a vision of God that makes a human being happy or blessed). Nevertheless, he argues, comprehending God (seeing God) is possible for a mind that is elevated by "supernatural grace."

In so arguing, Aquinas introduces a new concept of grace, one that elevates the mind above itself, so that it can see what no natural capacity is able to see. Grace, in this new sense, doesn't just come to our aid, doesn't just heal us so that our natural mind is strengthened to see God. Rather, supernatural grace actually enables humans to do what they cannot do by nature. This gift of grace, when given, is said to reside in one's soul, making it habitual—a habit of the soul—to see God. Aquinas, influenced by the Greek philosopher Aristotle, comes to understand grace as a skill or habit that enables one's heart and soul to see what is beyond their inborn capacity to see and comprehend. Hence, it is possible to look directly at God and find in that brightness, not dazzlement or blindness, but rather happiness and beatitude. While the beatific vision—the ultimate goal of human life—cannot be achieved independently, such experience, such finding, requires faith, hope, and charity, supernatural gifts of divine grace. One, alone, however, is not sufficient. Knowing God requires all three gifts simultaneously.

The Spirituality of the Icon

Of the three major divisions in Christianity today—Roman Catholicism, Eastern Orthodoxy, and Protestantism—the least known in the West is Eastern Orthodoxy. Most Protestants, if they think of Orthodoxy at all, think of it as a kind of Roman Catholicism without the Pope. The differences, of course, are far greater, including the starting questions. While Protestants and Catholics generally ask the same questions—How is a person saved? What is the church? Where does religious authority lie?—Orthodox Christians start elsewhere, with holy images called icons. Found on church partitions called the iconostasis, the wall of paintings that separates the sanctuary from the nave, or hanging on walls in Orthodox homes, these images of Jesus and the saints serve as a kind of window between the earthly and the celestial realms. Viewed less as aids to worship and more as ways the heavenly beings manifest themselves to the faithful on earth, it is impossible to understand Orthodox worship apart from icons.

For both Eastern and Western Christianity, beatific vision is the goal of human existence—what makes us eternally happy or blessed. Eastern Orthodoxy has a unique and distinct view of vision and grace. We start our discussion with physical vision, for this is where Eastern Orthodoxy begins—seeing with our physical sight. And what they see are icons (from a Greek word meaning "image"). When Orthodox Christians speak of icons, they often refer to "holy images," typically pictures of saints, often of Christ, his mother, the apostles, and so on.

Icons are part of Eastern Orthodox theology, not just Orthodox culture. The theology of icons reaches a classic formulation in the seventh ecumenical council, the Second Council of Nicaea in 787. The fundamental doctrine of that council is the veneration of icons. The issue is controversial, because in the Christian tradition there is a strong prohibition against using graven images in worship, as we find in the Ten Commandments and in Judaism as a whole. The same holds true in Islam, a religion then pressing in on the eastern borders of the Byzantine Empire. Prior to the seventh ecumenical council, there is also the movement of iconoclasm, an effort hostile to icons and religious images in general. For a while, all images are banned in worship, and many such aids to worship are destroyed. The main argument of the iconoclasts is Christological: whoever makes an image of Christ makes an image of God, who cannot be pictured or represented. Mixing divinity with humanity, thereby reducing Jesus to one nature, is something Christians already condemn. If images reduce Jesus solely to his humanity, that too is condemned, for it separates Jesus' divinity from his humanity. In either case, such worship is considered theologically corrupt. And if icons of Christ are forbidden, by implication this holds true for all icons.

The seventh ecumenical council responds by arguing from the Catholic use of crucifixes, noting that such representations of the crucified Christ do not diminish Jesus' divinity but rather that they divinize his flesh, thereby giving unity to Christ's two natures. This argument brings out an important distinction between the Eastern and Western churches: the East, when it takes a Christological risk, leans toward the unity of Christ's natures, whereas the West leans toward their distinction. In its use of icons, the East is not seen to deny Christ's two natures, but rather to heighten the deification of his flesh. Hence, when one gazes on an icon of Christ, it is not his divinity one sees—for divinity is invisible—but his divinized flesh. Therefore, his flesh is worthy of veneration.

For the sake of clarity, it is important to distinguish between veneration and worship. The Eastern Orthodox do not worship icons, for no images are to be worshipped. Rather, they venerate icons, because icons represent something holy. When someone venerates an icon, they are said to be communing with the holy individual thus represented, in such a way that one's desire and love are extended to the person thus pictured. This is a way of knowing Christ or the saint being pictured.

The veneration of icons is so important to Christians in the East that it comes to be identified with Orthodoxy itself. For that reason, there is in the liturgical calendar of Eastern Orthodoxy a Sunday called "The Sunday of the Triumph of Orthodoxy." This event, observed on the first Sunday in Lent, celebrates the restoration of icons by the seventh ecumenical council. Interestingly, the Roman Catholic Church, utilizing statues rather than images, accepts the teaching of this council, while most Protestants do not accept the authority of this council or the piety represented by status or images, which requires not only the veneration of icons but devotion to the saints. This is one of the reasons why Protestant churches are generally bare of images. They display crosses, but not crucifixes, and the cross is empty, in keeping with the Second Commandment.

Nevertheless, as a Protestant, I find something profoundly beautiful and true for spirituality in the Eastern veneration of icons. To understand this, we need to examine the theology behind the veneration of icons, and this gets us to the heart of Orthodox theology, for underlying this theology is an understanding of the Transfiguration of Christ, an event found at the center of the Synoptic Gospels (see Matt. 17:1–8; Mark 9:2–8; and Luke 9:28–36).

As we note above, when Eastern Orthodox gaze upon an icon of Christ, they physically see deified flesh, like Peter, James, and John viewing the Transfiguration of Jesus. The Transfiguration is the glory of God, shining like light from the very flesh of Christ. Think of that picture—incandescent flesh shining with a light that is divine. For Eastern Orthodoxy, this is deified flesh, and from that flesh shines a light—an uncreated light, according to the fourteenth century Greek theologian Gregory Palamas, perhaps the most distinctive and influential late medieval Orthodox theologian. This "uncreated light," shining from the flesh of Christ, must be the Holy Trinity itself, for only the Trinitarian God is uncreated. The stirring notion here, according to Palamas, is that though this light is divine, it can be perceived both sensibly (with the physical eyes) and with the intellect.

If we go back to Plato's distinction between intelligible and sensible perception, which is about two kinds of being—natural and supernatural—Greek Orthodoxy collapses that distinction. The Eastern perspective on the Transfiguration does not distinguish between physical light and the divine uncreated light shining forth, perceptible both to the senses and the intellect, for even though the light of the Transfiguration is "brighter than the light from the sun," as one Orthodox scholar puts it, no one at the bottom of the mountain seems to have seen it. The reason is that both the physical eyes and the intellect need to be purified in order to see this divine, uncreated light. The astonishing thing is that the light of the icon—known as the Light of Tabor, after the mountain of the Transfiguration—transforms, beatifies, and deifies those who see it, thereby overcoming the Platonic distinction between sensible and intelligible things, between the natural and the supernatural.

The Eastern Orthodox theology of transfiguration makes Christ central to the way Orthodox Christians think about God. The beatific vision, for the Orthodox, is the vision of the transfigured Christ. This episode at the heart of the Gospels is a foretaste of the beatific vision that is said to be the ultimate joy and fulfillment of human nature. When one gazes on an icon, it is not the divine essence one sees, but the uncreated light flowing from the human flesh of Christ. According to Eastern Orthodoxy, the Light of Tabor is not a one-time occurrence, but something experienced by the holy saints, those believed to have experienced this light, not merely by the eyes, but also by the ears, the heart, or the intellect, for the transformative Light of Tabor can enter one's being through many avenues. Furthermore, when the glory of this light spills from the souls of the saints and transforms their bodies, for a pious believer to behold an icon of a saint is to experience the deifying effects of the Transformation.

From this understanding of Christ's transfiguration comes the doctrine of *theosis*. In Orthodoxy, the idea of "image" is essential to understanding how God and humans relate. Humans are created "in the image of God," bearing within the icon of God. Unlike Western Christians, inclined to understand the fundamental relationship between God and humanity in legal terms, the great theme of Orthodox theology is the incarnation of God and the re-creation of humanity. According to Orthodoxy, when humans sin, they do not violate the legal relationship between themselves and God; they diminish the divine likeness.

Salvation, therefore, consists in restoring the image of God within humanity. The major themes of Orthodoxy, then, are the rebirth, recreation, and transfiguration of human beings. This takes place within the church, viewed not as a formalized institution but as the mystical body of Christ constantly renewed by the Holy Spirit flowing through it. It is within this fellowship of love that human beings are made ready to join the preexisting communion among Father, Son, and Spirit. Orthodox believers call this process *theosis*, what Athanasius means when he pictures Jesus fully sharing in the corrupted world of humans so that we might fully share in the incorruptible fellowship of God: "Christ became human so humans could become god." Understandably, the language of "becoming god" troubles Western Christians, but the language is less about humans becoming God and more about humans becoming fit companions for an eternal communion with and in the triune God.

According to Symeon the New Theologian, an Eastern medieval theologian, this inner radiance, which the saint receives, can be transmitted to the body as well, just as physical fire transmits its effect to iron; and from the saint, it can be experienced by others as well. In ancient Greek philosophy, there are four elements in the material world, "fire" being the highest. When iron, which is made of the lower element "earth," is joined with fire, it is transformed from a base metal into something shining and glorious, glowing with an incandescent light as a result of being heated. For this reason, fire is a metaphor of spiritual transformation. Like fire, the recipient of iconic vision is afire with the light of God. You can call this glory, but also grace, for this is the Eastern Orthodox doctrine of grace, and this explains why Eastern Christians venerate icons. When one gazes at an icon of a saint, one is contemplating the transformed flesh of a saint, someone who has the divine transfiguring light within. This experience is said to be a foretaste of the eventual beatific vision.

An attractive exemplar of this form of spirituality in the West is the seventeenth-century French mathematician and philosopher Blaise Pascal (1623–1662), who demonstrates in his life and thought how to connect head and heart, intellect with conviction. A child prodigy, Pascal gains the admiration of mathematicians and scientists in Paris for his invention of the calculating machine and for his discoveries of the basic principles of atmospheric and hydraulic pressures. Committed to the scientific method, his writings on geometry and probability theory strongly influence the development of economics and social science. A person of vast intellectual ability, he becomes an avid student of the Bible, finding in it principles for inner spiritual transformation.

Due to his premature death at the age of thirty-nine, he is unable to complete a projected book on the evidence for Christianity. After his death, friends find portions of his writing on faith and reason, which they publish under the title *Pensées* (Reflections). At the time of his death, a servant notices a curious bulge in the great scientist's jacket. Opening the lining, he finds a folded parchment written in Pascal's hand. The words speak of a religious conversion he experiences on the night of November 23, 1654: "Fire! God of Abraham, God of Isaac, God of Jacob, not of the philosophers and the scholars. Certainty, certainty, feeling, joy, peace. God of Jesus Christ . . . May I never be separated from Him." The words record Pascal's mystical experience in the presence of God.

Fully immersed in the "age of reason," Pascal knows he cannot ignore the domain of the heart; "the heart has reasons that reason cannot know" he writes. According to this conception, faith and reason belong to different orders, but they need not be opposed to one another. In his view, Christian faith is not a leap *within* the order of the intellect—a leap that violates the essence of that order—but a leap *from* the order of the intellect to the order of the heart. Pascal understands the human condition so deeply yet so clearly that Christians in our own time still gain perspective from him for their own spiritual pilgrimage.

We conclude this chapter with a distinction between Roman Catholicism and Eastern Orthodoxy. In the Roman Catholic view of the beatific vision, as found in Thomas Aquinas, it is possible for a believer to gain a vision of the divine essence, when that individual is elevated by supernatural grace. The Eastern view follows Denys (Pseudo-Dionysius), who argues that the essence of God cannot be seen by any created being. The Eastern tradition follows Palamas, making a further distinction. What one sees, through the uncreated Light of Tabor, is not the essence of God but rather the energies of God. These "energies" or "workings" of God, often identified with God's glory, are the means whereby creatures participate in the life of the Triune God. The essence of God, however, remains incomprehensible to all but God. Like light flowing from the sun, humans can experience the light, enjoying the light and its benefits without looking directly at the sun, which is not humanly possible without risking severe damage to the retina. Like glimpsing an eclipse with a safe filter, humans can look at God only by looking at Christ—that is, at his flesh. And we can do this by contemplating an icon. In this respect, Eastern Orthodoxy is profoundly Christocentric; it is seeing the glory of God in the face of Jesus Christ (2 Cor. 4:6).

Grace, for Eastern Orthodox, makes humans gods, that is, children of God, giving us everlasting life, which makes us immortal. Moreover, it is the life of the Triune God that is shared with us by adoption. *Theosis* is said to happen when the uncreated light flows from the flesh of Christ into our eyes, flesh, and intellect. It is a deifying light, which transforms the faithful into immortal gods, giving them a share in the life of the Father, Son, and Holy Spirit. For a person dedicated to Christian devotion, there is no higher depiction of spirituality.

Questions for Discussion and Reflection

In addition to the questions listed at the end of the preface, answer the following questions, writing your answers in a journal. If you are in a group study, be prepared to share your answers with those in the group.

1. In our quest for truth, should experience trump authority? Explain your answer.
2. Describe and assess the contributions of monasticism to the development of second-half-of-life spirituality.
3. The Christian mystical tradition produces numerous spiritual mentors. Is there one you find more attractive than others? If so, whom? Explain your answer.
4. In your estimation, is God knowable or unknowable? Explain your answer.
5. If God is unknowable to humans, is God also incomprehensible?
6. In your estimation, what is the greatest difference between Eastern and Western Christianity? Explain your answer.
7. In your own words, explain the meaning of Athanasius's famous dictum, "God became human, that humans might become god."
8. In your own words, explain the meaning of the term *theosis*.

9. Of Evagrius's four deterrents to spirituality (*gnosis*), which do you find most difficult to subdue or defeat? Explain your answer.

10. Which of Denys's three forms of spirituality or "theology" do you find most attractive at this point in your spiritual journey? Explain your answer.

11. After reading this chapter, what did you learn about the spirituality of the icon? Explain your answer.

9

Sectarian Spirituality
Baptists, Quakers, Pietists, and Revivalists

Two worldviews mold medieval intellectual and religious culture: the Greek and the biblical traditions. The Protestant Reformation of the sixteenth century brings profound changes to European culture, for the Reformers seek to repudiate the synthesis mentality that dominates Christian thought for centuries, with its reliance upon reason. In their opinion, medieval thinkers consciously attempt to fuse radically different traditions into one theological system. The Reformers begin questioning doctrines and practices established during the medieval period, including ecclesiastical hierarchicalism, the authority of the pope, the estrangement between laity and clergy, sacramentalism, monasticism, the veneration of relics and saints, the emphasis on good works as meritorious for salvation, and the sale of indulgences. In so doing, most Protestants are not rejecting church authority, but rather attempting to return the church to its biblical foundation. Their cry becomes *ad fontes*, "back to the sources," meaning that they wish to return to the scriptures of the Old and New Testaments. While retaining the ancient creeds and the theological formulations of the great ecumenical councils of the fourth and fifth centuries, mainline Protestants reject doctrines, practices, and ceremonies for which no clear warrant exists in the Bible, or which seem to contradict its letter and intent.

While economic, political, and social issues inspire the major transformations of sixteenth-century Europe, spiritual and moral issues are the primary forces advancing the development and course of the

Reformation. Above all else, the Reformers seek to correct the doctrine and life of the Christian church. Unfortunately, the focus is on first-half-of-life spirituality, concentrating on an antiquated sin-salvation paradigm fashioned from a limited reading of scripture.

It takes early Christianity several centuries to create a systematic understanding of Jesus and his mission, one that, in my estimation, it gets wrong. When I think of Jesus, it is not how he is dissimilar from other human beings that I seek to understand, but rather how he serves as the model and metaphor for all humanity. In my estimation, the historical Jesus embodies the universal Christ, the Reality that gives all humans final meaning and definition. As a biblical scholar and a lifelong follower of Jesus, I consider my conception of Christian faith and practice to be closer to that of Jesus and his earliest disciples than that defined by later orthodoxy (as shaped by canon, creeds, and episcopacy [that is, governance by bishops and male hierarchy]).

The historic creeds and dogmas of Christianity reflect less an incorrect view of Christian teaching than a limited and incomplete view, the church's attempt to define its organizational first-half-of-life identity. Later, during the fifteenth and sixteenth centuries, Reformers begin questioning doctrines and practices established during the medieval period, including the role and interpretation of scripture. Unfortunately, the Protestant Reformation, charting a new organizational identity for Christianity, also focus on first-half-of-life issues, including statements of belief (creeds and confessions) and a closed canon, further fragmenting the church.

Designed to reform the church, the Reformation gives birth to Protestantism, challenging papal leadership of Western Christendom.[1] Four major traditions mark early Protestantism: Lutheran, Anabaptist, Reformed, and Anglican Christianity. Shortly thereafter, Roman Catholic Christianity regroups and, led by the Jesuits, recovers its moral zeal. Bloody struggles between Catholics and Protestants follow, and Europe is ravaged by war before it becomes obvious that Western Christendom is permanently divided. While the Protestant Reformation further fragments Christendom, the idea of Christendom, in the form of state

---

1. The term "Christendom" represents the view that church and state work cooperatively for the benefit of earthly order and welfare. After the schism of 1054 and until the Protestant Reformation, historians speak of two such overarching networks in the former Roman Empire, Eastern Christendom centered on the patriarchate in Constantinople and Western Christendom centered on the Vatican in Rome.

churches, survives the Reformation practically unscathed. The first Protestant Reformers hold to the idea of Christendom as firmly as the Catholics. What they seek is a reformed Christendom, not the possibility of opting out.

One Protestant principle that greatly affects the relationship between church and society is the Lutheran principle of the priesthood of all believers. The church, Martin Luther teaches, does not need a priestly class to mediate between believers and God. Rather, each believer has immediate access to God through Christ. By virtue of one's faith in Christ, each believer stands before God as priest, needing no human institution as intercessor.

While Luther in Germany and John Calvin in Switzerland are the leading Protestant Reformers during the sixteenth century, they are not viewed as infallible, and some of their followers begin modifying their views. One group, later called Anabaptists or Radical Reformers, disagrees with the notion of a reformed Christendom altogether. Led by the Swiss Reformer Ulrich Zwingli (1484–1531), they disagree with Luther, who allows in worship and in practice whatever the Bible does not prohibit. Zwingli establishes the principle that whatever the Bible does not commend should be discarded. For this reason, the Reformation in Zurich strips away traditional symbols of the Roman Church such as candles, statues, music, and pictures. Later, in England, people call this behavior Puritanism. In one matter, however, Zwingli, is inconsistent, for he commends the ancient Christian practice of baptizing infants, even though there is no clear example in scripture. Zwingli thinks that baptizing infants is crucial for holding a community together, the basis of good citizenship. He says that infant baptism is a Christian version of the Jewish ritual of circumcision, a sign of the people's covenant with God. Not all of Zwingli's followers agree.

Conrad Grebel and Felix Manz, both well-educated men of standing in Zurich, support Zwingli's initial reforms. But in their study of the Bible they come to see obvious differences in the apostolic churches and those of their own day. In 1525, the city council of Zurich arranges a public debate on the question of baptism, and after hearing arguments on both sides, the council sides with Zwingli and his followers. As a result, the council requires all parents to baptize their children. Failure to do so results in banishment. A few days later, a group of individuals meet at the Manz house to decide how to respond. George Blaurock, a former priest, goes to Conrad Grebel and askes to be baptized as an adult, upon confession of personal faith in Jesus Christ. Grebel baptizes him on the spot and Blaurock proceeds to baptize the others. Thus, Anabaptism (rebaptism) is born.

Shortly after, the small company of believers relocates to the nearby village of Zollikon, where they establish the first "free church," a church free from state jurisdiction. In 1526 the Zurich council decides that Anabaptists are threatening the very fabric of society, and it decrees that anyone practicing rebaptism be put to death by drowning. During the Reformation years, between four and five thousand Anabaptists are executed by fire, water, and sword. In 1527, Felix Manz becomes the first Anabaptist martyr. That same year, an early conference of Anabaptists takes place at Schleitheim, marking the first synod of the Protestant Reformation. The group adopt the Schleitheim Confession, a shared set of belief and values based on the following principles:

- *Discipleship.* To be a Christian one must have a relationship with Jesus Christ. Such faith transcends doctrines and leads to a transformed style of life. For the Anabaptists, discipleship refuses participation in worldly power, including bearing arms, holding political office, and taking oaths. In the sixteenth century, such abandonment of citizenship constitutes treason.
- *Love.* The principle of love, logically developed from discipleship, requires pacifism. Anabaptists are not to go to war, defend themselves against attacks, or participate in any coercion by the state.
- *Congregationalism.* Decision-making rests with the entire membership, not with bishops, priests, or other church officials. In Anabaptist assemblies, all members are baptized as adults, upon profession of faith in Christ. In deciding matters of doctrine, the authority of scripture is primary, its interpretation given by the consensus of local members. In matters of church discipline, the believers also act corporately.
- *Separation of church and state.* The church, according to the Anabaptists, is distinct from society, even if society claims to be Christian. Christ's true followers are a pilgrim people, perpetual aliens in a sinful world.

Many of these beliefs are now accepted by other Christians. The distant relatives of the Anabaptists today include Quakers, Baptists, and, to some extent, Congregationalists. The first Anabaptists, wishing to restore apostolic Christianity, desire radical social change. Their goal is to restore apostolic Christianity. Unlike Lutherans, who follow the notion of the "territorial church," considering the population of a given territory members of their church, Anabaptists follow the notion of the "gathered church," where individuals have the freedom to join the congregation of their choice. Such freedom begins with conversion, and for Anabaptists, it is this experience of spiritual regeneration that makes one fit for baptism.

The true church, the radicals insist, is always a community of saints, dedicated disciples in a wicked world. Like the missionary monks of the Middle Ages, Anabaptists wish to shape society by their example of radical discipleship.

Baptist Spirituality

The first Baptists are Puritan Separatists in England.[2] They originate in the seventeenth century, the century after the birth of the Protestant movement. They are not the same as the Anabaptists, though the two groups have much in common. Both groups reject infant baptism, insisting that only believers can properly be baptized.[3] More fundamentally, they see no basis for infant baptism in scripture, at least not explicitly. Both groups also insist on baptism by full immersion in water, not simply by sprinkling. Such beliefs reject the underlying Catholic notion of sacraments as instruments of grace, and for these and other reasons of nonconformity, both groups are persecuted. In fact, the Baptist church in England is illegal when it arises.

As Separatists, Baptists are illegal because they reject the concept of a state or national church, which in England means the Church of England.

---

2. The Puritans are Anglican Protestants who want to further reform the Church of England according to scripture, purifying their church of residual Roman Catholic customs such as making the sign of the cross, kneeling to receive communion, and observing holy days other than the Sabbath. Such practices are required by the government, and the crucial theological issue is whether the church has the right to make rules and customs not required in scripture. Puritan clergy who do not observe the regulations of the Church of England are called non-conformists. The great document of English Puritanism is the Westminster Confession of 1647, composed by an assembly of Puritan theologians at the request of Parliament during the English Civil War.

3. According to Baptist belief, "believer's baptism" contravenes the validity of infant baptism. Since, in their view, baptism does not regenerate, that is, make one a true Christian believer, baptism should occur after regenerating faith, which only a person of consenting age can proclaim.

In the late sixteenth century, for example, the period of Queen Elizabeth's reign, Anglican worship is mandatory. No other form of worship is legal, and violators can be fined and/or jailed. In early Baptist theology, as with Puritan Separatists, believers adhere to the pattern of a "gathered church," viewed as a local congregation of covenanted believers. Hence, no one is born a member, nor is membership automatic. This means the church follows congregational polity, signifying it is a voluntary society, not based on geographical parishes but on a regenerate church membership.

In the "territorial church" model, characteristic of state churches, it is difficult not to be a member, and non-members incur rejection, loss of status, and threats of damnation, whereas according to the Baptist model, it is actually difficult to join, for candidates must present evidence of personal regeneration (true conversion), a state requiring both correct belief and proper moral conduct. In sixteenth-century England, not being an Anglican means one cannot attend national public universities such as Oxford and Cambridge. However, not being an Anglican does not prevent one from paying taxes, which includes paying for the support of Anglican clergy.

From 1750 to 1850, it is increasingly difficult to be a religious Separatist in England, due to a marriage act that requires all valid marriages, except those for Jews and Quakers, to take place in the Church of England. Thus, if one's marriage is Baptist or Catholic or non-Christian, it is considered illegitimate. These practices are not as extreme as being burned at the stake, the earlier punishment for dissenters, but they force Baptists to stand for religious liberty. In their struggle to win freedom from government persecution, Baptists become leaders in the fight for religious liberty for all, both in England and in America. Their dissent, and the price they pay for nonconformity, paves the way for disestablishment and the religious liberty citizens prize in the United States.

Because there is a wide variety of religious belief across Baptist congregational lines, due to the value placed on congregational autonomy, it is difficult to define Baptist identity. Baptists include Calvinists (who emphasize such doctrines as unconditional election, predestination, particular redemption, irresistible grace, and perseverance of the saints) and Arminians (who emphasize conditional election, free will, hypothetical universal redemption, resistible grace, and the possible loss of salvation). Ultimately, authority is biblical, for there are no bishops or councils and no overarching institutional authority. Baptists tend to reject the notion of sacraments, taking a strong Zwinglian view of the Lord's Supper as a symbolic or memorial meal. While Baptists agree on biblical authority, they uphold the right of private interpretation, unmediated by hierarchical tradition. Baptist individualism is reinforced in America by national commitment to democracy, and by a congregational approach to worship. By opposing state churches and insisting on religious liberty for all, Baptists are ideally suited for American denominationalism.

Quaker Spirituality

The seemingly endless debate on dogma, and the intolerance of nonconformist Christians that arises in England and on the Continent in the sixteenth and seventeenth centuries, lead many Christians to seek refuge in inner piety. One such figure is George Fox (1624–1691), born of humble origin in a small English village. At the age of nineteen, disgusted by the licentiousness around him, he begins a life of wandering, seeking divine illumination. His study of the Christian scriptures and his attendance of varied religious meetings lead to the conviction that all religious sects are in error, and that public worship is an abomination.

Church buildings, clergy, hymns, sermons, sacraments, creeds, liturgies—all seem to him hindrances to life in the Spirit. Against all of these, Fox places the "inner light," a pathway common to all human beings, no matter their race, faith, or creed. True Christianity is not a matter of conforming to a set of doctrines or performing rituals led by a professional priest. Rather true believers are illumined by an inner light.

In religious gatherings across England, Fox declares he has been ordered by the Spirit to announce his spiritual version of Christianity. For disturbing the proceedings, he is repeatedly beaten, thrown out of meetings, and cast into jail. His followers grow rapidly, calling themselves "Friends," but others begin calling them Quakers, for their religious enthusiasm. Espousing their belief in equality, they speak out against war, violence, slavery, paying tithes, and swearing by oath. When he is not in prison, Fox travels throughout England and abroad, visiting Scotland, Ireland, and the European Continent, as well as the Caribbean and North America. In all these places he gains converts, and by the time of his death, his followers are counted by the tens of thousands.

Like Baptists, the Religious Society of Friends, as they call themselves, are inspired by the notion of radical immediacy, taking that notion much farther than the Baptists. Immediacy is a modern notion, which arises when one disagrees or finds irrelevant national churches, established churches, and governments that enforce religion through persecution. Citizens of modern nations find the notion of forced worship repugnant, not only for being undemocratic but because it actually suppresses religion.

According to the Quakers, there is only one requirement in religion, namely, one's relation with God. The central Quaker conviction, articulated by Fox and other early Quaker leaders, is that the same Holy Spirit that inspired the Bible also speaks today within the human heart. For that reason, Quaker meetings have no liturgy or clergy but only members of the congregation speaking as they are moved by the Spirit. When they speak, their words have the same authority as scripture. For Quakers, the scriptures are a declaration of the fountain, not the fountain itself. The Fountain is the Holy Spirit; the scriptures are merely an expression of that fountain, as is the testimony of a good Quaker at a Quaker meeting. The scriptures are secondary, always subordinate to the Spirit. This is radical immediacy. The Holy Spirit is the inner light in one's heart, and that is all one needs. Believers don't even need the Bible. They do, however, need to meet together, but they don't need a liturgy, the sacraments, or any external forms, because those who have the Spirit already possess the means they need for the spiritual life. While Baptists practice the ordinances of baptism and the Lord's Supper, Quakers find them unnecessary.

Quakers believe that the inner light of divine revelation is available to all; every human has the Holy Spirit. For this reason, everyone is equal. Like Arminians, Quakers believe that Christ died for every human being, even those who have never heard of Christ. Because Quakers are radical egalitarians, they are resolute pacifists. From the beginning, they refuse to take their hats off for anyone, since they recognize no one as their superior. Like the Baptists, Quakers are consistent advocates of religious liberty for all.

In America, the most famous Quaker is William Penn, after whom the state of Pennsylvania is named. In 1681 Penn receives a charter to found a colony in North America in which there is complete religious freedom. Other British colonies are in existence in the New World by then, but with the exception of Rhode Island, all are marked by religious intolerance. Despite his land grant, Penn is convinced that the Indians, and not the crown, are the legitimate owners of the land. And he hopes to establish such cordial relations with them that the settlers would have no need to defend themselves. The capital of this "holy experiment" is called

Philadelphia—the city of "fraternal love." Under the leadership of Penn, the first governor of the colony, relations with the Indians are excellent, and for a long time his dream of a peaceful settlement is a reality. In the seventeenth century, if you are a Roman Catholic in the American colonies, the only place you can celebrate the Mass freely in the British world is in Pennsylvania, because as a Quaker colony, it advocates freedom of worship for all. In England it is not until the "Glorious Revolution" that accompanies the accession of William and Mary that full religious tolerance for Quakers and all other dissenting groups is made into law.[4]

Pietist Spirituality

Modernity arises, in part, from the Protestant Reformation, which dissolves the unity of medieval Catholicism and results in competing churches or denominations. This movement fosters secularism, especially as national churches become less acceptable. As sectarian groups develop, they run into opposition from the national church in their region, often suffering persecution as a result. In turn, groups like the Baptists and Quakers become critical of the established churches, and for good reason, since the ruling churches often use the existing governments to suppress their rivals. So modernity tends to push against national or established churches, against conformity with authorities external to the individual, favoring secularized government, one with decreasing responsibility for the religious welfare of its people.

As Western society and politics become more secularized and fragmented, modernity provides an environment more suitable to low rather than high churches, favoring theologies of the Spirit and experience over theologies of word and sacrament. High churches are more hierarchical and institutionalized, affirming distinctions between laity and clergy, while enforcing doctrinal orthodoxy. Low churches, like Baptists and Quakers, are moving in the opposite direction, toward anticlericalism, though there is always the temptation toward holiness, purity, and withdrawal from social influences. In many ways, these groups represent the future of modernity, arguing for immediacy, a phenomenon called "inner

---

4. In 1688, the Catholic monarch James II is deposed and replaced by his daughter Mary II and her husband William of Orange, James's Dutch nephew. William and Mary rule together for five years. The Act of Toleration of 1689 is part of the Bill of Rights that confirms the primacy of parliament over the British crown. After Mary's death in 1694, William rules over England, Ireland, and Scotland until his death in 1702.

light" by Quakers and "soul competency" by Baptists, thereby opposing institutional mediation between the individual soul and God.

Most Protestants are not that radical, but as modernity unfolds, they, too, tend to oppose institutional mediation. Thus, modernity favors a turn toward experience, toward the inner self, a view that says, "I can find God on my own, with little or no help from clergy or the church." This turn away from sacraments toward the Holy Spirit tends to characterize many Protestants, certainly those opting for the "gathered church" and away from high-church liturgy and ritualistic forms of worship.

In the seventeenth century, this mindset is particularly prevalent in the Puritan movement in England, and then among German Pietists in the eighteenth century. At some point early in their development, Puritans encounter an issue that becomes all-consuming, namely, the question of how knowledge of salvation is possible, and in particular, how one can have assurance of salvation. This issue of skepticism concerning knowledge is a characteristically modern concern, both in philosophy and in theology. And the turn to experience is a typically modern way to answer that question, assuming that inner certainty is the solution.

Among early Lutherans and Calvinists, faith is regarded as a form of certainty, because it is based on the Bible, believed to be God's Word and therefore absolutely true. At a certain point, Pietists place an additional requirement on individual faith, namely, having the assurance that one's faith is adequate for salvation. Only those with true saving faith are said to be saved, and not those with merely acquired or intellectual faith. At this point, assurance of salvation comes to be based not solely on scripture, but rather on the inner evidence of grace in the heart, manifest through personal salvation. Of course, such evidence is fragile, susceptible to uncertainty and doubt.

In the seventeenth century, these concerns are taken to Germany, where they are adapted to the Lutheran tradition and become known as Pietism. The beginning of German Pietism is customarily traced to a German Lutheran pastor named Jacob Philip Spener (1685–1705), who in 1675 writes *Pia Desideria* (Pious Desires) because he is concerned about the lack of piety (sincere faith and practice) in his congregation and among his colleagues. He desires to promote personal piety, and he does so by gathering people together in small groups for the study of scripture—like small-group Bible studies today. Those small groups are meant to intensify Christian life. Spener's efforts are said to be based on a devotional book, *True Christianity*, written in 1606 by the German Lutheran pastor Johann Arndt.

The background to this problem of insincere worship and behavior by the majority of Lutheran clergy and laity in seventeenth-century Germany is a phenomenon called "Protestant Scholasticism," whereby Lutherans of that period turn faith into a mental exercise. This form of theology, modeled after medieval scholasticism, leads to formality in worship and turns faith into a matter of outward conformity, something Pietists reject. One of Spener's key complaints is that Lutheran ministers are mostly careerists, trained in German universities to become successful rhetoricians, proving the superiority of doctrine to Catholic, Anabaptist, or other forms of Christian belief. To accomplish this, university-educated pastors are trained in Latin disputations, that is, learning to argue the merits and logic of certain beliefs and practices. Pastors then translate these disputations into German, using such proofs for Christian doctrine as the basis for their sermons. Imagine going to church and listening to sermons that consist exclusively of intellectual argumentation. As a result, spirituality suffers, and worship turns into an extension of the classroom. Many pastors become careerists, lacking in pastoral care or in ability to help with the faith-formation of their parishioners.

The head-heart split seems to be a good way of describing what is taking place, an emphasis on head knowledge rather than on religion of the heart. By "heart" we do not mean simply the emotions, but rather the original Hebrew emphasis on unity of emotion, perception, and thought. As the eighteenth century progresses, however, those who emphasize head knowledge view heartfelt piety narrowly and pejoratively, whereas those who emphasize heart knowledge view theology as purely intellectual and irrelevant to the Christian life.

That split becomes most evident in the work of the Protestant theologian August Hermann Francke (1663–1727), an early eighteenth century Lutheran pastor and a protégé of Spener. Francke is one of those Lutheran ministers in training who enrolls in a German university with the intention of training for a good career. At this point, theology is still the "queen of the sciences," still the reigning academic discipline. That changes shortly, as modern science enters the curriculum. As a careerist, filling his head with knowledge, Francke finds that theology hardly affects his spirituality. For a while, he questions whether he is a Christian. He lacks the "true Christianity" Arndt speaks of decades earlier, and fears he might be an atheist. This is perhaps the first time in Christian history when that worry arises. Luther's struggle with God concerns whether God was merciful, but Francke's struggle is new, the struggle over whether God exists. This phenomenon grows virally in the eighteenth century, especially when Christianity is evaluated solely through the lens of reason, where it is found unconvincing.

Francke narrates his own conversion experience as follows: "One day I fell on my knees. When I did so, I did not believe there was a God, but when I stood up, I believed it to the point of giving up my blood, without fear or doubt. Reason stood away: victory was torn from its hands." Reason, here, becomes the enemy of faith, for reason can only produce arguments in the head, not true piety in the heart. To grow spiritually—to live authentically—one needs to put reason aside, so that one can fall to one's knees and experience the Holy Spirit, who makes one a new person. Unlike Luther, who finds regeneration in baptism, Franke finds regeneration in a conversion experience, where one is fully committed—body, heart, and soul—rather than through a sacrament like baptism, where the infant remains passive and uninvolved. For Pietists, one knows one is Christian through experience, by turning inward, into one's heart.

Pietism makes an enormous contribution to Christianity. It shifts emphasis from theological controversy to the care of souls. It makes preaching and pastoral visitation central to Protestant ministry. It enriches Christian music and underscores the importance of the laity for a vital church. Perhaps its greatest legacy, however, is its emphasis on small groups and the devotional reading of the Bible. Supporting all these emphases is regeneration, the Pietist's dominant theme, by which they mean not doctrinal renewal but experiential renewal. The intensely personal way that Pietists describe regeneration often turns Christianity into a drama of the human soul, the scene of a desperate struggle between good and evil. In this sense, Pietism is the foundation of all modern revivals.

Revivalist Spirituality

Our examination of Christian revivalism begins in the American colonies during the seventeenth century. At this time, New England Puritans are predominantly congregationalists in church governance and worship. Interestingly, revivalism arises in the Reformed (Calvinist) tradition, a response to problems that emerge in Puritan churches. The first great revivalist is the Puritan theologian Jonathan Edwards (1703–1758), a Congregationalist

Protestant pastor widely regarded as one of America's most important and original theologians. His work directly leads to the Great Awakening of the 1740s, the first great period of revivalism in America.

Edwards is a staunch Calvinist, and this is striking because of the inference that revivalism is associated with free will—an important aspect of later revivalism—but Edwards, the first great theorist of revival, is a Calvinist, and thus committed to divine predestination, whereby God from eternity foresees and chooses to save some undeserving sinners rather than others. As we think of New England Puritans, congregationalists fleeing from the Church of England, we ponder an anomaly, for though these Puritans affirm congregational autonomy, they become the established church in Massachusetts and Connecticut, meaning their ministers are paid by the state and only church members have full citizenship.

In the mid-seventeenth century, these Puritans begin requiring profession of faith as a condition of membership in the church. Unlike English Congregationalists, such a profession means not simply demonstrating knowledge of basic Christian doctrine, but rather producing evidence of the experience of Christ having worked in your life proper conversion and true saving grace. In Edwards's congregation in Northampton, Massachusetts, in 1734 and 1735, many individuals experience conversion. This is what Edwards means when he uses the word "revival." A revival is not a one-time event but a protracted period in which the activity of the Holy Spirit results in many conversions.

Revivals, for Edwards, are God's solution to the problem that conversion cannot be accomplished by human efforts but solely by divine action. Unlike Armenians, who affirm free will and believe conversion requires human effort in addition to divine grace, Edwards articulates a Calvinist theology of conversion and revival, leaving unregenerate sinners no resource but to wait for God to convert them. And there is no guarantee of conversion, since in Calvin's theology only some humans are predestined for salvation.

Conversions in Edwards's church follow an experiential pattern that reflect his theology. Conversion begins with what Puritans call conviction or awakening. Sinners need to be convicted of their sin—of their lack of love for God and others. As Edwards sees it, God is angry at human sin and intends to damn some sinners while rescuing others. The first stage of awakening is what Luther calls preaching the Law for conviction. Luther follows that with the second stage, preaching the gospel, which involves the gift of grace for all humans, since Christ died for all.

However, as a Calvinist, Edwards cannot agree with this stage, since, according to Calvin, grace is only limited to the predestined, for whom alone Christ dies.

Let us recreate the scenario of Edwards's revivalist preaching. When sinners hear the Law preached, they become anxious and fearful, for they know they fall short of God's standards. They try to bargain with God, but they do so by relying on their own strength to change their ways, aiming to convert themselves, which they are unable to do. Thus, they find themselves in a vicious circle. However, this brings them to the turning point, when they stop struggling against God. Giving up the struggle to convert themselves, they say, in effect, "God, if you damn me, you are just. If I am one of those predestined for damnation, you are right to do so. The mercy of Christ is wonderful and beautiful, even if it is not for me. And your damnation of sinners is also just and wonderful, and I acknowledge it."

At this moment, sinners give up all selfish hopes, and this becomes the turning point. Having accepted the mercy of God unselfishly, they resign to the justice of God, loving God for God's own sake and not for selfish reasons. Sincerely rejoicing in the judgment of God, they realize their heart has changed. And this becomes the moment of conversion. The pastor's role is to proclaim the Law, and create fear in the sinner's heart. This becomes the premise of Edwards's most famous sermon, "Sinners in the Hands of an Angry God." Based on a text from Deuteronomy about the ground falling beneath your feet, sinners find there is nothing to prevent them from falling directly into the abyss. They are like spiders dangling on a precarious thread over the fire, and only God's mercy keeps them from falling. Death can come momentarily, and they can awaken in hell; and there is nothing they can do about it.

While this approach doesn't appear loving, Edwards's sermon is intended to be helpful, within the constraints of his theology. Even Edwards's delivery of the sermon is passionless, lacking any attempt to influence the free will of his parishioners, since the work of conversion is solely God's. In 1737, Edwards writes a book narrating the conversionist revival in Northampton, a book that is read avidly by John Wesley and others in England soon to be involved in New England's Great Awakening of 1740 to 1742.[5]

---

5. Wesley is an Armenian, meaning that later revivals in the colonies shifted from a Calvinist to an Armenian theological setting.

Edwards has a profound influence on later New England theology, arguing for divine determinism, contending that the fallen human will is unable to obey or believe in Christ. However, contrary to traditional Calvinism, Edwards makes a subtle but influential distinction between natural human ability and moral (psychological) inability. Natural ability means that nothing within or even external to the human will can prevent humans from obedience to and relation with God. Nevertheless, moral inability means that humans are unwilling and in a sense unable to obey God.

Later followers of Edwards, like the prominent American revivalist Charles Finney (1792–1875), reject the concept of moral inability but retain the concept of natural ability. A Calvinist like Edwards, Finney teaches that the only factor preventing conversion is human unwillingness—but he does not call this an inability. Rather, Finney's new measure provides an alternative to waiting for God to convert people. He resorts to emotionalism, unlike Edwards, who preaches quietly from a text, and yet has parishioners squirming in their seats, begging him to stop. Finney is willing to shout, and is pleased when listeners shout back, groaning and sighing in despair. Finney even prays for people by name, inviting them forward to the anxious bench. Finney is not shy about using all means available to elicit conversions in his hearers. In his revivals, everyone can participate and pray, including women. Under Finney, revivalist spirituality becomes democratic and egalitarian—the individual prominent. "Choose now," he preaches, and it works! Called the Father of Modern Revivalism, Finney helps lead the Second Great Awakening in the United States. In 1851, he becomes president of Oberlin College in Ohio, one of the first American colleges to accept both women and black students.

At the same time as Edwards's followers are leading American revivals, a parallel movement is taking place in England. It is based on Armenian, not Calvinist theology, and it is led by Methodists, who come from a rival tradition led by John Wesley. In England, the dramatic spiritual renewal associated with Pietism comes to be known as the Evangelical Awakening. Evangelicalism is associated with the spirituality of John and Charles Wesley, founders of the movement known as Methodism. In the American colonies the movement leads to the first Great Awakening, associated with Jonathan Edwards and the revivalist preacher George Whitefield (1714–1770).

In the early decades of the eighteenth century, England is a most unlikely place for a nationwide revival of vital faith. Among the rich and the educated, the Enlightenment shoves religion from the center of life to its periphery. In the established Anglican Church and in the nonconformist denominations such as the Baptists and Congregationalists, the zeal of the Puritans seems to be outdated. The order of the day is moderation in all things.

The fifteenth of nineteen children, John Wesley (1703–1791) is reared in a god-fearing home, the son of an ordained Anglican pastor. While at Oxford University, he and Charles become leaders of a band of students who wish to take religion seriously. Alarmed at the spread of deism at the university, they draw up a plan of study and a rule of life that stresses prayer, Bible reading, and frequent attendance at Holy Communion. The small group attracts attention and some derision from the lax undergraduates, who call them the Bible Moths, Methodists, and other names. The Methodist label sticks.

John and Charles receive an invitation to visit the newly chartered American colony of Georgia, but other than an encounter with Moravians, the entire episode proves to be a failure, and the brothers soon return to England. On his way home John writes in his journal, "I went to America to convert the Indians, but, oh, who shall convert me?" Two years later, on the evening of May 24, 1738, he attends a Moravian prayer meeting in Aldersgate Street that forever changes his life.[6] While listening to the reading of Luther's preface to the epistle to the Romans, he feels his heart "strangely warmed," and that becomes the moment of his conversion. Finding the assurance of salvation he lacks, he embraces a new sense of purpose that sustains him for a half century of evangelistic ministry. He discovers his life's message, but he lacks a method.

George Whitefield, nine years younger than John, goes to Georgia in 1738 but returns to England in the fall of that year to be ordained. Not satisfied with the opportunities given him in church pulpits and eager to reach the masses of people, he begins preaching in the open fields to coal miners who seldom care to enter a church. His voice is clear and strong,

---

6. Sometimes grouped among the Pietists, the Moravians are known for their emotional heart religion. Persecuted for their faith, early Moravians find asylum on the Herrnhut estate of German Lutheran pastor Count Nikolaus von Zinzendorf (1700–1760). Under Zinzendorf, the Moravians carry the pietistic concern for personal spirituality around the world, with important missions in India, the West Indies, North America, and elsewhere. In 1753, the English preacher John Wesley encounters a company of Moravians during his voyage to the New World colony of Georgia. What he sees of their behavior and what he learns of their faith contribute directly to his own evangelical awakening.

and he discovers that his fervent preaching moves the hardened and weary men to tears. When the miners plead for divine mercy in great numbers, Whitefield urges Wesley to follow his lead. The results are amazing. On one occasion, John preaches to over three thousand people in the open air, and conversions take place readily. The Methodist revival has begun. Encouraged by the initial response, John preaches in jails, in inns, on vessels, wherever people gather; "I look upon all the world as my parish," he writes. He travels across England, mostly on horseback, logging some 250,000 miles in his lifetime, the equivalent of ten times around the world. For his part, John's brother, Charles (1707–1788), who itinerates almost as actively for many years, becomes well known as a hymn-writer, composing over six thousand hymns to spread the good news of God's grace. To this day, when English-speaking Christians gather to worship, they often sing his hymns. Perhaps his best loved is "Jesus Lover of my Soul." It is sung in societies all over Britain and America.

In 1739 George Whitefield brings his powerful voice and magnetic style to the American colonies, preaching his way through Georgia, the Carolinas, Virginia, Maryland, Pennsylvania, and New York. By 1740, at the invitation of Boston ministers, he moves northward, preaching in Boston and at Northampton, where Jonathan Edwards is leading revivals, and through the towns of Connecticut, attracting massive crowds wherever he appears. The regional revivals unite into the first national Great Awakening. From 1740 to 1742 the Awakening sweeps 25,000 to 50,000 members into New England churches alone, resulting in the formation of thousands of new congregations.

To be sure, George Whitefield and the Wesleys do not act alone. They are only the most visible English leaders in the more general movement of pietistic renewal that, from the late seventeenth century, eventually encompasses Europe and North America. The impact of Methodism carries far beyond the Methodist Church. It renews the religious life of England and her colonies, elevates the life of the poor, and stimulates missions overseas and the social concern of evangelicals in the nineteenth and twentieth centuries. In both style and message, the adjustments made by John and Charles Wesley and their fellow Anglican George Whitefield prove to be the single most important factor in transforming the religion of the Reformation into modern Protestant evangelicalism.

As the work grows, John decides to employ laymen from the religious societies as preachers and personal assistants. He carefully avoids calling them ministers and he refuses them any authority to administer the sacraments. Throughout his life he resists all pressures from his followers and all charges from Anglican clergy that suggest separation from the Anglican Church. "I live and die," he says, "a member of the Church of England." In America, however, the needs of the Methodists lead him to take significant steps toward separation. The American societies need ordained leaders, but when Wesley's appeals to the Bishop of London prove fruitless, he takes matters into his own hands. He appoints two of his lay preachers for the American ministry and commissions Thomas Coke as superintendent of the American Methodists. The Methodist Church in America become a new, distinct denomination in 1784, and after John's death, the English Methodists follow their American brethren into separation from the Anglican Church.

Methodist preaching has no hesitation in promising grace to all. Believing everyone has free will, meaning every person has the ability and responsibility to choose God's salvation, Methodists teach that grace is available equally to everyone. The Methodist doctrine of prevenient grace means that all who hear the gospel are able, by grace, to choose faith in Christ and salvation. Grace comes first—that is the meaning of "prevenient"—but it is ultimately up to each person to choose whether to accept Christ.

When it comes to practical spirituality, John Wesley leaves as model an ideal way of living that focuses on attitudes toward wealth and on the use of one's resources. Called "the Wesleyan Trilateral," the model promotes the following ideals: "Gain all you can; save all you can; give all you can." Wesley believes that when it comes to economics, Christians should be industrious and clever, working hard and long in order to gain all they can. Wesley follows his advice, becoming one of the highest earning preachers of all times. Based on current dollar amounts, he earns the equivalent of $1.4 million in a single year. Despite his entrepreneurial spirit, Wesley cautions that money should not be illegally gained, and never at the expense of one's health or by taking advantage of others. Given these cautions on wrongful gain, Wesley encourages Christians to be thrifty and industrious, not in order to hoard their money but in order to be generous.

His second concept is about saving. What he means by this is not that we should squirrel as much as possible into saving accounts, but rather that we should be frugal, careful in spending. Rather than squandering money on extravagance and sensual living, Wesley calls for simplicity and plainness. His third concept is about giving "all you can." This is the motivation of his entire view of life, including personal economics. The trilateral stands on giving: we gain and save in order to give. How should we give, and to whom? Generosity begins with ourselves, meeting basic needs. Then we give to family and employees what is their fair share. Third, we gives to other Christians, beginning with our home church. Finally, we give to all in need, even if they are not believers.

Wesley practices what he preaches. In the year he earns the equivalent of $1.4 million, he lives on 2 percent of his income and gives 98 percent of it away. During his lifetime, he earns the equivalent of $30 million, but when he dies he leaves only a few miscellaneous coins and a couple of silver spoons. He has given away all the rest. What a way to die . . . and live!

Holiness Spirituality

Wesleyan revivalism, unlike Puritan or Calvinist revivalism, is not focused exclusively on salvation versus damnation of the human soul, but rather primarily addresses the problem of nominal Christianity, focusing on people who believe the doctrine of Christianity but who are lukewarm believers, not serious about the Christian life. As it turns out, revivalism focuses more on Christians than on unbelievers or people of other faith traditions.

As an Arminian, Wesley does not believe in predestination. A positive corollary of the doctrine of predestination is the notion of eternal security, namely, the belief that once saved, forever saved. Arminians, having no such security, rely on sanctification, with its impetus to deepening one's spiritual life (one's personal holiness). Such motivation, they feel, is undermined by the notion of eternal security. People can just coast, Wesley thinks, believing that this characterizes Calvinism and predestinarians in general. Such security leads to antinomianism—to not taking God's law seriously enough, and to backsliding.

It turns out that Wesley is wrong about Calvinists such as the Puritans, who take sanctification seriously, though for a different reason, Pietists feel that backsliding might indicate that someone is unsaved all along, and therefore not among those predestined for salvation. The bottom line for all Christians, it seems, is confidence in one's sanctification as a precondition to confidence in one's salvation. Thus, Wesley is committed to the spiritual life, particularly to loving God unconditionally and one's neighbor as oneself. The word for this form of spirituality in

Wesley's theology is "perfection." While previous Protestant theologians, including Reformed thinkers, agree on the need for sanctification, taking sanctification to perfection is Wesley's direct contribution.

In this context, perfection means one is perfectly loving and never sins intentionally. For Wesley, perfection does not mean one is morally or intellectually perfect, incapable of failure or error in wisdom and knowledge. It doesn't mean one always get things right, is perfectly wise, or has perfect judgment. Such persons still need forgiveness, but they no longer live in a state of sin.

Luther insists that all human deeds, even those of the best Christians, remain mortal sins. For Luther, believers are made righteous by grace, yet remain sinners in their hearts. In this respect, Wesley's disagreement represents a major departure from classic Protestantism. While Wesley insists that true holiness in the hearts of believers is due to the grace of the Holy Spirit, for him the eventual result can be entire sanctification. Holiness, for Wesley, is obligatory for Christian spirituality; for Luther, such holiness makes no sense. Reformed theology agrees with Luther that sanctification in this life is never perfect, but agrees with Wesley that Christians ought to experience an increase in holiness throughout their lives.

In the nineteenth century, the tradition of holiness becomes normative for Methodism, especially in America, where it is known as the Holiness Tradition. This phenomenon is associated primarily with Phoebe Palmer, who teaches at camp meetings and revivals, but also at the famous "Tuesday Night Meetings for the Promotion of Holiness," conducted in her home in New York City for nearly forty years, beginning in 1836. In this respect, Palmer is part of the pre-history of American evangelicalism. She is a Methodist who desires to live an entirely sanctified life, to experience sanctification truly and fully, but she seeks what she calls the "shorter way" to complete sanctification. Traditionally, sanctification means a lifetime of hard work, when by effort and good works one cooperates with the Holy Spirit. However, Palmer seeks a "shorter way"—holiness now!

She begins what she calls "a season of waiting on the Lord," and she decides not to get up from her knees until she receives such holiness from the Lord. In preparation, she consecrates herself, surrendering her entire life to God, including all her hopes, fears, desires, and needs. Convinced that God had accepted her sacrifice, she acknowledges by faith that she now belongs entirely to God and that as a result, God has granted her the blessing of holiness. This she accepts less on experience and more on trust.

"Faith alone" becomes a distinctive aspect of the Holiness movement. Justification by faith alone is one of the principles of Luther and of the Protestant Reformation as a whole, and it characterizes Wesley as well. However, sanctification—by faith alone—this is unique to the Holiness movement. It is something one receives passively—through yielding and surrender—trusting that God has done it. For Protestantism in general, it is faith alone that sanctifies, but the result is always works of righteousness, which the epistle of James calls "pure religion" (1:27). For the Holiness Tradition, holiness does not require greater effort, but greater surrender—naming and claiming the blessing; God offers good things, and believers claim them by faith.

Palmer devotes her life to listening for what she calls the "Spirit's leading" in her heart. The practice requires discernment, since some suggestions of the heart might actually be temptations rather than promptings of the Spirit. Palmer teaches the practice of listening for this leading, which becomes influential for evangelical Protestantism. One need not be part of the Wesleyan Holiness Tradition to benefit from its influence.

Questions for Discussion and Reflection

In addition to the questions listed at the end of the preface, answer the following questions, writing your answers in a journal. If you are in a group study, be prepared to share your answers with those in the group.

1. In your estimation, how does the Protestant Reformation influence and change the development of Christianity as a religion and as a way of life?
2. In your own estimation, how does the Protestant Reformation change Western society?
3. Assess the significance of the Lutheran principle of the priesthood of all believers for the development of Christian spirituality.
4. Assess the significance of the Lutheran principle of salvation by faith alone for the development of Christian spirituality.
5. After reading this chapter, what did you learn about Baptist spirituality?
6. After reading this chapter, what did you learn about Quaker spirituality?

7. After reading this chapter, what did you learn about Pietist spirituality?
8. After reading this chapter, what did you learn about Revivalist spirituality?
9. After reading this chapter, what did you learn about Holiness spirituality?

10

Liberal Protestant Spirituality

The Middle Ages and the Reformation are centuries of faith in the sense that reason serves faith and the mind obeys authority. To Catholics it is church authority, to Protestants biblical authority, but in either case, faith comes first, not reason. The Enlightenment changes that orientation; reason replaces faith, and concerns for this life replace preparation for the next. Science, prosperity, and reason become the best guides to happiness, not emotions, myths, or superstition. The spirit of this age is nothing less than an intellectual revolution, a new way of looking at God, the world, and oneself. The Enlightenment gives birth to modernism and its twin, secularism. If hatred of religious bigotry, coupled with a devotion to religious pluralism, has a familiar ring, it is because the modern ethos is not outdated. It lives today in the values of the Western world.

The seeds of the Enlightenment lie in the Renaissance, a movement that also gives impetus to the Reformation. Renaissance means "rebirth," and refers to the recovery of the values of classical Greek and Roman civilization expressed in literature, politics, and the arts. In one sense, the Reformation is not possible without the influence of Renaissance humanism, which seeks human flourishing.

Another root of the Enlightenment emerges from the century of religious conflicts between 1550 and 1650, including the English Civil War, the persecution of the French Huguenots, the Spanish Inquisition, and the Thirty Years' War (1618–1648), the deadliest religious war and one of the most destructive conflicts in human history. Religious prejudice seems like a far greater danger than atheism. Thus, a thirst for tolerance and truths common to all people spreads.

Modern science arises in the sixteenth and seventeenth centuries, filling humans with visions of an age of peace and harmony. The pioneers of modern science create new ways to think about the universe. Nicolaus Copernicus (1473–1543) insists that the sun, not the earth, is the center of our universe. Johannes Kepler (1571–1630) concludes that the sun emits a magnetic force that moves the planets in their courses. Galileo Galilei (1564–1642) makes a telescope to observe the moons of Jupiter, adding further support to the Copernican theory of the universe. Isaac Newton (1642–1727), the most illustrious scientist of the Enlightenment, unites all the laws of motion in his monumental work, *Mathematical Principles of Natural Philosophy* (1687). The universe, he argues, is one great machine operating according to unalterable laws, harmonized in a master principle of the universe, the law of gravitation.

Though a devout Christian, Newton's concept challenges the medieval notion of unseen spirits—angels and demons. His theory considers such beliefs superstitious, replacing them with a universe operated by physical laws, explained by mathematics. The sudden access to the mysteries of the universe seems to magnify the role of human reason while minimizing the role of divine revelation. If the universe is a smooth-running machine with all its parts coordinated by one grand design, this frees humans to find meaning and happiness on their own.

This, then, is the fundamental idea of the Enlightenment, that humans are able to find truth by using the scientific method—an experimental approach that combines reason with the senses—rather than rely upon ancient values and beliefs, rooted in superstition and ignorance. The theological implications of such humanistic optimism are significant. In this environment, God seems less necessary to sustain the world. In the new model, the sun displaces the earth as the center. Some believe that humanity is displaced as the crowning apex of creation in the center of God's world. Others feel that God is displaced as well.

Modern philosophers are primarily concerned with epistemology, that is, with the concept of knowledge, not simply with factual knowledge (what can be known), but with the process of knowing (how one acquires certainty). Until the 1600s, philosophy is concerned primarily with the nature of God and with existence itself. However, that concern changes dramatically in the seventeenth century. During modernity, philosophers and intellectuals in general become obsessed with epistemology.

At this time, the concern of philosophers is directed toward finding a new source of certainty. Protestant and Renaissance rejection of church authority, humanistic optimism in society, and the birth of modern science, all shake the foundations of medieval faith. Consequently, seventeenth-century epistemologies explore two basic alternatives: rationalism (that certainty arises primarily from human reason), and empiricism, (that certainty arises principally from human sense perception).

The figure who perhaps best exemplifies modern rationalism is René Descartes (1596–1650). Descartes, above all, seeks to know what is certain. He lives in a rapidly changing world in which long-held foundational principles are being challenged, including religious and scientific teachings. Skepticism flourishes. Descartes, however, is not a skeptic. He is a devout Catholic who contends that human beings are capable of attaining certainty in knowledge, but that before people can obtain certainty, they must first become aware of how dubious or uncertain most of their accepted beliefs are. Descartes begins his *Meditations on First Philosophy* with what he calls "methodical doubt," and on the basis of this methodology he concludes that there is only one thing that he cannot somehow doubt, and that is his thinking self. This discovery of an innate idea, clear and distinct to reason, he summarizes with the Latin phrase, "*Cogito ergo sum*," which means "I think, therefore, I exist."

The important result of Descartes's approach is that knowledge in every case begins with knowledge of one's existence. Self becomes the starting point for knowledge, not God, and its justification is reason. Thus, human autonomy replaces divine sovereignty as the foundation of modern thought.

Thomas Hobbes (1588–1679), another great thinker of the seventeenth century, makes significant contributions to the fields of political theory and philosophy. His father, a cruel and ignorant man who serves as vicar of a British parish, abandons his son after engaging in a fistfight with one of his parishioners at the church door. Fortunately, an uncle takes care of Thomas, sending him to Oxford University.

Hobbes becomes a follower of British scientist and philosopher Francis Bacon (1561–1626). Hobbes is particularly influenced by Bacon's emphasis on the superiority of the physical sciences over any speculative inquiry of the supernatural. Like many seventeenth-century skeptics, Hobbes is not a thoroughgoing or consistent naturalist, since he believes in a supernatural being. His God, however, is not the Christian God of the Bible, whom we worship or with whom we can establish personal relationship, but rather is the God underlying nature, "the first of all causes." In Hobbes's view, God is totally transcendent and apart from nature, not having intervened in the world since its creation. This theological perspective becomes known as deism.

Deist Spirituality

Deism becomes the primary religious belief of intellectuals during the Enlightenment. After Hobbes and Descartes, as confidence in reason soars, many intellectuals begin dismissing appeals to scripture as superstitious nonsense. A group of French thinkers and writers known as the *philosophes* bring the Enlightenment to its climax. These are not philosophers in the academic sense but rather men of letters, observers of society who analyze its evils and advocate reform. They aim to spread knowledge and emancipate the human spirit. These are not atheists, as we might call them today, for most believe in a supreme being but deny that he interferes in the affairs of the world. They are deists, believers in the watchmaker God: God creates the world as a watchmaker makes a watch, and then winds it and lets it run. Since God is a perfect watchmaker, there is no need to interfere with the watch. Hence the deists reject miracles and special revelations or anything that suggests God's interference in the world.

The most influential propagandist for deism is Voltaire (1694–1778), who personifies the skepticism of the French Enlightenment. He achieves his greatest fame as a relentless critic of the established churches, Protestant and Catholic alike, sickened by the intolerance and petty squabbles that seem to characterize organized religion. Voltaire, Jean-Jacques Rousseau (1712–1778), Denis Diderot (1713–1784), and other brilliant thinkers, champion tolerance, denounce superstition, and expound the merits of deism. They hold Jesus in high regard, urging contemporary Christians to emulate the morality of the ancient master and to discard the theological trappings.

While metaphysical and ethical questions formulated during the Christian centuries continue to preoccupy European intellectuals, the great philosophical influences of the nineteenth century—like Immanuel Kant (1724–1804) and Georg Friedrich Hegel (1770–1831) in Germany or John Stuart Mill (1806–1873) in Britain—labor to replace traditional dependence upon revelation and religious tradition with what they believe are more secure foundations of the good, the true, and the beautiful. Kant's argument in his 1793 work *Religion within the Limits of Reason*

Alone becomes an intellectual charter for many great minds of the nineteenth century: "True religion," he argues, "is to consist not in the knowing or considering of what God does or has done for our salvation but in what we must do to become worthy of it."

Enlightenment thinkers use the distinction between natural and revealed religion to understand the diversity of religions, especially Christianity. "Revealed religion" means any religion based on a purported revelation from God, such as Judaism based on the Torah and the Talmud, Christianity on the Bible, and Islam on the Qur'an. "Natural religion" means religious beliefs that are based on reason, which Enlightenment thinkers consider universal and common to all humanity. Later thinkers question these premises, but during the eighteenth century, intellectuals favor natural religion.

The reasons are clear. They are looking back to the seventeenth century, a century filled with religious wars in Europe. These are enough to convince intellectuals that religious zeal is fanatical and dangerous. Many intellectuals conclude that being religious is a bad thing, State churches, whether Catholic or Protestant, viewed as oppressive, authoritarian, and dogmatic, are falling out of favor. The very words "dogma" or "dogmatic" become negative concepts, associated with repression and narrow-mindedness. The conflicting diversity of denominations within Christianity, from Catholic to Anglican to free churches, makes revealed religions questionable and unappealing, by contrast with the rising modern sciences, which are improving people's lives and making significant progress. Theology, by comparison, is looking increasingly less reliable and helpful.

Modern physics, based on Newtonian science, is presenting nature as a closed system, functioning solely on the basis of predictable and knowable natural laws and leaving decreasing room for divine intervention, that is, for the supernatural. A new concept for the supernatural is needed, filled by deism and later by atheism. The eighteenth century becomes the first time in Western history when many seem content to call themselves atheists. Earlier, a few may have wrestled with the possibility, but not it is becoming acceptable, even fashionable.

Many theologians become anti-Trinitarian at this time, leading to the spread of Unitarian views critical not only of Trinitarianism but also of related Christian doctrines such as the incarnation. If Jesus is neither God nor divine, he comes to be seen instead as a great teacher and as a model human. Many intellectuals take satire and ridicule to an exalted literary level, using language that Protestants had previously used of Catholicism, such as superstition and priest-craft, and turning it into criticism of Christianity as a whole. When not criticizing state churches, they also criticize the experiential churches, regarding Quakers, Baptists, Wesleyans, and revivalists in general as fanatical, emotionalists, enthusiasts (a bad word for eighteen-century intellectuals), and deluded, as neglecting reason and misusing passion. Authority in general comes under criticism at this time, especially religious authority, particularly when backed by ruling authorities. Reason comes to stand for autonomy, freedom, and independence, as something opposed to institutional and religious authority in general. On the other hand, belief becomes private, and no one can tell another person what to believe.

Deists focus attention on the difference between natural and revealed revelation, because they advocate natural religion, using it as the criterion with which to judge revealed religions. The content of natural religion, according to Benjamin Franklin, one of its famous adherents, is belief (1) in the existence of God, (2) in providence (that is, in God's governance of the world), (3) in morality as the best way to worship God and live with one's neighbor, and (4) in the afterlife, with punishment or reward based on one's life on earth. By focusing on the relationship between God and morality, the advocates of natural religion have no room for divine intervention; no place for supernatural mystery; no need of priests, dogmatic authority, or incomprehensible dogma; and no need for traditional worship, based on superstitious beliefs and sacraments. Early deists view Christianity as transmitter of the universal truths of natural religion and the Gospels as vehicles for the religion of reason, correcting the accretions of organized religion. Later deists view Christianity as representing the very accretions they despise, and by the end of the eighteenth century, Thomas Payne, expressing the views of the "Age of Reason," speaks of Christianity as corrupt and in need of rejection.

Nevertheless, deists tend to admire Jesus, believing that by eliminating the theological and institutional accretions, the figure of Jesus would emerge as a teacher of natural religion. This becomes the view of Thomas Jefferson, who, while president, takes the time to cut and paste what becomes known as the "Jefferson Bible," which eliminates all miracles and dogmas such as the resurrection and incarnation from the Gospels. The result is a thoroughly human Jesus, the proclaimer of natural religion, a view found primarily in the parables and in teachings such as the Sermon on the Mount; gone is Jesus the Savior, the Messiah, and the resurrected Lord.

Friedrich Schleiermacher's "Liberal" Spirituality

In the nineteenth century, a movement of theology arises that is much more theologically sophisticated about history than deism, and that gives a more plausible picture of Jesus, while maintaining a non-dogmatic faith. It is based neither on reason nor the authority of the church but rather on experience. The name for that movement, especially as it flourished in Germany, is Liberal Theology, initially a movement within Protestantism, though in the twentieth century it also influences Catholicism.

The demise of rationalism in the second half of the eighteenth century leads to dramatic changes in sensibility. Instead of viewing reality as rational and ordered, people turn to mystery, imagination, and feeling as the basis of truth. The new sense of the human self that captures the imagination of influential Europeans often goes under the name "Romanticism." This romantic worldview is initiated by the German secular philosophies of Johann Wolfgang von Goethe (1749–1832), Friedrich von Schiller (1759–1805), and Gotthold Ephraim Lessing (1729–1781). Rebelling against the rationalist thought of the Enlightenment, these authors emphasize emotion. Their view becomes integrated into all aspects of European society and culture. This sense of human transcendence flourishes in such English Romantic poets as Wordsworth, Coleridge, Shelley, and Byron. It inspires Goethe, drives the musical compositions of Beethoven, Mendelssohn, and Wagner, and undergirds the spectacular rise of the novel as the dominant form of European literature.

Like rationalism, Romanticism is a form of humanism, elevating the human being to a position of prominence in knowing and valuing. Unlike Enlightenment thought, which emphasizes reason as the means of knowing, the Romantics stress spontaneity, creativity, imagination, and intuition, attempting to reclaim the deeper dimensions of life. Whereas Enlightenment intellectuals view nature as orderly and mechanical, functioning independently of humans and solely according to natural laws, Romantics look to nature with eyes full of wonder, pointing anew to the mystery of life. They value relationships with others and with nature, seeing individuals as part of an organic whole.

Perhaps the best spokesperson for a Romantic view of Christianity is the German theologian Friedrich Schleiermacher (1768–1834). Called "the father of modern theology," he not only summarizes the theological insights of progressive Protestantism for his time but he sets the course for subsequent Christian thought. He attempts to rehabilitate religion among intellectuals, insisting that the great debates over proofs of God and the abstract doctrinal descriptions of faith are, at best, a secondary expression of religion. The theological task, he argues, cannot be separated from the great movements and concerns in society. He believes that theology no longer has the luxury of being isolationist. From now on, theology has to come to grips with society, culture, and technology, and with the growing authority of science. In particular, theology has to embrace the scientific method, with its stress on experience, observation, and experimentation.

In 1799, ordained as a pastor and serving a church in Berlin, Schleiermacher falls in with a group of Romantic thinkers, for whom feeling, rather than reason or even morality, is central. Schleiermacher agrees that feeling is at the heart of true piety, yet he also wishes to retain much of his Christian conviction. Throughout his life, therefore, he seeks to harmonize Romanticism and theism. At one point, his Romantic friends ask him to clarify his thought, and he does so in his *Speeches on Religion to Its Cultured Despisers*, his first influential work and the first great document of Liberal theology. There he pleads with his friends not to discard religion, but to realize that the rationalism they disdain distorts religion by subordinating it to reason and conscience.

The title alone tells us a great deal about Liberal theology. First, it addresses the cultural elite, to whom Schleiermacher says, in effect, "We Christians can show you how what you desire as the cultural elite is best represented in Christianity. The feeling that you Romantics cultivate, the awareness of unity and continuity with the universe, the awareness that the self exists not for its own sake but rather as part of the whole—as representative of the Infinite in your lives—is actually at the heart of Christian spirituality." This perspective—that religion is not primarily about dogma, ritual, or morality, but rather about intuition and mystery, about the innate sense of the Infinite behind the finite—lies at the center of Schleiermacher's argument. For Schleiermacher, the human sense of feeling, of dependence upon something ultimate and Infinite, is preconceptual and religious in nature. Christian spirituality is this experience of the Infinite in all things. To seek and find this eternal factor in our lives, and to experience it directly, in the present—something all humans sense by nature—that feeling, says Schleiermacher, is what we mean by religion.

In arguing against the opponents of religion, Schleiermacher views religion as basic to human existence. Contrary to the rationalists, who view reason (the mind) as the source of certainty, religion is not about knowledge or knowing. Contrary to the Kantians, who view conscience (the human will) as the seat of religion, religion is not about morals or doing. Going beyond the dialectic of knowing and doing, Schleiermacher carves out for religion a third dimension of human consciousness, prior, independent, and more essential than knowing and doing. In addition to knowing and acting, humans also feel. According to Schleiermacher, the essence and source of religion lies in the realm of feeling—the aesthetic realm.

For Schleiermacher, the deepest feeling of one's heart aims at the Infinite, by which he means what we call "God," even if he doesn't always make this clear. In his *Speeches*, Schleiermacher avoids using the term "God," preferring instead terms such as "the Universe," "The One and Whole," or the "World Spirit." Not surprisingly, his theological language leads to charges of pantheism. His language, however, is typically romantic usage. Schleiermacher is uncomfortable with personalistic descriptions of God, not wishing to confuse God with ideas about God. At the same time, he recognizes the inadequacy of impersonal or non-personal descriptions of God. They, too, remain ideas, abstract and religiously empty. Schleiermacher's point, however, is that without religion as a vital and living awareness, neither personal or impersonal descriptions of God have value. Ultimately, experience is necessary.

Schleiermacher's hesitancy with "God language" is best understood by looking at the predominant Kantian philosophical background of the era. German philosophy at that time is in the shadow of Immanuel Kant, who argues for a turn to philosophical experience, and for whom the structure of human consciousness is the structure of human knowledge, which in turn is the structure of the world. In other words, if one wants to know the structure of the universe, one has to examine human consciousness and experience, because that is what structures our world.[1] For Kant, knowledge is based on experience.

---

1. As students of modern philosophy know, Kant performs a task similar in scope to that of Plato. However, whereas Plato provides a synthesis in cosmology (combining the rationalism of Parmenides with the empiricism of Heraclitus), Kant provides a synthesis in epistemology, showing how knowledge takes place. Kant views the mind as a pseudocreater rather than a knower. Kant's fundamental premise is that although all knowledge begins with sense experience, not all knowledge arises from experience. The mind receives simple sensations from the world, but then it imposes organization and structure upon those impressions to create knowledge. The world, as it exists apart from our experience of it, is unknowable. For Kant, humans cannot know the essence of an object in itself (*ding an sich*).

The Romantics take Kant one step further: the root of all experience is not reason, which our mind constructs, nor is it moral or ethical action, which Liberals find compelling, but rather it is feeling. What feeling provides is immediate, unmediated contact with the Infinite in the finite. Thus, when a Romantic poet looks at a waterfall or writes a sonnet, its beauty opens up the very essence of the universe, which religion calls "God." That sense of immediacy and awe, says Schleiermacher, is the source of religion, of which the rituals, dogmas, and morality of Christianity are external expressions. While some might argue that belief gives expression to experience, Schleiermacher and the Liberal tradition argue the reverse view, that it is experience that gives form to outward expression. For this reason, Liberalism is revisionist, making doctrine conform to experience.

At this point, some background on Schleiermacher is helpful. He is raised in an extremely religious atmosphere. His parents send him to a Moravian boarding school, where he has a conversion experience and cultivates a heartfelt, Christ-centered piety. However, despite their efforts, the Moravians fail to protect him from modern ideas. Schleiermacher and his friends start a philosophy club and read prohibited books by Goethe and Rousseau. At age twenty-one, Schleiermacher writes to his father saying he no longer believes in the incarnation (the deity of Jesus) and vicarious atonement (the substitutionary death of Jesus on the cross). This results in a loss of faith in orthodoxy, but not in spirituality. In his schooling he awakes, he writes later, to "the consciousness of the relation of man to a higher world. Here it was that that mystical awareness developed that has been so important to me, and has supported and carried me through all the storms of skepticism. Then it was questioning, now it has attained its full development, and I may say, that after all I have passed through, I have become a Herrnhuter (a Moravian in piety) again, only of a higher order." In this way, Schleiermacher does not actually claim to be a Moravian, but he is doing his theology in order to provide the intellectual scaffolding for the spirituality he learns among the Moravians.[2] What is valid about his experience among the Moravians was not their doctrines or their Lutheran theology in general, but rather their sense of piety. Schleiermacher's aim as a theologian is to give outward

---

2. Those familiar with my writings might recognize here an example of what I call "postcritical understanding" or "secondary naiveté"; see Vande Kappelle, *Adventures in Spirituality*, 33, and *Beyond Belief*, xxii–xxiv.

doctrinal expression to that inward experience of piety, an approach he calls "a science of theology."

Interestingly, Schleiermacher becomes one of the founders of the University of Berlin, where he serves as professor of theology. There, he becomes one of the most famous and influential professors in Germany. In German higher education, one's discipline is a science, and Schleiermacher is committed to making theology a science. Beginning with Romanticism, it is this science that articulates the meaning of Christian feeling of piety. His approach becomes "systematic theology," a perspective he lays out in *The Christian Faith* (1821), his *magnum opus*. As the first great systematic theologian of Liberal theology, Schleiermacher rethinks Christian epistemology, soteriology (sin and salvation), and Christology (the person and work of Jesus Christ). If in his *Speeches* he answers the question, What is religion?, in *The Christian Faith* he answers the question, What is Christianity? (that is, what is theology?). Religion, he argues in his *Speeches*, "is nowhere so fully idealized as in Christianity."

Central to Schleiermacher's epistemology is his understanding of scripture. Rooted in his definition of religion is his view that true Christianity is not a set of dogmas but an inner individual experience. Building on this notion, Schleiermacher understands the Bible as simply the textbook of Christian dogma and doctrine. The scriptures, being only a reflection of the original Christian feeling, are subordinate in authority to human feelings or intuitions about God, religion, and truth. On this account, Schleiermacher denies that the Bible provides truth revealed by God. The only absolute truth in Christianity comes from our inner experience; objective theological knowledge does not exist.

Because of the centrality of Jesus Christ to his theology, Schleiermacher's approach is called "Christocentric Liberalism." Jesus is central to Schleiermacher because Jesus has perfect "God-consciousness," that is, the awareness of absolute dependence upon God, viewed as the ground of all existence and being.

Unlike Jesus, other humans have a problem with "sin-consciousness," because our consciousness is attracted to finite things and to passions such as greed, power, and lust, to anything but God. Our sin-consciousness is our over-attachment to finite things. While piety and spirituality should always be directed to God, we live autonomously, falling prey to temptation and moral weakness.

Though he is a theological Liberal, Schleiermacher has a strong doctrine of sin. For him, there is a tension in every human being between what the apostle Paul calls spirit (God-consciousness) and flesh (sensual self-consciousness). Sin, for Schleiermacher, is "forgetting God," that is, giving in to autonomy and selfishness; because sin is related to human finitude, it affects all persons. In arguing that sin is a matter of the will, Schleiermacher sides with Augustine and the Reformers. Unlike rationalists, Kantians, and humanists in general, humans are unable to save themselves. Furthermore, reason cannot alter our will, but can only serve it. Schleiermacher understands this serious and deep understanding of sin as something that makes Christianity unique among world religions. Schleiermacher agrees with Christianity that even the best human piety—the best first-half-of-life spirituality, we might say—is inadequate and in need of reconciliation.

However, there is in Schleiermacher a twist to the traditional Christian doctrine of sin, for in his estimation, sin (moral evil) need not be viewed negatively. The Fall of Man (called "original sin" by Augustine and his followers) is not a step downward, but actually a step upward. While sin in itself is not praiseworthy, awareness of sin and admission of guilt actually lead to grace. In this sense and only in this sense, sin becomes the precondition to reconciliation with God, nature, and others, a *felix culpa* ("blessed fault").

Can anything overcome humanity's sin-consciousness? Schleiermacher's answer, again, sounds traditional: redemption in Christ. But how does redemption work? Humans need to have contact with Christ's perfect God-consciousness, something that can occur through preaching.[3] What clergy should convey in worship is an impression of Christ's perfect God-consciousness; this should be the focus of every sermon. Redemption, for Schleiermacher, does not consist in dogmas such as vicarious atonement or in events such as the incarnation or resurrection, but rather in Christ's perfect God-consciousness, something modeled for believers in scripture and through preaching. According to Schleiermacher, what is crucial about Jesus is not his deity but rather the central idea he teaches and lives, "that all finitude requires higher mediation in order to gain union with the deity." For Schleiermacher, humans cannot save themselves. They need help (mediation), and the mediator (Christ) must not himself require mediation. In this way, subtly and gradually, Schleiermacher introduces what has been called his "reverse Christology," moving

---

3. We need to keep in mind that Schleiermacher, in his position as university professor of theology, is primarily teaching seminarians; clergy are undoubtedly his target audience in *The Christian Faith*.

from Christ's office of mediation to his divinity. However, lest we place Schleiermacher firmly in the orthodox wing of Christianity, several additional twists appear in his theology. For example, if we ask, "Is Christ the only mediator?," Schleiermacher would answer that for Christians he is, but not necessarily in an absolute sense for all humans.

Because he argues that Jesus never claims to be the sole mediator of God, Schleiermacher is accused of seeing Jesus as only one of "many Christs." Christians might question that assertion, arguing that in passages such as John 14:6, Jesus states that his ministry is uniquely mediatorial. The authenticity of that passage, however, is disputed by many biblical scholars, who see it as an interpolation (an addition) by the author of the Fourth Gospel, denying its authenticity by arguing that this claim is unlike anything found in the Synoptic Gospels.[4] For those who maintain the saying's authenticity, one interpretation is that Jesus is here speaking as a representative of regenerate humanity, that is, as one of those who has relinquished their false self (their first-half-of-life egocentricity) and replaced it with their True Self (their second-half-of-life spirituality).

Schleiermacher's greatest contribution is his attempt to move Christianity into the realm of the heart. To be human, he argues, is to be religious, for at the heart of human experience lies the awareness of humanity's absolute dependence upon God. After Schleiermacher, it becomes commonplace to view religions as differing expressions of a common inner religious experience shared by all people. The uniqueness of Christ, Schleiermacher argues, is not some doctrine about Jesus or in his miraculous nature. The real miracle is Jesus himself. In him we find a person who demonstrates the sense of God-consciousness to a supreme degree. The church is the living witness to the fact that down through the centuries individuals have come to a vital God consciousness through their contact with the life of Jesus. Religious practice, focused on God-awareness, can lead to the true reunion of humanity. Schleiermacher is the "father of modern theology" primarily because he shifts the basis of the Christian faith from the Bible to "religious experience."

Schleiermacher seems to have taught that Christianity was only temporary, and that it could one day be transcended by a more adequate faith. Part of the glory of Christianity, he believes, is its humble recognition of its own relativity. As he writes in *The Christian Faith*, "It is possible to hope ... that some day, the human race, if only in its noblest and best, will pass

---

4. While every Gospel contains editorial bias, most biblical scholars view the Synoptics as reflecting a more primitive and hence more accurate view of Jesus.

beyond Christ and leave him behind." This hope, however, contributes to Schleiermacher's dilemma: "But this [hope] clearly marks the end of Christian faith, which on the contrary, knows no other way to the pure conception of the ideal than an ever-deepening understanding of Christ."

Will all humans ultimately experience salvation (perfect God-consciousness)? Yes, this is Schleiermacher's hope, the hope of universal salvation. However, for that to happen, each person must gradually relinquish sin-consciousness, which requires divine mediation.

The climax of a century of progressive European Liberal theology is reached in 1900 in a series of lectures titled *What is Christianity?* In these lectures, the learned scholar Adolf von Harnack (1851–1930) argues that the simple gospel preached by Jesus is largely lost when it is translated into a Hellenistic idiom. Harnack thinks that the original teaching of Jesus can be summarized as the fatherhood of God, the brotherhood of man, and the infinite value of the human soul. Such views are labeled "liberal" by conservative Christians, for they appear to betray the core biblical values upon which Protestantism is founded.

Liberalism, or modernism, as it is sometimes called, is an attempt to adjust religious ideas to the needs of contemporary society. Harry Emerson Fosdick, minister at the influential Riverside Church in New York City, puts it well when he says the central aim of Liberal theology is to make it possible for a person "to be both an intelligent modern and a serious Christian." Protestant Liberalism engages a problem as old as Christianity itself, attempting to make faith meaningful in a changing world without distorting or destroying the gospel. The apostle Paul tries and succeeds. The early Gnostics try and fail. Gnostic Christians such as Clement of Alexandria, Origen, Evagrius of Pontus, and Denys the Areopagite try. The jury is still out on Liberalism.

Questions for Discussion and Reflection

In addition to the questions listed at the end of the preface, answer the following questions, writing your answers in a journal. If you are in a group study, be prepared to share your answers with those in the group.

1. In your estimation, how does the Enlightenment influence and change the development of Christianity as a religion and as a way of life?

2. In your estimation, how does the Enlightenment influence and change Western society?
3. After reading this chapter, what did you learn about deist spirituality?
4. In your own words, explain the meaning of "Liberal" spirituality.
5. Why is Friedrich Schleiermacher called "the father of modern theology"? Explain your answer.
6. Assess the merits of Schleiermacher's definition of piety (spirituality) as one's experience of the Infinite in all things.
7. Do you agree with Schleiermacher that the essence and source of religion lies in the realm of "feeling"? Explain your answer.
8. Why is Schleiermacher's approach to Christian theology called "Christocentric Liberalism"? Assess his idea of "many Christs."

11

Christian Existentialist and Neo-Orthodox Spirituality

SØREN KIERKEGAARD (1813–1855), A nineteenth-century Danish Christian philosopher and Lutheran theologian, is often seen as the founder of existentialism, not because he uses the term, but because of his focus on the concept of existence, by which he means *human* existence. Kierkegaard is interested in how human existence differs from the existence of non-human things such as trees, rocks, or chairs. For the latter, existence is not a task, nor do such objects think about death or worry about existence.

For humans, existence is a task, one that produces anxiety, even guilt and despair. Kierkegaard explores all those aspects of existence because for him, the task of human existence is ultimately the task of being a Christian. What it means to be a Christian becomes the key to his thought. Hence, he is called, not simply an existentialist, but a Christian existentialist. He is not, like Sartre and Camus, an atheistic existentialist who presupposes and acts as if there is no God, but a theistic existentialist, who, like Dostoyevsky and Berdyaev, believes God to be the ultimate source of reality in the universe, arguing that humans discover their essence through commitment to God.

Kierkegaard's nineteenth-century setting helps us understand his task. In that century, Christianity fares better than in the previous century. In the nineteenth century, Western civilization is spreading throughout the world, and it is Western Christian civilization that is spreading. Many Christian theologians are heartened by Christian spread and success, viewing these as proofs that Christianity is the true religion, the most advanced and progressive form of religion because it is replacing older, more superstitious religions. In that century, Christianity is seen to be on the side of progress, enlightenment, and civilization, as opposed to paganism, animism, and the outmoded religions it is replacing. Of course, this mindset is chauvinistic and Eurocentric, and Kierkegaard doesn't accept it.

He sees institutional Christianity spreading, and he realizes that head knowledge of Christianity does not make one a Christian. Indeed, at one point he utters his famous dictum, "It is impossible to be a Christian in Christendom." Not only can institutional or corporate Christianity not make him a Christian, such Christianity can actually become an impediment to the existing individual, for, according to Kierkegaard, one can only become Christian through individual action, that is, by the passionate inward decision of faith. How, then, does one become Christian? Certainly not by proving its truth or superiority, for such rationality actually replaces faith. When a professor delivers a lecture or a scholar writes a book that simplifies truth or makes it understandable, the result is not faith. Faith, for Kierkegaard, is a passionate inward subjectivity, not objective proof. Faith is what gives authenticity to human existence. Faith doesn't simply eliminate anxiety or produce steady inward peace, but rather faith is what helps us deal authentically with uncertainty and despair.

This focus on the negative in existentialism, on anxiety, guilt, and despair, is Lutheran in origin, and like Luther, Kierkegaard believes that terror, guilt, and despair can drive us to the gospel. The negative aspect of existentialism is not an accident. Viewed as a component of all individual human existence, anxiety can help us deal authentically with human existence and can lead to a faith that honestly confronts the problems of human existence.

Examining how Kierkegaard arrives at his perspective is important, for it reveals the strong correlation between his life and his writings. Known as "The melancholy Dane," Kierkegaard is no ivory-towered speculative thinker. Largely, his thought is shaped by his life. His major works include *Fear and Trembling*, *The Concept of Dread*, and *The Sickness Unto Death*. These titles remind us of the macabre in Edgar Allan Poe's short stories, indicating Kierkegaard's preoccupation with the negative and the subjective dimensions of life.

Born in Copenhagen in a time of great social change, Kierkegaard preserves his interpretation of his life in a work published posthumously under the title, *The Point of View for My Work as an Author*. In that work, Kierkegaard calls attention to three key events that shape his thought: (1) the influence of his father on his early life; (2) his relationship with Regina Olsen; and (3) his relationship with institutional Christianity. All three relationships are turbulent.

Introduced into Lutheran doctrine by an intensely intellectual yet guilt-ridden father, Kierkegaard is also slightly deformed by an early accident, which leads to unconventional behavior in his youth and a profound sense of social isolation. This seclusion is undoubtedly enhanced by the fact that only he and his older brother survive childhood, unlike his other five siblings, all of whom die in their youth.

In 1830 he enrolls in the University of Copenhagen, where he studies theology and the philosophy of G. W. F. Hegel (1770–1831). Hegel's influential philosophy attempts to explain rationally all of reality, but it seemingly ignores the actual existence of the individual. Kierkegaard reacts strongly against the abstractness of Hegel's system, which teaches individuals to *think* rather than to *be*. Kierkegaard distinguishes between the uninvolved spectator in the audience and the involved actor on the stage, arguing that only the actor is authentically involved in existence.

Kierkegaard's university experiences begins a stormy period in his life. He almost discards Christianity, and he becomes estranged from his father. His wit and taste for food and drink form his reputation. His favorite places to visit are the café and theater, and he later refers to this period as the aesthetic stage of life. Eventually he re-establishes his relationship with his father, and in 1836 he experiences a kind of moral conversion, followed two years later by a conversion to Christianity.

At one point he begins courting Regina Olsen, winning her from another suitor. However, after their engagement, he reneges, feeling it cannot lead to marriage. While longing for a home and family, he eventually breaks his engagement, which he attributes to incompatibility, his own melancholy, and eventually, to a special call from God to forego his security and happiness, a sacrifice he compares to Abraham's call by God to sacrifice his son, Isaac.

Kierkegaard becomes a polemical author, writing *Either/Or* in 1843, a code message to Regina, in part to break her from merely romantic and finite attachment to himself, but also opening a way for mature ethical choice. His writing career leads to an attack on Christendom, criticizing church officials for not presenting New Testament Christianity in its full vigor. According to Kierkegaard, the central fact of the nineteenth century is that civilization that has been Christian is no longer so. He finds the church of his day so thoroughly institutionalized and self-serving that it has become complacent and convenient rather than demanding total commitment to God.

Kierkegaard's one passion becomes Christianity, not philosophical or theological Christianity, but personal Christianity. His main purpose is to demonstrate through his life and writing what it means to be Christian. This, for Kierkegaard, and not the other questions that pastors and theologians are discussing and philosophers debating, is the great fork in the road for the whole of humanity. Most of the other questions and concerns are frivolous, mere pastries rather than the main course. On October 2, 1855, only forty-two years of age, Søren is stricken with paralysis of the lower limbs, and he dies soon thereafter.

Kierkegaard makes an important contribution to the religious journey in his formulation of three levels or realms of existence, three progressive stages of life through which humans go in their ascent toward God. On the first level, which he labels the aesthetic stage, individuals are ruled by their senses. Such persons live solely for the present, and particularly for self-gratification. The second level, the ethical stage, requires that one abandon attitudes of selfishness and embrace universal standards, making commitments to others. Here moral standards and obligations are adopted. The third and final stage, which Kierkegaard calls the religious stage, entails a life of faith.

He further distinguishes between Religiousness A and Religiousness B, associating Religiousness A—a natural form of religious life we call first-half-of-life spirituality—with the ethical sphere or stage, and Religiousness B—an ethical life lived in relation to God—with the religious sphere or stage.

In each stage, Kierkegaard selects a figure from literature or history as an example. For the model of the religious stage of life, the highest level through which humans go in their ascent toward God, he selects Abraham, whose trust of God and unwavering obedience lead him to choose to sacrifice his only son Isaac, even in the face of absurdity, for to question God is to place reason over faith. In selecting this example, Kierkegaard is not denying the validity of ethics. He states that the individual who is called to break with the ethical must first be ethical, that is, must first subordinate to universal morality. The break, when one is called to make it, is made in "fear and trembling" and not arrogantly or proudly. In this final stage, the ethical is not abolished but dethroned by a higher purpose or end, a phenomenon he describes as the "teleological suspension of the ethical." The key to this final stage is not the commendable humanistic goal of universal duty to others, but the unqualified giving of oneself to God. For Kierkegaard, if one doesn't go beyond the ethical realm, beyond moral obligation, one cannot properly say one is related to God, or obedient to God. Ethical duty, he believes, must ultimately lead to God, but since it usually leads to humanity (i.e. to humanism), then this stage must be transcended. An absolute relationship to an absolute (God) requires a relative relationship to relative ends. And for Kierkegaard, everything other than God is relative.

Feeling life to be fragile and frequently despairing of his purpose in it, Kierkegaard believes himself unable to take the acceptable path of a prosperous career. Rejecting both the established Lutheranism of his day and the dominant Hegelian philosophy of the intellectual world, he turns his attention to the ambiguities and uncertainties of his own life as an "existing individual," and this becomes the central feature of his thought. If Hegel is correct in his diagnosis of the nineteenth-century malaise as "spiritless," then the correct prescription for that way of life is not a passive immersion of the self into the Hegelian Absolute Spirit or World Soul, but rather the active, continuous vocation to a spiritual journey of the self before the personal God, life's essential being.

The essential longing of the soul to escape from the social swamp is for Kierkegaard "the umbilical cord of the higher life." And the biblical precursors of that path of salvation are lonesome knights of faith such as the beleaguered Abraham and the suffering Job. Since Kierkegaard is not ordained by any denomination and has serious doubts as to whether institutional Christianity represents the original gospel of Jesus Christ, he does not believe that his words hold any intrinsic authority. Hence the modesty of some of his titles—"Philosophical Fragments," "Concluding Unscientific Postscript," and of his homilies, written largely on the occasion of festivals in the church's liturgical year—intended not as sermons to be preached but as "edifying discourses" to be read individually. He does not expect the success of his words to be dependent on persuasive eloquence but rather on the free response of the believer who learns to make the proverb personal, "Drink water ... from your own well" (Prov. 5:15).

One of Kierkegaard's familiar homilies, "Purity of Heart is to Will One Thing," an extended meditation on Luke 10:42 and James 4:8, is written for the Feast of Confession. Characteristic of Kierkegaard's spiritual writing is the opening prayer: "Father in heaven! What is a man without Thee? What is all that he knows, vast accumulation though it be, but a chipped fragment if he does not know Thee! What is all his striving, could it even encompass a world, but a half-finished work if he does not know Thee: Thee the One, who art one thing and who art all! So may Thou give to the intellect, wisdom to comprehend that one thing; to the heart, sincerity to receive this understanding; to the will, purity that wills only one thing."

While Kierkegaard's piety is simple, as opposed to his philosophy, often complex and convoluted, yet there is a high degree of intensity in his prayers, and the central paradox of creature in common with Creator remains. The possibility of such communion, though implanted by the Creator, requires the free initiative of the individual, who must come to see, often by bitter experience, that his or her life is inadequate without the spiritual element. As Kierkegaard prays in his homily, "Whenever a man may be in the world, whichever road he travels, when he wills one thing, he is on the road that leads to Thee." This does not mean, however, that the wrong thing can be the object of one's desire or devotion. As he writes, "The person who wills one thing that is not the Good [that is, God], he does not truly will one thing. It is a delusion, an illusion, a deception, a self-deception that he wills only one thing. For in his inmost being he is bound to be double-minded." To will one thing, namely, God alone, is the heart's purity.

If the will to do one thing is the true Christian's spiritual goal, then the corresponding temptation is "double-mindedness"—a wavering of the will between the good and the evil, or between two goods, which makes for a divided self. For it is indecision that is at the root of the despair Kierkegaard faces before his decisive turn to Christian faith, and it is ever the fatal accomplice to disbelief.

Kierkegaard writes to free people from illusion, and the worst illusion, he feels, is the view that truth is objective, such that it can be compressed into a creed, doctrine, or dogma. Unlike mathematical truth, which is impersonal, religious truth must penetrate our own personal existence, becoming our own. For Kierkegaard, the task of philosophy is to convert people to the subjective. Objective truth make us observers, subjective truth makes us participants. Hence, for Kierkegaard, faith and truth cannot be universal, one size fitting all, as for Schleiermacher. Religious truth must be personal and individual, not driven by conformity. Such truth cannot be inherited or passed on. In that regard, faith is always characterized by objective uncertainty. For Kierkegaard, objectivity is a myth, and as he states in his *Concluding Unscientific Postscript*, "an objective acceptance of Christianity is paganism or thoughtlessness" (note how modern, even postmodern, this sounds).

For Kierkegaard, truth is not something cold and objective, a system of ideas to be grasped intellectually, but rather is personal and emotional. Truth is whatever an individual believes intensely. Such truth is active, not passive, and is paradoxical, for it is characterized by objective uncertainty. Active truth entails "a leap of faith," for it requires trust and commitment before it can be known. To be valid, religious truth must penetrate one's personal existence, for if it does not become one's own, it is meaningless. Truth must be lived, passionately.

Kierkegaard's lasting contribution to spiritual thought lies in his exploration of the relationship between each individual and the realm of the Eternal. This necessary relation is established in the area of "inwardness" where individual humans fully discover the one true source of their being and true goodness. For Kierkegaard, the means to nurture this inward life is prayer (contemplative devotion in general), which he describes as a person's "greatest earthly happiness."

Through the experience of his short life, he forges the foundations of an existential theology in which the struggle and crises of the self become the focus of the search for God. Although his ideas may seem dire or desperate to outsiders, Kierkegaard has no doubt that he "lived with God as one lives with a father." That strong spiritual conviction of intimacy with God is the anchor of his existentialist thought.

Karl Barth's Neo-Orthodox Spirituality

At the start of the twentieth century, an influential movement emerged in Protestant Christianity known as Neo-orthodoxy. The key figure in this movement is the Swiss theologian Karl Barth (1886–1968), considered the greatest Christian theologian of the twentieth century. In time, Barth becomes known for the manner in which he applies the theological concerns of Reformed Protestantism to the prevailing Liberal theology. Barth gives his ideas systematic exposition in his *Church Dogmatics* (1930–1969), one of the most significant theological achievements of the twentieth century.

Neo-orthodoxy, sometimes called Religious Existentialism, has its roots in the existentialist thought of Kierkegaard, which initially profoundly influences Barth. In the late 1920s, Barth begins writing his *Dogmatics* and completes one large volume. When critics point out that it is dependent upon existentialist philosophy, Barth begins over again. This becomes a decisive turning point in his theological development. Henceforth he determines to build his theology upon orthodox Christian thought, taking the incarnation of Christ as his starting point. Neo-orthodoxy is usually dated to 1919, with the publication of *Römerbrief*, Barth's commentary on the New Testament letter of Paul to the Romans. Seen as a synthesis of Christian orthodoxy and Protestant Liberalism, Barth's theology later becomes a repudiation of many tenets of theological Liberalism.

Barth starts his career as a Liberal theologian, hoping that modern values and human progress could revolutionize society, building the long-awaited Kingdom of God on earth. In 1911, he begins a ten-year pastorate in a small town in Switzerland. Trained by Liberal theologians, for a time he repudiates theism. As a young pastor, he quickly realizes that his training in theology has not prepared him adequately for his primary task as pastor. Preaching twice each Sunday, he questions the role of preaching. He faces what Kierkegaard must have faced in Denmark, a Christianity that accommodates with secularism. As pastor, Barth faces classism among his parishioners, that is, tension between factory owners, managers, and common laborers. Barth experiences deep disappointment in August of 1914 when German intellectuals, including most of the theology teachers he confidently respects, sign a published statement endorsing the military and war policy of Kaiser Wilhelm II. Feeling betrayed, he senses he can no longer adhere to their ethical and dogmatic formulations, including their exposition of the Bible or presentation of history. Like Kierkegaard, he wonders whether there is any future for nineteenth-century theology.

Finding no help in theology, Barth turns to the Bible, where he finds a "strange new world" that is more alive than the latest philosophy. He does not intend to become a theologian, hoping only to offer a biblical correction to the theology of others. But after his commentary appears, he is catapulted to the center of theological discussion.

The First World War comes as a shock to Barth's optimism, causing him to question the human capacity for goodness. As he watches the civilized nations plunge into an orgy of destruction, Barth feels the human situation is too desperate to be solved merely by changing political and economic structures. In 1921 he becomes a professor in Sweden, and in 1929 he relocates to Germany, where he teaches at Bonn. He watches the rise of Hitler with concern and becomes one of the founders of the Confessional Church in Germany, which resists attempts to unite Christianity with Nazism. He helps to draft the famous 1934 Barmen Declaration, which repudiates Hitler's totalitarian dictatorship, declaring that the church's allegiance is to God alone. In 1935, refusing to take a loyalty oath to Nazism, he flees from Germany, accepting a professorship at the Swiss university in Basle, from which he retires in 1962.

Initially, Barth calls his approach "dialectical theology," referring to the give and take in an argument or conversation, especially in God's "No" and "Yes," because Barth is interested in the way in which God communicates with humans, first the negative and then the positive side of revelation. When Barth's biblical commentary appears, it hits the public like a bombshell. Interestingly, Barth uses the image of a bombshell regularly. Speaking of revelation as an "event" caused by God, Barth views God's communication with humanity the explosion. The crater left behind by the explosion of God's revelation is religion—the institutionalized Christian church, religious consciousness (so central to Schleiermacher's theological approach), and all other human religiosity. Revelation, for Barth, is an event through which God says both No and Yes to humanity, shaping the dialectic in Barth's theology.

Building his theological perspective, like Augustine, on the principle of "faith seeking understanding," Barth notes in his commentary on Romans that faith, which he defines as "knowledge of God," is an "impossible possibility." Knowledge of God is impossible for humans because human faith cannot reach God, but such knowledge becomes possible because God is able to reach humanity. Theology (faith), for Barth, is one-way communication, from God outward, and authentic faith must see things from God's point of view rather than from human perspective. This approach leads to Barth's rejection of Liberal values and perspectives such as the emphasis on human experience. For Barth, the event of revelation shatters human efforts and perspectives, and what it leaves behind (including human consciousness and awareness) is but the crater. Eventually, Barth's perspective resonates with a diverse group of thinkers, all of whom gather around his understanding of revelation as "existential event."

While Neo-orthodoxy is said to have been founded by Barth, most Americans first learn about the movement from Emil Brunner

(1889–1966), whose works are translated into English earlier than Barth's. Like Barth, Brunner is born in Switzerland. After an eight-year pastorate, Brunner joins the theological faculty at Zurich in 1924. Like Barth, he is known as an exponent of "dialectical" or "crisis theology." For dialectical theology, God's revelation is paradoxical, because theology is an incomplete and finite expression of the paradoxical relationship to God that can never be fully expressed in human terms.

This position is called "crisis theology" because it teaches that a crisis occurs whenever God confronts a human being. In medicine, for example, a crisis is the turning point at which a patient turns either toward death or toward better health. Similarly, for Brunner, when God confronts human beings, their future hangs in the balance. Humans can say No to God and turn to death or say Yes and become new beings.

Neo-orthodoxy parts ways with Liberalism on many fronts, but especially on the issue of revelation. In the biblical tradition, God's self-revelation to humanity takes two forms—general revelation, available to all people, and special revelation, given to humans in unique historical events such as the incarnation and resurrection. Besides Christ, the living Word of God, God's self-revelation occurs through scripture, which interprets and clarifies revelatory events in history, giving them meaning.

As its name implies, general revelation is available to all humans regardless of time, place, culture, or other historical factors. General revelation is non-verbal. It is God's self-disclosure in nature, the human mind (or conscience), and through the events of history. The purpose of general revelation is clear: all humans live in nature (viewed as God's created order) and in history, and through such experience humans can know God and gain insight into the qualities that give meaning and purpose to life. According to the Bible, if humans were not sinful, general revelation would be sufficient for them to know God accurately and relate to God authentically. However, as Paul indicates in Romans 1, sinfulness leads humans to "suppress the truth," distorting the truth about God's sovereignty, providence, and standards, resulting not only in ignorance but also in idolatry and autonomy.

Protestant Liberals, it seems, stress general revelation almost exclusively. Stressing God's immanence rather that God's transcendence, they limit revelation to what comes through nature, history, and the human mind, as well as to what is ideally exemplified in Jesus, who, though the exemplar of God's character, will, and nature, is merely mortal. Neo-orthodox thinkers such as Barth stress God's transcendence, focusing on special revelation, though some, like Brunner, argue that a fragment of general revelation remains available.

In claiming that the Bible is God's Word, orthodox Christians affirm that God inspires the authors of the Bible in such a way that what they write is what God intends for humans to know about salvation and spirituality in general. Most Neo-orthodox theologians, however, distinguish between verbal revelation (that God speaks to humans by means of propositions or statement) and revelation through encounter (through existential, spiritual encounter that cannot be fully or even accurately conveyed in words), arguing, like Brunner does, that religious truth is neither objective nor subjective but something that occurs through encounter. Thinking dialectically, Brunner maintains that God does not reveal information or doctrine but rather reveals Godself, thereby overcoming the subject-object dilemma. God's revelation is not objective, that is, not an idea or object of thought, but rather self-revelation, as a person encounters another, establishing relationship with the other.

This view, popularized by Barth and Brunner, maintains that divine inspiration applies only to the *activity* of receiving revelation from God, and not to the *content* of the words themselves. Hence, believers should not directly equate God's Word and the Bible. According to Barth, the Bible is fallible—it contains errors, historical and scientific inaccuracies, and theological contradictions. However, despite its fallibility, the Bible *can become* the Word of God, but only in those parts and at those times when God chooses to reveal Godself. Consequently, the Word of God is not something humans can possess, not something that resides permanently in the Bible, for the Word of God resides only with God.

While the Bible can become a means of revelation, for Barth, revelation occurs only in Jesus Christ, and scripture is a witness, attesting to this revelation. However, although Christ is the primary form of revelation, there are actually three forms of the Word of God, (1) the written Word—scripture, (2) the preached Word—including proclamation and the sacraments, and (3) the revealed Word—Christ. Thus, scripture, preaching, and the sacraments may become the Word of God, but they only acquire this function as they reveal Christ. The first two forms—indirect witnesses—are primarily pointers to revelation.

In classic Christin formulation, the Trinity consists of three persons—Father, Son, and Holy Spirit. To understand God, Augustine, the great orthodox Trinitarian theologian, uses the analogy of love: the Father is the Lover, who loves the world through the Son; the Son is the Beloved of the Father; and the Spirit is the bond of Love that binds all three. In Augustine's Trinity, knowledge of God is inseparable from love of God.

To understand God, Barth uses the analogy of revelation: the Father is the Revealed, the Son the Revealer, and the Spirit the Interpreter of God's self-revelation. Unlike Aquinas, whose theological starting point for understanding God is proofs for the existence of God, Barth begins his theology with the assumption of God's revelation; for Barth, God is a self-revealing God. The emphasis is on concrete relationship: God reveals Godself in relationship. However, what is significant about God's revelation is that it is never direct but always indirect. Like the proponents of apophatic theology, for whom God is Subject and never Object, God's revelation is always one of concealment. Barth's primary illustration for this is taken from Exodus 33, Moses' confrontation with God. "Face-to-face" encounter with God, the desire of every Jew, is also Moses' desire, but even Moses does not see God's face; God remains incognito. However, for Barth, scripture is the message of the "passing before" of God; even the events of Christ represent God's secondary objectivity—at best a veil or sign of God's work. Whether it be "the crib of Bethlehem" or "the cross at Golgotha," revelation remains indirect, for that is how God intends it. Nevertheless, for that very reason, revelation is "real," for divine revelation requires faith. As Barth notes, "faith either lives in this sphere, or it is not faith at all," a view reminiscent of Paul's famous declaration, "now we see in a mirror, dimly, but then we will see face to face" (1 Cor. 13:12).

Barth breaks with other dialectical theologians by rejecting any foundation for theology that arises from theories of human nature or existence rather than exclusively from the revelation of God in Christ. For Barth, Christian theology is not fundamentally about experience, human consciousness, or human existence, but rather exclusively about God. Hence, whatever theology has to say about human experience, it must primarily be from God and about God. If humans wish to look within, they must begin with a divine vantage point. Looking within comes second. What comes first is looking at Jesus Christ, for he is the crucial event of revelation.

Barth's break with natural theology comes when he writes a printed reply to his old friend Emil Brunner. The title of Barth's 1934 pamphlet, *Nein!* (No, with an exclamation mark), is a response to Brunner's essay "Nature and Grace." Although Brunner disparages the role of natural theology in its Liberal guise, that is, as a purely philosophical or humanistic attempt to know God, Barth criticizes Brunner's insistence that the image of

God is still found in sinful humanity, meaning that God is still adequately revealed in nature. Against Barth, Brunner argues that if humans are no longer in the image of God and if there is no longer revelation of God in nature, humans cannot be held responsible for their sin. For Brunner, human responsibility makes possible human response-ability. While accepting the Augustinian doctrine of sin, namely, its pervasiveness, Brunner disagrees that sin is inherited. Perhaps what Barth finds most objectionable is Brunner's methodology, whereby he uses reason to demonstrate the reasonableness of Christian faith. Barth takes the Christian doctrine of sin to its logical conclusion, what in Augustinian terms is called the noetic effects of sin,[1] namely, that sin both cripples human will and clouds human knowledge, leading humans to deny what they know innately to be true—that God exists and expects our worship and obedience.

The primary illustration that Barth uses for the bankruptcy of natural theology is the situation against which the Barmen Declaration speaks in 1934, the alliance between the church and state in Hitler's Germany. Hitler considers himself a Godsend, demanding obedience and trust. Barth insists that this be seen as a veiled form of natural theology, thereby viewing an alliance between God's revelation in Jesus Christ and anything else as heresy (whether that something else be reason, conscience, emotion, history, nature, culture, or race). This, for Barth, is the error of natural theology, displayed by the church's acceptance of reason (Enlightenment), conscience (Kant), emotion (Schleiermacher), and experience (Kierkegaard) as pathways of God's revelation. For whenever it has done so, the church adds an "also" to an "only," with the result that the "also" often becomes the "only," thereby perpetuating the "camel's nose in the tent" syndrome. Adding anything to revelation by the word "and," such as "Christian and German," or combining Christianity with "social" or any other concept, points in Barth's mind to the presence of a "Trojan horse" within which the enemy is already drawn into one's domain. For Barth, even the word "religion" becomes suspect; as he states, "in faith, man's religion as such is shown by revelation to be resistance to [revelation]; for in religion man bolts and bars himself against revelation by providing a substitute."

For Barth, nothing human or natural is capable of knowing God or even of adequately receiving divine revelation. Such reception requires not mere restoration of an organ or capacity, but rather complete re-creation, as in being reborn or resurrected from the dead. This is what the

---

1. The term "noetic" relates to the human mind (*nous* in Greek), and to the mind's ability to reason.

event of revelation is for Barth. Jesus' word is God's word; it gives people ears to hear, because it replaces death with life. There is no point of contact, no seeing or hearing, in a dead person, but God's Word can raise the dead. That, for Barth, is what happens whenever someone comes to faith. The foundation of theology is also the foundation of faith, namely, what God has done in Jesus Christ: "I was blind, but now I see" (John 9:25); "I was dead, but now I live" (see Rom. 6:11; 8:10; Eph. 2:5; Col. 2:13).

Such points of emphasis lead to what has been called Barth's Christocentrism, meaning that Christ is the only place where humans can experience God's grace. Human beings don't want to admit they are helpless, believing there is still goodness and righteousness within, or that they are unable to find God or grace on their own, but for Barth, there is nothing humans can do to gain salvation, that is, to come into a right relationship with God.

Unlike Schleiermacher, whose Christocentrism is about Christ's consciousness, Barth's Christocentrism begins with the Father. For Barth, God's revelation is the act of the triune God. In thinking about the universe and God's purpose in history, Barth begins with God's essence as Revealer. When God reveals, the revelation is of the Father, but the means is through Christ, and the content of that revelation in human beings is the Holy Spirit. While it is the Father who is revealed, that revelation remains hidden, because humans cannot see the Father; only the Son can. The Holy Spirit is the effective power that brings that revelation into our lives and changes us. So God—Father, Son, and Holy Spirit—is the structure of revelation.

Because God is by nature One who cannot be unveiled to humans, God does what humans cannot do. God the Father reveals Godself in the Son, in the form of what God is not (in the form of a human being), and the Holy Spirit takes this outward form and brings it into our lives by grace. There is a self-knowledge of God in the Trinity, we might say, where the Father is known in the Son. That, for Barth, is God's primary revelation; then the Son presents God to humans, which, for Barth, is God's secondary revelation.

The difference between the primary objectivity (the inner Trinitarian revelation, which is essential to the Being of God) and the secondary knowledge or objectivity of God (which God does not need to make known), is marked by the doctrine of election. For Barth, the person and work of Christ are one and cannot be separated. Christ is the sole mediator (reconciler) between God and humanity because he is fully God and fully human (see 1 Tim. 2:5). Hence, for Barth, it is the incarnation that is the truly crucial aspect in reconciliation, not the biblical emphasis on the cross. In Jesus, God is both electing Creator and elected creature—both the giver and receiver of grace. In essence, Jesus is the elected man. As the elected man, Christ's atoning work—the salvation he accomplishes—is not partial or limited but rather universal in intent. It is for all humans. To understand Barth's doctrine of salvation, we must understand his doctrine of election.

To begin with, Jesus is the elected human. As the representative of every human being, he is the only condemned or rejected human. If the positive side of election is blessing (salvation), the negative side is reprobation (judgment). As we note earlier when speaking of dialectical theology, in revelation God always speaks "No" as well as "Yes," but only one is ultimate. Behind God's No is always God's Yes. If God's No to human sin is penultimate, God's Yes to humans is always ultimate.

The doctrine of election, as formulated initially by Augustine and later by Calvin, involves predestination and atonement. Are some people chosen by God for salvation and others for damnation, as Calvin taught? For Barth, there are no frontiers to cross from rejection to election. There is only non-recognition and recognition of election. In his view, God is free to be gracious to every human. There is nothing in God's grace, or even in God's justice, that keeps God from electing every human being.

Neo-orthodoxy is criticized on a number of fronts, particularly for its emphasis upon the otherness of God, which leads to God being viewed as distant and potentially irrelevant. Some find Barth's approach fideistic;[2] others fault him for dismissing other religions as distortions or perversions of God's truth, or for his unorthodox perspectives on predestination and the atonement. However, his doctrine of election may be his most controversial concept.

Building on the contributions of Augustine and Calvin, Barth uses a unique Christological approach to arrive at a startling conclusion. For Barth, predestination refers not to the election of select humans for preferential treatment but rather to God's election of Jesus Christ to serve as mediator between humanity and deity. Barth's starting point is with God's free and sovereign decision to enter into fellowship with all humanity. Because Christ is elected to redeem humanity, it is he who is rejected, not humanity. The cross, representing God's judgment upon sin, is God's

---

2. Fideism, or "blind faith," is a belief system that so emphasizes faith as to drive an irreparable wedge between faith and reason.

"No" to humanity. However, this "No" does not result in the exclusion and rejection of humanity, for God's "No" to sin is borne by Christ, who died for all. In Christ, then, we find God's judgment *and* God's redemption, God's "No" to sin and God's "Yes" to grace. Because Christ is the sole elected individual, his mediatorial role leads to God's final word to humanity, which remains "Yes." Barth's doctrine of predestination, pointing to universal restoration and the salvation of all humanity, eliminates condemnation of humanity. The only one who is predestined to condemnation is Jesus Christ, who from all eternity wills to represent humanity.

Barth, in effect, takes Calvin's doctrine of election and says, "Why not suppose that this is about Christ? What happens if this doctrine is fundamentally about God's choice to reveal Godself to humanity in Jesus?" Barth pursues this idea through his *Dogmatics*, which comprise thousands of pages and fourteen volumes, placing election at the heart of his argument. Election, for Barth, is always good news, because in Christ, God chooses to be *for* humanity. Election always serves blessing rather than condemnation. We see this in chapter 2 in the election of Israel, whose election as the chosen people is intended for the blessing of all nations. Likewise, Abraham's call is not for his own sake, but for the blessing of all nations (see Gen. 12:3; 26:4; Ps. 72:17).

The biblical doctrine of election is not that some are chosen *instead of* others, but that some are chosen *for the sake of* others. Like Abraham and Israel, God chooses Jesus to bless (save) others. In this respect, Barth is not an advocate of limited atonement, espoused by the Arminian opponents of Calvinism. In electing Jesus, God is declaring good news for the human race. In electing one human, God is electing all humanity. In some sense, all humanity is saved in Christ. In Christ, one sees deeply into God's character and eternal purpose: God chooses, at the beginning of time, to be for humanity, not as our antagonist, but as our Savior. This is the Good News of the gospel, and it is the best of all possible news for a struggling, confused, and suffering humanity.

Barth's perspective, though hopeful, is rejected by many evangelical and fundamentalist Christians, who consider that his methodology and conclusions compromise the traditional Christian doctrines of human nature, sin, and grace. While accused of universalism (that all humans will be saved by God's grace), Barth rejects the title, though he leaves the possibility open, arguing that while everyone might be saved in theory, this does not mean salvation is automatic. It still requires the response of faith. Nevertheless, while encounter is necessary, such intimacy is totally

Christian Existentialist and Neo-Orthodox Spirituality   207

in the hands of God, else it would be based on human effort and not exclusively upon grace. In this respect, Barth is wholly Augustinian.

This conclusion leaves us with more questions than answers, but one thing becomes clear. For Barth, there is no private, that is, no exclusive Christianity. As a result, no person is more beloved or special than any other. Is Barth's theology an alternative orthodoxy, a new orthodoxy, or simply Neo-orthodoxy? The answer, like Barth's dialectical theology, is Yes and No. In the final analysis, Barth's theology demonstrates the resilience of Christian spirituality.

Paul Tillich's Neo-Orthodox Spirituality

Perhaps the most important Neo-orthodox theologian in the mid-twentieth century is Paul Tillich (1886–1965), a German Lutheran minister and existentialist philosopher who, though trained in Germany, enjoys an influential teaching career in the United States, beginning in 1933. Educated under the influence of nineteenth-century Liberalism, Tillich is a chaplain in the German army during World War I. After the war he becomes a professor of theology and begins to work with the Religious Socialist movement, an activity that makes engagement with Nazism impossible. In 1933 he flees from Germany to become a professor at Union Theological Seminary in New York City. There, with the support of the influential American Neo-orthodox professor Reinhold Niebuhr, he becomes known as one of America's greatest theologians. In 1955, after retiring from Union, he teaches theology at Harvard and later at the University of Chicago. Speaking to both undergraduates and graduates, his classes are always packed, and his sermons, aimed at urban audiences, attract overflow crowds, including many who consider themselves atheists, humanists, and secularists.

Tillich is called the "theologian's theologian." While his writings are never easy reading, he is completely at home in many fields of thought, including history, philosophy, psychology, and art, in addition to theology. In this regard, he is typical of German scholarship at its best. During his teaching career, he occupies a strange position in theology. In Europe, he is perceived as a Liberal theologian in opposition to Brunner and Barth. He sometimes refers humorously to himself as the "last Liberal." However, when he comes to America, he is considered a representative of Neo-orthodoxy. He frequently claims to stand on the boundary between

Liberalism and Neo-orthodoxy. He joins Liberals in their insistence that religion must be subjected to the scrutiny of reason. He accepts the higher criticism of the Bible and is deeply concerned to relate religion and culture. On the other hand, he aligns with Neo-orthodoxy in his insistence that the final criterion of revelation is the picture of "Jesus as the Christ" that we find in the Bible. Nevertheless, he combines faith in the finality of revelation in Christ with a sympathetic appreciation of revelation in other religions. Like Schleiermacher, he agrees with the concept of "many Christs," meaning, specifically, the possibility of the replication of the phenomenon of Jesus in many cultures and religions. Over time, Tillich develops a theological system that defies categorization.

Central to Tillich's system is what he calls the "principle of correlation," in which theology takes Christian symbols like "the cross," "the Christ," and "God," and uses them to answer existential questions. Taking these concepts as symbols only, he applies them to the unavoidable task of every theologian, which is to relate the biblical message to the contemporary situation. Tillich insists that individuals cannot process answers to questions they are not asking. Therefore, if modern individuals are to understand the revelation of Christ, there must be a preparation that enables them to comprehend revelation, a correlation between the thoughts and problems of modernity and the answers given by religious faith. It is the task of theology to demonstrate this correlation. In other words, Christian theology must speak the language of the culture in which it finds itself.

Hence, each section of Tillich's *Systematic Theology* begins with an analysis of a particular problem in terms of philosophy. When the problem is probed fully and its relation to human existence clarified, Tillich shows how the Christian revelation provides an answer. The answer is always symbolic and even paradoxical, but it is ultimately more satisfying than any alternative.

Unlike Rudolph Bultmann (1884–1976), the famous Neo-orthodox New Testament scholar best known for his 1941 essay, "New Testament and Mythology," Tillich does not believe we should demythologize scripture; rather, the interpreter must use myth and symbols, remythologizing rather than demythologizing, in order to provide answers to existential questions. Tillich's approach is not literalistic, not taking literally biblical events such as Jesus' resurrection from the dead, since that is something for historians to deal with. Whether the resurrection happens as historical event is not relevant for Tillich. What matters is the symbol of "the cross," of "the resurrection," and of "the Christ." Hence, Tillich regularly speaks of "the Christ" as symbol, disagreeing with Christians who associate Jesus with Christ. "The Christ" is a symbol, addressed to existential needs. As symbol, "the Christ" can appear in other humans, not exclusively in Jesus.

What faith does is create authentic existence, overcoming alienation and estrangement. Faith establishes what Tillich calls the "new being," a new relationship to one's own existence. Faith accomplishes this, and hence, the task of Christian theologians is to apply these symbols to existential needs. The historical objectivity of biblical events, irrelevant to our existential needs, is not significant to Tillich's theology.

By his method of correlation, Tillich is not implying that the answers to the questions and problems of life can be deduced through philosophical analysis. The answers must be supplied "from beyond." By this approach, Tillich attempts to stand midway between what he considers to be two false methods: (a) naturalistic philosophy, which attempts to answer existential questions humanistically, and (b) supernaturalistic theology, which views the Christian message as consisting of a set of sacred truths that fall into the human situation from an alien world.

Tillich's method of correlation becomes clearer when we understand three terms he uses constantly: heteronomy, autonomy, and theonomy. All thinking, according to Tillich, is an expression of one or more of these. Interestingly, these also correlate with the three stages of understanding I describe in my books as precritical, critical, and postcritcal.

Heteronomy (meaning "other law") is the imposition of an external law upon oneself. This standard appears in world religions but also in secular form. When a religion dictates belief and action, it is heteronomous, for it stifles reason and ignores and destroys creativity. Heteronomy often justifies itself by claiming to speak for God, who is pictured as supreme lawgiver. It is also used by parents and others in authority to enforce rules and legislation, thereby insuring acceptable behavior and cooperation. Such externalized authority is typical of precritical consciousness, the first phase of the faith journey, and first-half-of-life spirituality.

When children (and some grownups) are exposed to heteronomy, sooner or later they rebel, and when they do, they rebel in the name of autonomy (rule of the self by itself). In autonomy, people follow the logic of their own mind and rationality, establishing their own boundaries and standards. Autonomous individuals are "captains of their fate" and "masters of their soul." Autonomy corresponds to critical understanding (and to the second phase of the faith journey); together, autonomy and heteronomy characterize first-half-of-life thinking and living.

Theonomy repudiates both heteronomy and autonomy. According to Tillich, it asserts that the superior law, rooted in God, is simultaneously the innermost law within human beings. This law, given by God, does not come through external agencies, since it resides within each human. Heteronomy calls us to be what we are meant to be. It does not diminish or destroy us, but rather fulfills us. The law of God is not to be obeyed because it reflects God's sovereign power over us, but rather is obeyed because it expresses the deepest and most essential relation of an individual to self, others, nature, and God.

As Tillich examines history, he finds that different periods are characterized by one or other of these laws: the early medieval and early Reformation ages being periods of theonomy, the late medieval and late Reformation ages periods of heteronomy (when theonomous periods lose their power, they normally become heteronomous), and the Renaissance and Enlightenment ages periods of autonomy (the normal reaction to heteronomy). While Tillich welcomes the autonomous revolt against the demands of heteronomy, he finds that autonomy cannot satisfy the deepest existential human needs. Autonomy leaves humans without depth or cohesion. Autonomy, whether individually expressed or as a historical movement, lacks global and corporate vision. Viewing life as a series of unrelated activities, autonomy is unable to provide a stabilizing center for life. Lacking depth and direction, autonomy grants neither certainty, security, nor an adequate foundation for life.

When an autonomous period collapses, as is occurring today, it tends to go in one of two directions. The lure of heteronomy is strong at such times, whether in its more fundamentalist religious version or its totalitarian secular version, where personal freedoms are relinquished under promises of increased prosperity and security. The other alternative is that a new theonomy may arise, whereby humans, instead of abandoning their freedom, find meaning, wholesomeness, and depth of life in God, however understood. In such theonomy, God, however conceived, is not an outside force or power that breaks into nature and history to rescue humanity. Rather, this God is the depth and foundation behind those aspects of truth and goodness that autonomy has already discovered. In such theonomy, humans no longer have to live in anxiety or fear, trying harder or pretending to be other than what they already are.

Building on what he calls the Protestant principle, growing out of Luther's rediscovery of the biblical message of justification by faith, Tillich argues that faith is the paradox that humans, though finite and sinful, are accepted by God as if they are righteous, the unholy becoming holy. The faith by which we receive the forgiving, reconciling grace of God gives us a power not our own.

Because of its understanding of grace, Protestantism, as Tillich understands it, represents the eternally necessary protest against everything that takes the place of God. To Protestantism, only God is holy, and no church, doctrine, institution, rite, or individual is holy in itself. Protestants thus insist on the priesthood of all believers, that is, that God's grace is not channeled through any particular group of clergy but is open to all. The duty of Protestantism is not to condemn secularism, because when humans choose this option, the church is called to encourage secularists to look more deeply into their perspective and to find its ground and depth, for whatever is of ultimate concern to any individual or system, that is its religion. Such religion, Tillich believes, will be the midwife to new birth and revitalized faith.

For Tillich, religion (what we are calling "spirituality") is not a matter of specific beliefs or practices, nor should it be identified with traditional institutional forms. Only individual people can be religious (that is, spiritual), and people are religious (spiritual) at the point where they are ultimately concerned, which occurs when they experience what Tillich calls "the unconditional," by which he means God. The experience of the unconditional is the experience of that which has absolute authority for us, before which we bow in awe and humility. When we encounter our "ultimate concern," it lifts us out of ourselves and requires our undivided allegiance.

When we understand religion in these terms, it is evident that such spirituality may be found among secularists and even atheists, particularly if their irreligion arises from a commitment to truth. Loyalty to truth is itself a relationship to God, though atheists do not recognize it as such. In light of his view of "ultimate concern," Tillich finds that the popular idea of God as personal, sovereign, omnipotent, and so forth, is idolatrous and unworthy of our ultimate concern. Thus, Tillich startled his hearers by telling them he did not believe that "God" exists, suggesting that we dispense with the term "God" for the twenty-first century.

For Tillich, God dos not "exist," for existence is a quality of dependence. A god who exists is simply another being; even if we call God the

Supreme Being, God is still on the same level of other beings. Hence, instead of looking outside nature for a supernatural being called God, Tillich looks through nature to its transcendent ground and depth. God, according to Tillich, is not a being but Being itself, or better yet, the "Ground of Being," the power of being that enables all existence.

When we speak of God, according to Tillich, we must speak symbolically. The only non-symbolic statement we can conceptualize about God is Being itself, and even such terminology takes us to the realm of symbol and myth. Hence, anything we say about God, such as God is male, personal, powerful, loving—all is symbolic. Similarly, when we speak of God causing certain things, this, too, is symbolic. Ultimately, the world cannot be conceived as something separate from God, for this world is the medium of God's continuing activity, an extension, so to speak, of God's Being.

When speaking of God, it is evident that Tillich relies on a deep sense of mysticism. Though God is experienced as the unconditioned in life, as the power from which life derives, God can never be an object beside other objects. In this respect, we must agree with Tillich: God is the depth of reality from which all objects draw their reality.

For Tillich, the Christian claim that Christ reveals the truth includes the claim that wherever truth appears, it is harmonious with Christ. While Tillich views all religions, including Christianity, as preparatory for Christ, what they are said to offer is the preparation to comprehend the "New Being" that comes in Christ. Jesus as the Christ is a "New Being" in the sense that he portrays fully what God intends humans to be. Humans, as they exist in this world, fall short of what God creates them to be. In Jesus we find a person in complete unity with God, meeting life's temptations and misfortunes with the grace of God. Jesus is not the Christ by nature, but becomes Christ because God is present in him, in a full and revelatory manner. This does not mean that revelation ceases in the year 33, but rather that all revelation is to be tested and weighed by the revelation that comes through Christ.

If we can speak of Christ as the first, cosmic, incarnation of God in creation, we can speak of Jesus as the human incarnation of the Christ. For Tillich, any "Jesus-centered" religion is idolatrous. He believes that Liberal theology often falls into this error. It is not Jesus the man whom we worship, but the mystery of God—what Tillich calls "the Christ"—that shines through him.

As a religion, Christianity has no superiority over other religions: Christians are no more righteous than members of other faith traditions. Nevertheless, that to which Christianity witnesses—the Christ—is final. Christians should not set up Jesus as a heteronomous authority who demands obedience. Rather, in Jesus as the Christ we find the answer to the questions asked in other religions about the relationship of humans with the ultimate and with one another. In Christ we find—not a new law—but the true nature of existence.

Questions for Discussion and Reflection

In addition to the questions listed at the end of the preface, answer the following questions, writing your answers in a journal. If you are in a group study, be prepared to share your answers with those in the group.

1. Describe how Kierkegaard's spirituality is existentialist.
2. What, for Kierkegaard, does it mean for someone to be Christian?
3. Explain the merits of Kierkegaard's three stages or realms of existence. Explain his distinction between Religiousness A and Religiousness B.
4. Explain what Kierkegaard means when he described progression from the ethical to the religious stage as the "teleological suspension of the ethical."
5. Explain Kierkegaard's distinction between "double-mindedness" and "willing one thing."
6. Discuss the Liberal and Neo-orthodox views of general and special revelation.
7. Explain and assess Barth's view of the doctrine of election.
8. Explain and assess the influence of Tillich's theology and spirituality to modern believers and non-believers alike.

12

Current Progressive Spirituality
Matthew Fox and Richard Rohr

PROFESSOR OF THEOLOGY JOHN Haught argues that when it is wholesome, religion maintains four components: sacramental, mystical, silent, and active. Each of these dimensions suggests a distinct "way" of being religious, he argues, "but religion is most healthy and alive when it blends all four ways harmoniously. And it begins to dissolve into something other than 'religion' whenever any of the four aspects is isolated from contact with its three partners. In the actual world of religious life, such sundering of one aspect from the others is not unusual. But when this splintering occurs, religion rapidly decays into magic, escapism, or obsession with esoteric teachings, or into cynicism, iconoclasm, or vacuous activism."[1] When, on the other hand, religion concretely preserves the four components in a balanced way, it functions in an ecologically supportive way.

Of these, I am fascinated by the sacramental dimension. Religion is sacramental in the sense that it can speak of unspeakable mystery only through the use of symbols, or what theology calls sacraments. A sacrament, in its broadest sense, includes any object, person or event through which religious consciousness is awakened to the presence of sacred mystery. Historically, most of religion's sacraments have been closely related to nature. For example, the luminosity of sunshine, dawn, and dusk; the experience of wind or breath; the purifying power of clean water; the

---

1. Haught, *Promise of Nature*, 73–75.

fertility of soil and life—all of these natural phenomena, and many more, are used by religions to symbolize the way in which ultimate mystery affects us.

Since nature provides many of the fundamental sacraments of human religion, it is easy to see how the conservation of nature is indispensable for the survival of religion. If we lose the environment, we lose God as well. And it is equally true that when religion loses touch with its sacramental origins, it begins to grow indifferent to the natural world. A sacramental vision, Haught reminds us, makes nature transparent to divinity. In this sense it concedes to nature an inherent value without allowing it to become a substitute for God. According to this Christian perspective, nature is worth saving not because it is sacred, but because it is sacramental.

Matthew Fox's Creation Spirituality

In his seminal work *Original Blessing*, former Dominican scholar Matthew Fox[2] calls for a paradigm shift in religious thinking about human origins and the nature and destiny of human beings, from the fall/redemption paradigm to creation spirituality. The reasons for his appeal are compelling, intellectually and spiritually, and they are harmonious with the view of nature as sacramental.

Fox argues that the fall/redemption paradigm, based upon the doctrine of original sin, develops during medieval times and is essentially foreign to scripture. This tradition, dualistic and patriarchal, considers all nature "fallen" and does not seek God in nature. This tradition does not teach believers about creativity, justice-making, and social transformation, or about the God of play, pleasure, and delight. This tradition proves unfriendly to artists, prophets, science, and women.

Creation spirituality, on the other hand, begins with original blessing, embodying the biblical emphasis on the goodness of creation. Fall and Redemption theology begins with original sin and ends with redemption. Creation theology begins with original blessing and flows to all subsequent blessings, including those we share with our loved ones and those we affirm in creativity, compassion, birthing, and justice-making; all are prefigured in the grace of creation. Creation spirituality does

---

2. Joining the Episcopal Church following his expulsion from the Dominican Order in 1993, Fox is now an Episcopal priest.

not ignore sin, but views it differently. Boredom, depression, arrogance, violence, addictive behavior—these occur when we get cut off from the sense of grace and blessing. Original sin is not "original" or primary in time or in biblical theology but derived. Evil is conceived as neither original nor eternal, but rather as something good gone bad.

Hope for humanity and the future of our planet must be based on a proper understanding of the doctrine of creation, one that is not antithetical to science but rather is the subject of the scientist's search, the source of the prophet's vision, and the subject of the mystic's commitment. According to Fox, the universe loves us every day, and the Creator loves us through creation. The following quotation captures his perspective beautifully:

> Creation is the source, the matrix, and the goal of all things—the beginning and the end, the alpha and the omega. Creation is our common parent, when "our" stands for all things. Creation is the mother of all beings and the father of all beings, the birther and the begetter. It is all-holy; it is awe-filled . . . Creation is never finished, never satisfied, never bored, never passive. Creation is always newly born, always making new . . . How can such a drama be jeopardized as it is today? Only because our species, with its religions, education, moralities, governments, and economics, has lost the sense of creation. When that happens, nothing is holy; nothing seems worth the struggle for justice that is necessary to preserve it. Community dies, and relations no longer exist.[3]

In his writings on creation spirituality, Fox describes spirituality as a way of life characterized by four paths: (1) The Via Positiva: Befriending Creation; (2) The Via Negative: Befriending Darkness; (3) The Via Creativa: Befriending Creativity; and (4) The Via Transformativa: Befriending New Creation. For each path he provides a signpost or commandment (italicized below):

- Via Positiva: *Thou shalt fall in love at least three times a day*. This applies to human beings, to nature in all its magnificence, and also to activities such as music, poetry, and dance. Creation has much to do with falling in love. The first commandment, one of praise, flows from the awe of being alive.

---

3. Fox, *Creation Spirituality*, 10–11.

- Via Negativa: *Thou shalt dare the dark*. Every spiritual journey moves from the surface to the depths, and there is no moving from superficiality to depth without entering the dark. "Daring the dark" means entering nothingness and letting it be nothingness while it works its mystery on us. "Daring the dark" also means allowing pain to be pain and learning from it. Being at home in the dark involves relinquishing control—letting go and letting be.

- Via Creativa: *Do not be reluctant to give birth*. Spiritual discipline in the creation tradition is focused on the development of the aesthetic. Beauty, and our role in co-creating it, lies at the heart of the spiritual journey. Such creativity wrestles with the demons and angels in the depths of our psyches, embracing our "shadow" side as well as our visions and dreams. "To give birth" is to enter the Creator's realm. The work of co-creation engages the image of God (*imago dei*) that is in every person, essential for assisting nature and history in carrying on the creativity of the universe.

- Via Transformativa: *Be compassionate, as your Creator is compassionate*. This commandment, the summation of Jesus' ethical teaching (Luke 6:36), corresponds in meaning to Matthew's passage from the Sermon on the Mount, translated "Be perfect, as your heavenly Father is perfect" (Matt. 5:48). A better rendition of Matthew's Greek word *teleios* is: "Be mature" or "Be complete." As Luke's version makes clear, for humans to be perfect or complete is for them to be compassionate to all creatures (Luke 6:36). In this understanding, compassion is not about the actions that flow from a superior to an inferior, but as a result of our interdependence. True compassion, therefore, involves a deep respect for other cultures and traditions and the willingness to work together in our need for mutual wisdom.

If spirituality can be defined as "meeting with God in history," as Leonardo Boff defines it, and if a new spiritual era is emerging, then a new meeting with God is also upon us, providing a self-disclosure of God that is less warlike, less patriarchal, and more concerned with compassion, justice, celebration, beauty, and creativity.[4]

Such spirituality requires a paradigm shift in traditional Western thought. To implement fully the implications in paradigms shifts, we

---

4. Ibid., 18–23, 31.

consider the contributions of Thomas Kuhn in his classic work *The Structure of Scientific Revolutions*, Kuhn offers the following characteristics of paradigm shifts in science:

- They see nature in new ways
- They require a shift of vision
- They require transformation of vision
- They require conversion
- They require a switch in visual gestalt

Like worldviews or visions, paradigms are community issues, not private ones. Kuhn believes reeducation is greatly needed during the period of a paradigm shift. Such shifts require different roles of different persons—indeed they may require an entirely different kind of person.

Richard Rohr's Lessons on Spiritual Maturity

Citing Thomas Aquinas's observation that "Whatever is received is received according to the mode of the receiver," Richard Rohr, a Franciscan priest and founder of the Center for Action and Contemplation in Albuquerque, New Mexico, notes that whatever one teaches or receives is heard on at least nine different levels, according to the inner, psychological, and spiritual maturity of the listener.[5] Level 1 people misuse scripture, sacraments, and any other spiritual tool that is presented to them, whereas Level 7–9 people "make lemonade out of even sour or unripe lemons." While discerning these levels from his own pastoral and teaching experience, Rohr is quick to note that his levels serve a didactic purpose; real life is much more subtle.

Rohr's list includes:

1. *My body and self-image are who I am.* Such a view represents dualistic/polarity thinking and leads to dominance of security, safety, and defensive needs.
2. *My external behavior is who I am.* People at this level need to look good to others, and in so doing hide or disguise contrary evidence from themselves and from others. This stage is common among conservatives.

---

5. Rohr's list of nine levels, found below, is adapted from *Naked Now*, 164–66.

3. *My thoughts/feelings are who I am.* People at this level develop intellect and will in order to have better thoughts and feelings, and in so doing control them to the extent that neither they nor others see their self-serving character. This education as a substitute for transformation is common among liberals and the educated.

4. *My deeper intuitions and felt knowledge are who I am.* This level, while a breakthrough from previous levels, keeps people stymied, for it substitutes individualism, self-absorption, and inner work for true encounter with otherness.

5. *My shadow self is who I am.* People at this level are overwhelmed by their own weakness; without guidance, grace, and prayer, many go back to previous identities.

6. *I am empty and powerless.* At this level most attempts to save the self by superior behavior, techniques, morality, positive roles, or religious devotion lead to regression. All one can do is wait, ask, and trust. People at this level learn faith and discover the superior mentoring qualities of darkness. Such people are discovering for themselves the reality of God.

7. *I am much more than who I thought I was.* People at this level undergo the death of the false self and the birth of the True Self. Since such people are not yet fully yielded to the loss of ego, their experience feels like a void, even if a wonderful void. Such people, embarking on the second-half journey, are learning the meaning of "dark splendor."

8. *"I and the Father are one"* (John 10:30). At this level there is only God—or as Teresa of Ávila states, "One knows God in oneself, and knows oneself in God." All else is seen as passing ego possession, which need not be protected, promoted, or proved—to anyone.

9. *I am who I am.* At this level one accepts oneself fully, warts and all; no window dressing is necessary. This level represents the most radical critique of religion, viewed now as just a pointer to reality and not reality itself. People at this stage need not appear to be anything but who they are. Fully detached from self-image, such people live in the image of God for themselves, which includes and loves both the good and the bad. Here one experiences total nonduality, the serenity and freedom of the saints.

For Rohr, the goal is to keep people moving deeper into faith, knowing they receive all necessary information and experience at each level to travel onward.

Like Fox, Rohr's spirituality is comprehensive and progressive, yet engages fully with orthodox Christian doctrine and the contemplative tradition. For a helpful introduction to his life-affirming yet challenging concept called "falling upward," based on his 2011 book by that title, in which he speaks of the spiritual role of suffering, pain and setbacks in our lives, I summarize a weeklong series of presentations taken from his daily online meditations during the COVID-19 (coronavirus) pandemic in the spring of 2020.[6] In that series, titled "The Patterns That Are Always True," Rohr discusses five concepts that reality reveals to us in times of suffering—universal patterns that are always true. These principles, the planet's lessons regarding what matters and what lasts, are likened to ancient initiation rites of passage from childhood to adulthood, and they are helpful in transitioning from first-half-of-life thinking and living to second-half-of-life spirituality. Rohr's five essential messages of initiation are:

1. life is hard
2. the individual is not important
3. your life is not about you
4. you are not in control
5. you are going to die

These five lessons, shockingly negative initially, are transformative when taken together with life's underlying message that all living creatures on planet earth co-exist as a global family created and loved unconditionally by God. These five lessons are truths for the soul. We typically flee from anxiety, grief, and pain, but these truths provide meaning and a sense of God's compassionate presence within the chaos of life.

According to Rohr, life's two primary spiritual teachers are great love and great suffering. Only love and suffering are strong enough to decentralize the ego and superego, break down our dualistic (individualistic, autonomous, and hierarchical) thinking, and open us to divine Mystery. Ironically, to find our True Center, we must first go to life's edge. That is what Rohr does with these five messages. However, they don't exist alone. They require divine love as a precondition. With that

---

6. March 29–April 4, 2020.

preunderstanding—that each of us is loved unconditionally with eternal love—we proceed with Rohr's message of cosmic initiation into the second journey, what I call postcritical understanding or the "third phase" of the faith journey.[7]

Lesson One: life is hard. This lesson addresses individual and global crises as a collective initiation experience. It stands first because without it, we cannot progress spiritually. All great spirituality is about what we do with our pain. According to Rohr, death and resurrection are lived out at every level of the cosmos, but only the human species thinks it can get to renewal—to resurrection—without death.

People like us, living in the modern Western world, don't have time for pain. So we try to avoid it—whether through selfishness, denial, mediation, or even therapy—but in so doing, we ignore the obvious: we don't handle suffering; suffering handles us. Only suffering and certain kinds of awe lead us into genuinely new spiritual experiences. The rest of life is a reshuffling or repackaging of first-half-of-life spirituality.

This is the meaning of the cross in Christianity. The cross is not just a symbol of an impersonal or distant doctrine of substitutionary atonement, but the reality of love's undergirding presence. God does not wish or need to punish us *for* our sins; rather, we are punished *by* our sins (such as blunders, illusion, egocentricity, or pride). Such things keep us from growing into our spiritual destiny. They dwarf us and keep us from the joy of acceptance and the bliss of discovery. It seems that nothing less than the death of our false self—our egocentricity—can release our grip on our trivial explanations and our self-serving illusions. Resurrection to second-half-of-life living and thinking will always take care of itself, whenever death is trusted. It is the cross—the journey into necessary night—of which we must be convinced, and then resurrection is offered as a gift.

In time of suffering and deprivation, we must ask, "What is pain teaching us?" If we do not learn from our pain, we invariably transmit it onto others, either directly, by ignoring human need, or indirectly, through blame or shame.

Lesson Two: you are not important. This lesson teaches us that our ego—our temporary or false self, manifested by egocentricity—is not important. When we are willing to be transformed spiritually, we stop

---

7. The first-phase way of thinking occurs during childhood; the second is a critical non-religious or anti-religious phase; the third is the locus of encounter with the living God. For additional information, see my *Into Thin Places*, 320–21.

wasting time theorizing, philosophizing, theologizing, projecting, denying, or avoiding our own ego resistance. True spirituality is never afraid of a dose of humility. If we balk at some minor blow to our ego, this is a sign that no basic transformation into our True Self has yet taken place. Hence, pain's mentoring includes the lesson that we are not important. If we don't learn this from our spiritual leaders, painful life situations will dismantle our ignorance and resistance, brick by brick, year by year.

Typically, it is the prophet who deconstructs the ego, while pastors and priests, as representatives of the "body of Christ," are supposed to reconstruct the individual in preparation for union with Christ. As God says in the inaugural vision to Jeremiah, the prophet's task is to uproot and demolish, and then to start again, rebuilding and planting anew (Jer. 1:10). Jesus knows that he needs to destabilize his follower's false, separate selves before they can understand they have a more permanent True Self. In this regard, Jesus declares, "What does it profit [persons] if they gain the whole world, but lose or forfeit themselves?" (Luke 9:25). Destabilizing people's security systems and egos is never an easy sell, but it is something that true teachers, like Jeremiah, Jesus, and contemporary prophets and teachers must do. Their job is to deconstruct and reconstruct. Thus, the only reason they must tell us that we are not important is because they also must inform us of our infinite worth.

Thus, every parable and spiritual riddle, every one of Jesus' confounding questions, is intended to bring up the limitations of our minds, our personalities, and our self-images. If scriptures and spirituality signify issues or problems to be figured out or mastered, we will never discover our true essence, but remain caught up in building and defending our temporary ego structure.

Global suffering and pandemics teach us two powerful lessons: our vulnerability as individuals and our greatness in community and resolve. When we think globally, we perceive no individual more important than another, and no country greater than another. This must be true for God, for when God looks at humanity, God sees no borders or boundaries, and no divisions by gender, race, or class. Powerlessness is the beginning of wisdom, as Twelve-Steppers in recovery acknowledge. Recognizing one's fragility and vulnerability leads to worship, prayer, and contemplation. Such spiritual disciplines release the flow of God's Spirit, and the desire for such divine power in our lives, when stirred and recognized, changes us forever. Once we embark on the second journey, nothing less totally satisfies us again.

Lesson Three: your life is not about you. This lesson teaches us that we are part of a much larger whole. Life is not about us, but we are about life. We are not our own; a greater life, a more universal and even eternal life, is living within. We, however, substitute the part for the whole!

Believing that our life is not about us is a Copernican revolution of the mind, a discovery as difficult to accept today as when humans discovered that the earth is not the center of the universe. Such shifts in consciousness come as an epiphany—as pure grace—and never as rational or logical conclusions.

Understanding that our lives are not about us is expansive, not limiting, for such recognition becomes the connecting point with everything else. It lowers the mountains and fills in the valleys that we humans create and that so often divide us. It also helps us recognize that the myriad forms of life in the universe are essentially parts of the one life most of us call God. After such a discovery, we are glad to be a part—and only a part. We do not have to figure it all out, straighten it all out, or even do it perfectly by ourselves. We do not have to be God; all we have to do is participate.

After this epiphany, prospects such as promise, gratitude, and compassion come naturally—like breathing. True spirituality is not taught; it is caught, once our sails have unfurled and been filled by the Spirit. One of the reasons Christians misunderstand many of Jesus' teachings is because they miss his purpose. Is it to save us? Well, not as traditionally understood. Jesus saves us by educating us, by situating us in the larger life he called his "Father" and which we might call today God, the Real, the Infinite, or Life. In seeking a prize of eventual salvation, Christians miss the freedom of present fulfillment.

Our life is not about us; it is about God, about willing participation in a larger mystery. Our life is not about acquiring something more, but about letting go—of the false, superficial ego—and accepting the larger life pressing in to flow with us and through us to others and ultimately back to God, the source of life and fount of all blessing.

Lesson Four: you are not in control. This lesson counters most everything we know and value in Western society, psychology, and even religion. Taking control of our life is a foundational message in nearly every self-help program, and for first-half-of-life spirituality, it is necessary. On a practical level, it is true, but not in deeper spirituality. As we get older, our bodies, souls, and especially our failures teach us we are not in control. These, too, are the lessons from pandemics, super storms, floods, and extreme winds.

Learning we are not in control situates us correctly in the universe. It makes us better global citizens. This teaching appears in the mystical writings of all religions. External guidance—divine guidance—is precisely what allows authentic spirituality to flourish. In spirituality, such guidance is genuinely exhilarating and truly freeing—like riding the crest of a wave, cycling to a tailwind, or skiing downhill. What gives religion such a bad name are first-half-of-life spiritual distortions such as hierarchical power, doctrinal arrogance, egocentric hubris, and immature certainty. Such spirituality is pleasing to big egos, but it prohibits spiritual transformation and authentic spiritual growth.

Distinguished Christian psychiatrist Gerald May contrasts willingness with willfulness. Willfulness is setting oneself apart from others in an attempt to master, direct, control, or otherwise manipulate existence. By contrast, willingness implies surrendering one's individuality, immersing oneself in the deepest aspects of life, fueled by the desire to participate fully in that process. Such people are the ones that most appeal to us, those unconsciously full of life, almost to the point of self-relinquishment.

Pain, pandemics, and the storms of life can serve as incubators of such spirituality, for they reveal our powerlessness over our destiny and over that of those we love. This lack of control initially feels like loss, a stepping backward, an unwelcome vulnerability. However, as Rohr indicates, "recognizing our lack of control is a universal starting point for a serious spiritual walk toward wisdom and truth."

Lesson Five: you are going to die. As I reference Rohr's fifth point, it is the week before Easter, when many Christians worship Jesus so they don't have to follow him on the necessary three-day journey that Christians celebrate during Holy Week. Of course, the biblical reference to "three days" need not mean Friday to Sunday, for the expression "three days" is a classic initiatory phrase for going the distance or the full cycle. The transformational journey of death and resurrection is the only—and yet the most denied—message of Easter.

Death, of course, in any form, is perceived as the antithesis of life, and therefore as the great enemy of life. Most people are not ready to die until they feel they have really lived. Nevertheless, for second-half-of-life spirituality, those willing to face death are most alive. Ironically, the people most grounded in real life are the ones most able to let go. As Rohr notes, those who have lived fully are not the ones who fear death the most, but rather those who have not yet begun to live.

In initiation rites, some ritual of death and resurrection is the centerpiece. This is possibly why, in the Synoptic Gospels, Jesus speaks with his disciples about the necessity of going to Jerusalem—for him certainly a death journey—and why the disciples try to change the subject. It is undoubtedly why Jesus finally stops talking about it and simply does it.

The genius of primal spirituality and of others who practice initiation ceremonies is that this activity exposes seekers to the truth about pain and death, but always in a sacred space. In that setting, pain is no longer a scary unknown for adolescents questing adulthood, not something to avoid or change, but rather a gateway or point of entry. As young initiates discover, facing their own death—whether ritually or actually—leads to encounter with the sacred. Walking through our fear of life's final step leads to an encounter with life's next transforming step. Rites of passage, whether from adolescence to adulthood or from first- to second-half-of-life spirituality, free us to live, often for the first time, outside our head and our fear.

Death encounters seem to be the primary way to build or rebuild a real life. As a result, life itself—in all its depth and beauty—becomes the unquestionable blessing, the spiritual reality that keeps on giving. The second journey actualizes that gift.

Questions for Discussion and Reflection

In addition to the questions listed at the end of the preface, answer the following questions, writing your answers in a journal. If you are in a group study, be prepared to share your answers with those in the group.

1. According to John Haught, when religion is healthy, it displays four dimensions—sacramental, mystical, silent, and active. These resemble the four types of spirituality described by Urban Homes (see his typology in the appendix). Of these four forms of spirituality, which do you find best describes your own? Explain your answer.

2. Compare and contrast the fall/redemption paradigm with Matthew Fox's creation spirituality. Which approach do you find most compelling? Explain your answer.

3. In your own words, briefly explain Matthew Fox's four paths of spirituality. Which path most resembles your own? Explain your answer.

4. Of Richard Rohr's nine different levels or ways of thinking and living, which do you find best describes your faith journey? Explain your answer.

5. Of life's two primary spiritual teachers, which do you find most instructive in your life, great love or great suffering? Explain your answer.

6. After reading this chapter, what did you learn about transitioning from first- to second-half-of-life thinking and living?

Epilogue

SPIRITUALITY IS LIKE A multi-stage rocket mission. It begins with a solid launch pad, its rocket balanced and secure. As the engines are ignited, the thrust from the rocket destabilizes the forces, and the rocket travels upward. In its flight, the rocket goes through various stages, each requiring its own booster. Depending on their function, some rockets go into orbit, while others are directed toward a specific target.

Spirituality is for everyone and in everyone. It is not something human beings acquire during a crisis or at some distinct phase of life. Spirituality—like personality—is in our lives all along. For some, personality and spirituality are ill formed; for others, a strong foundation creates personal and spiritual equanimity, purpose, and vision. As *The Second Journey* indicates, there are two "halves" or phases in spirituality, sometimes flawed, sometimes overlapping, and other times distinct. While all people experience first-half-of-life spirituality, most people never get to second-half-of-life thinking and living. While the potential for second-half-of-life spirituality is ever-present, its influences are sometimes too subtle and other times too overwhelming. In either case, most people end up ignoring or rejecting them, settling for the comfort and security of partial truths.

Second-half-of-life spirituality is not monolithic or one-dimensional. While the goal is always to love and honor God and others, the means to this goal remain open and diverse. The second journey is personal and hence inclusive, multi-faceted, and multi-cultural. In second-half-of-life thinking and living, personality and individual interests, led by God and shaped by elements in one's personal story, determine the focus. Ultimately, it is not what we are or what we have been that counts, but what we want and need to be.

Richard Rohr speaks of three ways of seeing: with the eye of the flesh (with the first eye, which is good), with the eye of reason (with the second eye, which is better), and with the eye of true understanding (with the third eye, which is best). If the first eye represents *sight* and *thought*, the second represents *meditation* or *reflection*, and the third represents *contemplation*, a way of seeing that leads to genuine encounter because it sees coherence, spaciousness, and underlying mystery.

The third eye—the mystical gaze—builds upon the first two ways of seeing, and yet goes further. It is a different way of knowing and touching the moment. This happens whenever body, mind, and heart awareness are simultaneously open and nonresistant. This is what Rohr calls "presence" or "being present." The experience of "presence," manifests in moments of deep inner connection, makes us want to write poetry, create music, pray, weep, or be utterly silent. Some call these moments "conversion," others "enlightenment," "transformation," or "holiness."

Third-eye persons are saints, seers, poets, metaphysicians, or authentic mystics—gifted individuals who move "from mere belief systems or belonging systems to actual inner experience."[1] This experience is Paul's "third heaven," when "he heard things that are not to be told, that no moral is permitted to repeat" (2 Cor. 12:4). Consciously or not, too much organized religion keeps us in the first or second heaven, seeing with the first or second eye, where all can be articulated with proper language and where doctrine is deemed certain. The reasons for this may or may not be intentional, but rather may be due to a third possibility, namely that one can lead people only as far as one has gone.

An enormous breakthrough occurs when we honor and accept the divine image within ourselves, for we cannot help but see it in others as well, knowing it is just as undeserved in others as it is in us. That is when we stop judging and how we start loving unconditionally.

You may have heard the expression, "What you see is what you get." That axiom is as true spiritually as it is in other realms of life. The image of God in you calls forth the image of love in others. Wholeness sees and calls forth wholeness in others. Unconditional love in you calls forth unconditional love in others.

Another axiom holds equally true; "What you seek is what you get." If we want others to be more loving, we must choose to love first; if we seek peace in the outer world, we must create it inside first; if we seek a

---

1. Rohr, *Naked Now*, 29–30.

just world, we must start being just ourselves. As Rohr exhorts: "If you want to find God, then honor God within you, and you will always see God beyond you. For it is only God in you who knows where and how to look for God."[2]

---

2. Ibid., 161.

Appendix

A Typology of Spirituality

EACH PERSON IS UNIQUE, with a distinct personality. Despite their uniqueness, individuals share personality traits, qualities, and preferences that can be defined and typed into distinct categories. Insights from personality theory have a remarkable correlation with spirituality, as we discover in the following typologies.

Hindu Typology

Huston Smith, widely regarded as the foremost authority on the history of religions, notes in his classic text, *The World's Religions*,[1] that ancient Hindu scholars identify four basic spiritual personality types: some people are primarily reflective, some are basically emotional, others are essentially active, and yet others are experimentally inclined. While the types should not be regarded inflexibly, since human beings possess all four abilities to some degree, each person prefers one style over the rest. Carl Jung seems to have built his typology of personality on this Indian model, with some modifications. For each of these personality types Hinduism prescribes a distinct yoga or spiritual path that capitalizes on the type's distinctive strength:

---

1. This volume was first published in 1958 as *The Religions of Man* and then revised in 1991 under its current title.

- Karma yoga, intended for persons of active bent, is *the path through work*. The best way for persons on this path to express their spirituality is to perform action selflessly, for the sake of God and others instead of their own. In this way tasks become sacralized; work becomes worship. The aim is to channel the love that lies at the base of one's heart through disinterested action, detached from any consequences benefitting self-interest;

- Bhakti yoga, requiring a rare combination of rationality and spirituality, is *the path of devotion*. It is intended for those whose lives are powered primarily by emotion, the strongest of which is love. The aim is to channel the love that lies at the base of one's heart through relationship;

- Jnana yoga, intended for those who possess a strong reflective bent, is *the path of knowledge*. While thinking is important for such people, it has less to do with factual information than with insight or discernment regarding knowledge. The aim is to channel the love that lies at the base of one's heart through understanding;

- Raja yoga, intended for those who are scientifically or experimentally inclined, is *the path of liberation* (mystical union). Raja seeks freedom through self-actualization. The aim is to channel the love that lies at the base of one's heart through psychophysical (mental) experiments that culminate in harmony, freedom, and integration, leading the practitioner to direct personal experience of "the beyond that is within."

Holmes's Typology

Urban Holmes, dean of the School of Theology at The University of the South in Sewanee, Tennessee from 1973 until his death in 1981, presents a typology for the spiritual life in his insightful book *A History of Spirituality*. His book provides a tool and a method by which to conceptualize and name spiritual experience within a basic framework, particularly useful in helping to position one's own religious experience within the context of the experience of others.

Holmes suggests two appropriate ends for the spiritual life: a speculative spirituality that focuses on the illumination of the mind and an affective spirituality that focuses on the illumination of the heart. He

A Typology of Spirituality

further suggests two appropriate means toward those ends: a kataphatic means—an indirect way of knowing in which our relationship with God is mediated—and an apophatic means—a direct way of knowing, in which our relationship with God is not mediated.

Holmes calls his model the "Circle of Sensibility," and in it he delineates four styles of prayer, later configured as schools of spirituality. By "sensibility" he refers to the possibilities within individuals and communities as they seek to understand the experience of God and its meaning for our times. Holmes proposes the use of two intersecting lines placed within a circle. The vertical line creates a north-south axis, with Sensibility (Mind or Intellect) at the north pole and Affective (Heart or Emotion) at the south pole. The horizontal line creates an east-west axis, with Kataphatic (God as Revealed: known through images) at the east pole and Apophatic (God as Mystery: known mystically). Below is an adaptation of his circle, divided into four quadrants. Each quadrant contains one of the four schools of spirituality, which he labels "speculative-kataphatic" (Type I spirituality), affective-kataphatic (Type II spirituality), affective-apophatic (Type III spirituality), and speculative-apophatic (Type IV spirituality).

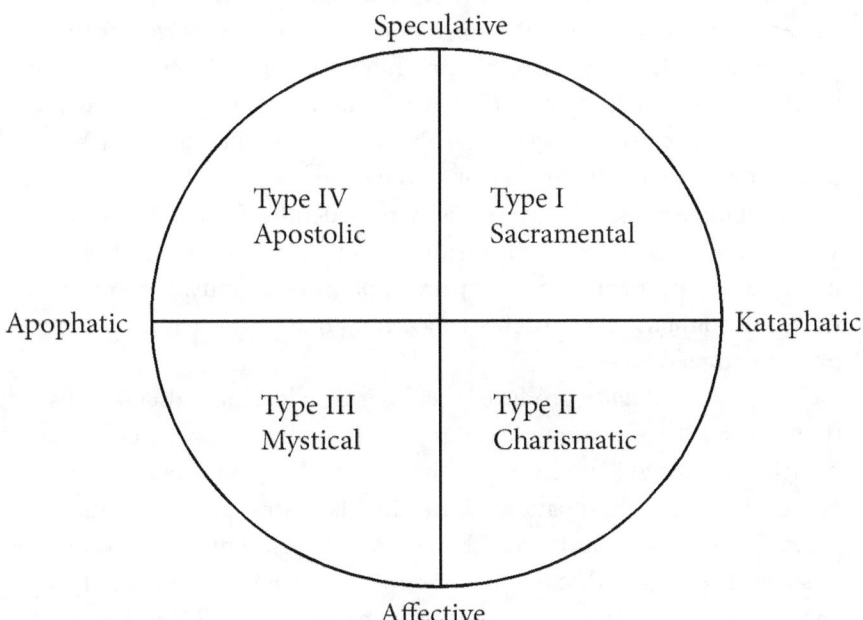

Type I spirituality, an intellectual "thinking" spirituality, is "sacramental." Its primary aim is to aid persons in fulfilling their vocation in the world. This spirituality favors what it can see, touch, and vividly imagine. Type II spirituality, a sensate, heartfelt approach to spirituality, is "charismatic." Its primary aim is to achieve holiness of life through personal renewal. Type III spirituality, which emphasizes being and direct experience of God, is "mystical." Its primary aim is union with the Holy, an unattainable goal, a journey that nevertheless continually impels the disciple onward. Type IV spirituality, a visionary, almost crusading type of spirituality, is "apostolic." Its primary aim is to obey God's will completely. Its major concerns are witness to God's reign and striving for justice and peace.

Type I spirituality (the speculative-kataphatic approach) falls prey to the "heresy" of rationalism (*an excessive concern for right thinking* that leads to dogmatism) if it denies the validity or counterbalance of Type III spirituality (affective-apophatic), its diagonal (opposite) approach. Each approach should look to its diagonal spirituality for growth and balance. Type II spirituality (the affective-kataphatic approach) risks falling into the "heresy" of pietism, *an excessive concern for right feelings* that leads to emotionalism. Type III spirituality (the affective-apophatic approach) is subject to the "heresy" of quietism, *an excessive concern for right internal experience* that leads to escapism or withdrawal; Type IV spirituality (the speculative-apophatic approach) may fall into the "heresy" of encratism, *an excessive concern for right behavior* that leads to moralism. Each approach needs to be held in tension with its opposite.

The understanding of spirituality provided by these typologies results in great benefit to one's spiritual identity as well to the level and nature of engagement with one's worshipping community. For example, from this fountain flow insights concerning one's approach to worship, prayer, and meditation.

Type I spirituality produces theological reflection and crafts position papers. Its practitioners are analytical, apprehending theology as doctrine. Divine guidance comes chiefly through scripture and sermons. Worship is orderly and patterned. Reading is central to this spirituality. Prayer in this quadrant is word-based and thought-out, whether aloud or silent. Theological discussion is common with this type, but if not balanced with other activities, can lead to a one-dimensional "head trips."

Type II spirituality uses an entirely different spiritual "vocabulary" in expressing its heartfelt intuition. Since experience must be shared, its adherents often emphasize evangelism, and personal transformation, sometimes of a sudden type. Witnessing, testimonials, and especially music mark congregational worship. Theologically this approach stresses immanence over the transcendence of God. Friendship with Jesus and an outpouring of the Spirit provide signs of God's presence in life. Type II prayer is often word-based but stated extemporaneously. Worship is full of feeling, energy, and bodily freedom of expression that Type I worship generally lacks. African-American churches have this capacity for spontaneity and enthusiastic worship. Not only in the U.S. but also worldwide, many Christians formerly concentrated in Type I mainline denominations are now leaving and, where they seek corporate worship, are moving to congregations that represent more affective (charismatic) types of worship.

Type III spirituality is dominated by contemplative prayer, the purpose of which is not to fill the mind or express the mind as to free the mind. The goal is to empty the self from all distractions so as to be fully receptive. Classic Christian congregational approaches may be found in Quaker worship, which silences the senses to create empty space, and Eastern Orthodox worship, which makes use of the senses as a means of eliminating their influence. While Orthodox utilize icons, music, and incense as vehicles for the mystery spiritually present but hidden, Quakers eliminate sermons, clergy, and sacraments altogether, emphasizing hearing rather than speaking. This form of worship attracts people who are by nature contemplative, introspective, intuitive, and inner directed. Representatives of this approach, often uncomfortable with organized religion, find simple life styles appealing. Historically, Type III spirituality pushes the frontiers of theology in the West, providing rich fodder for predominantly Type I spirituality.

Type IV spirituality, which combines mystic experience with an intellectual mode of gathering data, attracts single-minded visionaries with a deeply focused spirituality. Practitioners of this mode of spirituality care less than do others about affiliation with organized religion, certainly less than those in Types I and II. Their aim is to obey God. Theirs is a courageous idealism that takes responsibility for change, creating a passion for transforming society. Type IV practitioners equate prayer and theology with action. What other spirituality schools might consider a response to prayer (obedience), this school considers as actual prayer. Disciples on this path often participate in marches and rallies and seek to serve in the Peace Corps or locally in organizations such as AmeriCorps. Taking as their motto the words of Jesus in Matthew 25:40: "Truly I tell you, just as you do it to one of the least of these . . . you do it to me," they associate worship and prayer with the presence of God, particularly evident in situations of human need.

Bibliography

Armstrong, Karen. *Buddha*. New York: Viking, 2001.
Brakke, David. *Gnosticism: From Nag Hammadi to the Gospel of Judas*. Transcript Book. Chantilly, VA: The Great Courses, 2015.
———. *The Gnostics: Myth, Ritual, and Diversity in Early Christianity*. Cambridge, MA: Harvard University Press, 2010.
Brueggemann, Walter. *Theology of the Old Testament*. Minneapolis: Fortress, 1997.
Carmody, Denise Lardner and John Tully. *Mysticism: Holiness East and West*. New York: Oxford University Press, 1996.
Cary, Phillip. *Augustine: Invention of the Inner Self: The Legacy of a Christian Platonist*. New York: Oxford University Press, 2000.
———. *The History of Christian Theology*. The Great Courses Guidebook. Chantilly, VA: The Teaching Company, 2008.
Chopra, Deepak. *The Seven Spiritual Laws of Success*. San Rafael, CA: Amber-Allen, 1994.
Christian, William A. *Meaning and Truth in Religion*. Princeton, NJ: Princeton University Press, 1964.
Clement, Keith W. *Friedrich Schleiermacher: Pioneer of Modern Theology*. Minneapolis: Fortress, 1991.
Clifford, Richard J. *The Wisdom Literature*. Nashville: Abingdon, 1998.
Dunderberg, Ismo. *Beyond Gnosticism: Myth, Lifestyle, and Society in the School of Valentinus*. New York: Columbia University Press, 2008.
Ehrman, Bart D. *Lost Christianities: The Battle for Scripture and the Faith We Never Knew*. New York: Oxford University Press, 2003.
Erb, Peter. *True Christianity*. The Classics of Western Spirituality. Mahway, NJ: Paulist, 1979.
Fowden, Garth. *The Egyptian Hermes: A Historical Approach to the Late Pagan Mind*. Princeton: Princeton University Press, 1988.
Fox, Matthew. *Creation Spirituality*. New York: HarperSanFrancisco, 1991.
———. *Original Blessing*. Santa Fe, NM: Bear & Co., 1983.
Greer, Rowan A. *Origen: Translation and Introduction*. The Classics of Western Spirituality. Ramsey, NJ: Paulist, 1979.
Haught, John. *The Promise of Nature*. Mahwah, NJ: Paulist, 1993.
Heine, Ronald E. *Origen: Scholarship in the Service of the Church*. Oxford: Oxford University Press, 2010.

Hoffecker, W. Andrew, and Gary Scott Smith. *Building a Christian World View*. Vol. 1. Phillipsburg, NJ: Presbyterian and Reformed, 1986.

Holmes, Urban T. *The History of Christian Spirituality*. New York: Seabury, 1980.

Hordern, William E. *A Layman's Guide to Protestant Theology*. Rev. ed. New York: Macmillan, 1968.

Jonas, Hans. *The Gnostic Religion: The Message of the Alien God and the Beginnings of Christianity*. Boston: Beacon, 1958.

Jones, Cheslyn, et al. *The Study of Spirituality*. New York: Oxford University Press, 1986.

King, Karen L. *Images of the Feminine in Gnosticism*. Philadelphia: Fortress, 1988.

———. *What is Gnosticism?* Cambridge, MA: Harvard University Press, 2005.

Kushner, Lawrence. *God Was In This Place & I, I Did Not Know*. Woodstock, VT: Jewish Lights, 2016 (1991).

Leloup, Jean-Yves. *The Gospel of Thomas: The Gnostic Wisdom of Jesus*. Translated by Joseph Rowe. Rochester, VT: Inner Traditions, 2005.

Louth, Andrew. *The Origins of the Christian Mystical Tradition: From Plato to Denys*. 2nd. ed. Oxford: Oxford University Press, 2007.

Luittikhuizen, Gerard. *Gnostic Revision of Genesis Stories and Early Jesus Tradition*. Leiden: Brill, 2006.

Matt, Daniel Chanan. *Zohar: The Book of Enlightenment*. The Classics of Western Spirituality. Ramsey, NJ: Paulist, 1983.

May, Gerald G. *Addiction and Grace*. New York: HarperOne, 1991.

McGinn, Bernard M. *The Presence of God: A History of Western Christian Mysticism*. Vol. 1. New York: Crossroad, 1991.

Murphy, Roland F. *The Tree of Life: An Exploration of Biblical Wisdom Literature*. 3rd ed. Grand Rapids, MI: Eerdmans, 2002.

Newell, John Philip. *The Rebirthing of God: Christianity's Struggle for New Beginnings*. Woodstock, VT: Skylight Paths, 2014.

Noll, Mark A. *Turning Points: Decisive Moments in the History of Chris*tianity. 3rd ed. Grand Rapids, MI: Baker Academic, 2012.

O'Connor, Kathleen M. *The Wisdom Literature*. Collegeville, MN: Liturgical, 1990.

Pagels, Elaine. *Beyond Belief: The Secret Gospel of Thomas*. New York: Random House, 2003.

———. *The Gnostic Gospels*. New York: Random House, 1979.

———. *The Johannine Gospel in Gnostic Exegesis*. Nashville: Abingdon, 1973.

Pearson, Birger A. *Gnosticism, Judaism, and Egyptian Christianity*. Minneapolis, Fortress, 1990.

Perkins, Pheme. *The Gnostic Dialogue: The Early Church and the Crisis of Gnosticism*. New York: Paulist, 1980.

Rist, J. M. *Augustine: Ancient Thought Baptized*. New York: Cambridge University Press, 2003.

Robinson, James M. *Nag Hammadi Library in English*. New York: Harper & Row, 1977.

Rohr. Richard. *Falling Upward: A Spirituality for the Two Halves of Life*. San Francisco: Jossey-Bass, 2011.

———. *The Naked Now: Learning to See as the Mystics See*. New York: Crossroad, 2009.

———. *What the Mystics Know*. New York: Crossroad, 2015.

Ross, Nancy Wilson. *Buddhism: A Way of Life and Thought*. New York: Knopf, 1980.

Royalty, Robert M. *The Origin of Heresy: A History of Discourse in Second Temple Judaism and Early Christianity*. London: Routledge, 2012.

Bibliography

Rudolph, Kurt. *Gnosis: The Nature and History of Gnosticism.* San Francisco: HarperOne, 1987.

Shapiro, Rami. *Perennial Wisdom for the Spiritually Independent.* Woodstock, VT: Skylight Independent, 2013.

Shelley, Bruce L., and R. L. Hatchett. *Church History in Plain Language.* 4th ed. Nashville: Thomas Nelson, 2013

Smith, Huston. *Forgotten Truth: The Common Vision of the World's Religions.* New York: HarperSanFrancisco, 1976.

———. *The World's Religions.* San Francisco: HarperSanFrancisco, 1991.

Steere, Douglas V. *Quaker Spirituality.* The Classics of Western Spirituality. Mahway, NJ: Paulist, 1984.

Streng, Fred, et al. *Ways of Being Religious.* Englewood Cliffs, NJ: Prentice-Hall, 1973.

Thomassen, Einar. *The Spiritual Seed: The Church of the Valentinians.* Leiden, Brill, 2008.

Trigg, Joseph W. *Origen.* Atlanta: John Knox, 1983.

Turner, John D., and Ruth Majercik. *Gnosticism and Later Platonism: Themes, Figures, and Texts.* Atlanta: Society of Biblical Literature, 2000.

Vande Kappelle, Robert P. *Adventures in Spirituality: A Journey from Belief to Faith.* Eugene, OR: Wipf & Stock, 2020.

———. *Beyond Belief: Faith, Science, and the Value of Unknowing.* Eugene, OR: Wipf & Stock, 2012.

———. *Dark Splendor: Spiritual Fitness for the Second Half of Life.* Eugene, OR: Resource, 2015.

———. *Into Thin Places: One Man's Search for the Center.* Eugene, OR: Resource, 2010.

———. *Living Graciously on Planet Earth: Faith, Hope, and Love in Biblical, Social, and Cosmic Context.* Eugene, OR: Wipf & Stock, 2016.

———. *The New Creation: Church History Made Accessible, Relevant, and Personal.* Eugene, OR: Wipf & Stock, 2018.

Whaling, Frank. *John and Charles Wesley.* The Classics of Western Spirituality. Ramsey, NJ: Paulist, 1981.

Winston, David. *Philo of Alexandria.* The Classics of Western Spirituality. Ramsey, NJ: Paulist, 1981.

Young, William A. *The World's Religions; Worldviews and Contemporary Issues.* Upper Saddle River, NJ: Prentice-Hall, 2010.

Index

Abel (biblical figure), 70
Abraham (biblical patriarch), 23, 39, 92,
    250, 251, 252
  call of, 26–27, 206
Adam (biblical figure), 25, 54, 63, 66,
    70, 73, 121–22
  as originally androgynous, 73
aeon(s), 62, 65, 73, 74, 78, 105, 137
Albigensians, 60
Anabaptists, 156–58
Anselm, 101
Antony (desert monk), 130, 135
apatheia, 89, 93, 101, 138
Apocryphon of John, 59, 65, 73
apophatic spirituality, xiv, 140, 141, 142,
    143, 145, 202, 233, 234
Apostles' Creed, 53
Aquinas, Thomas, 43, 116, 117, 124,
    132, 133, 145–46, 151, 202, 218
archon(s), 62, 63, 68, 74
Arendt, Johann, 164
Aristotle, Aristotelian, xiv, 49, 83, 84,
    87–88, 102, 116, 146
Arminian, 159, 161, 166, 168, 172, 206
Athanasius, 131, 135, 136, 137
Augustine (bishop), xi, xiv, 2, 31, 37,
    42, 43, 60, 79, 101, 116–28, 131,
    132, 136, 138, 187, 199, 205, 207
  on evil, xiv, 79, 127
  on faith and reason, 123–24
  on free will, 124, 125, 127
  on grace, xiv, 120–28
  life of, 117–20
  on original sin, 121, 126, 187
  on predestination, xiv, 125–27
  on theology, 145–46

Bacon, Francis, 178
baptism, 55, 76, 121–22, 156–57, 158n3
Baptists, xv, 157, 158–60, 162, 163
Barth, Karl, xv, 7, 41, 197–207
Basil the Great, 111, 131
beatific vision. *See* God, vision of
Benedict of Nursia, 131
Berdyaev, Nicolai, 191
Bernard of Clairvaux, 132
Berry, Thomas, xi
Bible, biblical, 31, 107, 108, 186, 198,
    200, 201, 208
Black Death, 133
Boff, Leonardo, 217
Bonaventure, 133
bridal chamber, rite of, 68–69. 78
"brides of angels," 69, 72, 78
Brueggemann, Walter, 35
Brunner, Emil, xv, 199, 201, 202–3
Buddhism, ix, 139
Bultmann, Rudolph, 208

Cain (biblical figure), 70
Calvin, John, 37, 117, 125, 126, 132,
    156, 167, 205
Calvinism, 159, 166–67, 168, 172, 206
Campbell, Joseph, 2
Camus, Albert, 191
Cary, Phillip, 120

Cassian, John, 114, 131, 139
Catholicism. *See* Roman Catholicism
Chopra, Deepak, 7
Christendom, 155–56, 192, 193
Christian, Christianity, 48, 49
  See also orthodoxy, Christian
  and Judaism, 82
  and pagan philosophy, 82–84, 91
Christian, William A., 4
Christology, 16–17, 46, 137, 147, 148, 186, 187, 205
Cicero (Roman philosopher), 118
Clement of Alexandria (Christian philosopher), xiv, 49, 89, 92, 99, 100–102, 104, 114, 137–38
Cloud of Unknowing, 9, 134, 142
Congregationalism, 157, 159, 165, 166
Constantine (emperor), 59, 131, 135
conversion (religious), 125, 165, 166–67, 168, 228
Copernicus, Nicolaus, 177
corporate personality, 22–23
creation, doctrine of, 19, 24–25, 28, 46, 49, 79, 215–16
  evil and, 60, 79, 97, 110, 118, 127

Daoism, ix
D'Arcy, Paula, 13
David (biblical king), 22
deism, 179–81
Demiurge, 91–92, 107
demons (evil spirits), 138, 139, 177
Denys the Areopagite, 97, 111, 137, 140–43, 145, 151
Descartes, René, 95, 178
Dionysius. *See* Denys the Areopagite
docetism, 62n3
doctrine, 45
Dominicans, 132, 133
Dostoyevsky, Fyodor, 191
dualism, dualistic, 2, 17, 51, 67, 79, 84–87. 118, 127, 215
Duns Scotus, 133

Eastern Orthodoxy, xiv, 49, 111, 114, 116, 135, 136–44, 151–52
  veneration of icons in, 146–50, 152

Ecclesiastes, book of, 20, 109, 110
Edwards, Jonathan, 165–68
ego, egocentricity, x, xii, 7, 14, 39, 70, 71, 99, 188, 221–22, 224
election, doctrine of, 23, 26–27, 126, 204–7
  of Abraham, 26–27
Elijah (biblical prophet), 30
Eliot, T. S., 10
Enlightenment, 43, 176–78, 179, 180, 210
Epicureans, 130
Essenes, 130
Eusebius, 93
Evagrius of Pontus, 100, 111, 114, 137, 138–39, 140
evangelical(ism), 170, 173, 174
Eve (biblical figure), 63, 66, 70, 75
everlasting life. *See* immortality
evil. *See* creation, doctrine of, evil and
existentialism, 191
  Christian, xv, 191–97
Exodus, the (biblical event), 27–29

faith, 45, 138, 174, 176, 178, 192, 196, 202, 209, 219
false self. *See* ego
Finney, Charles, 168
Fosdick, Harry Emerson, 189
Fox, George, 160–61
Fox, Matthew, x, xv, 6, 215–17
Francis of Assisi, 132, 133
Franciscans, 132, 133
Francke, August Hermann, 164–65
Franklin, Benjamin, 181
free will, doctrine of, 55, 104, 107, 109, 114, 125, 129

Galileo Galilei, 177
Genesis, book of, 24–25, 63, 65, 73, 92, 107, 108
global warming, x
gnosis, 50, 54, 60, 62, 63, 66, 69, 70, 71, 75, 76, 77, 94, 97, 99, 100, 137, 138
  Christian, xiv, 49, 56, 102
  non-Christian, xiv, 49, 52, 56

Index

Gnostic(s), Gnosticism, xiv, 42, 49, 82, 91
- on body, 62, 67, 69, 70, 78
- Christian, xiv, 49, 61, 64, 99–114
- depiction by Irenaeus, 51–56
- dualism in, 67, 79
- ethics, 63
- gender roles in, 72–79
- and Judaism, 63
- literature. *See* Nag Hammadi writings
- non-Christian, 49, 52, 58–80, 94, 95, 99, 102, 104, 110, 114
- pneumatics in, 69, 72
- portrayal of Christ in, 62, 65–66, 71, 74
- portrayal of God in, 72, 74
- on salvation, 65–66, 68, 71, 76
- on sin, 68
- on soul and spirit, 62, 67–68, 69, 70
- worldview, 61–62

God, 29
- and creation, 24–25, 50, 79
- existence of, 211–12
- as "Ground of Being," 212
- hiddenness of, 30–31
- and humanity, 44
- incomprehensibility of, 54, 93, 96, 105, 135–46, 151
- intimacy with, 197
- justice of, 167
- knowledge of, 39, 44, 110, 127, 203
- love of, 15, 16, 18, 29, 107, 190, 220
- name of, 29, 91
- nature of, 35
- Selfhood of, ix
- union with, 74, 95, 97, 121, 137, 139, 152
- unity (oneness) of, 104, 108, 204, 219
- vision of, 55, 69, 93, 94, 139, 145–46, 147–52

Gospel of Judas, 58, 59, 65
Gospel of Mary, 76, 77, 78n9
Gospel of Philip, 76
Gospel of Thomas, 59, 70–71, 75, 76, 99
Gospel of Truth, 68, 137
Gospels, Synoptic, 46, 65, 148, 188, 225

grace, xiv, 145, 146, 152, 173, 187, 222
- *See also* Augustine, on grace
- doctrine of, 8, 150
- prevenient, 171
Gregory of Nazianzus, 111
Gregory of Nyssa, 107, 108, 111, 137, 143–44

happiness, 118, 124, 126, 145, 197
- definition of, 83
- for Philo, 93
- in Stoicism, 89
Harnack, Adolf von, 189
Haught, John, 214, 215
heaven, 14, 15, 106
Hebrew scriptures, 19–31, 44, 46, 47–48, 53, 92, 113, 119
- and the New Testament, 21, 31, 113
Hegel, G. W. F., 179, 193, 195
hell, 14, 15, 106
Heraclitus (Greek philosopher), 84, 87, 111, 184n1
heresy, heterodoxy, xiv, 48, 49, 50–51, 64, 89, 234
- definition of, 43n3, 48, 50
Hermes, Hermetic, xiv, 94, 99
heteronomy, 209–10
Hildegard of Bingen, 131
Hinduism, 231–32
Hitler, Adolf, 199, 203
Hobbes, Thomas, 178
Holiness Tradition, xiii, 172–74
Holmes, Urban, 232–36
Holy Spirit, 6, 52, 54, 105, 129, 150, 161, 163, 165, 166, 173, 174, 204, 222, 223, 235
Homer, 90
humanity
- dependence on God, xi
- love for God, xi, xiii
hypostasis, 95
Hypostasis of the Archons, 75

Ialdabaoth, 63, 66, 74, 75
icons, veneration of, xiv, 146–50, 235
immortality (everlasting life), 55, 83, 94, 120, 125, 136, 152

incarnation, doctrine of, 16, 54, 55, 205, 212
Irenaeus, xiv, 48, 50, 51–56, 61, 63–65, 66, 70, 99, 104, 107
Isis (Egyptian goddess), 75

Jabay, Earl, 14
Jacob (biblical patriarch), 23
Jefferson, Thomas, 181
Jerome (theologian), 93, 123, 132
Jesus Christ, 7, 14, 15–16, 38, 44, 45–46, 47–48, 54, 55, 122, 129, 155, 187, 188, 217, 222
    See also Christology
    as *aeon*, 62, 65, 74
    crucifixion of, 47
    deity of, 30–31, 33–34, 121, 137, 148, 152
    and discipleship, 34
    as divine Logos or Word, 83, 92, 101, 105, 106, 107, 108, 113, 201, 204
    humanity of, 200
    and kingdom of God, 46
    life of, 32, 34
    as "New Being," 212
    resurrection of, 47, 48, 54, 55
    and the second journey, 32–35
    transfiguration of, xiv, 46, 148–50
    as wisdom of God, 83–84
Jew, Jewish, 44, 45, 49–50, 91, 202
    Gnosticism and, 63
John, Gospel of, 16, 47, 48, 65, 83, 92, 100, 123, 188
John of the Cross, 98, 135, 144–45
Julian of Norwich, 11, 134
Jung, Carl, 79–80
Justin Martyr, xiv, 47, 48, 50, 51, 52, 99, 101

Kabbalah, 60
Kant, Immanuel, 179–80, 184, 185, 187, 203
kataphatic spirituality, xiv, 141, 142, 233, 234
Kepler, Johannes, 177
Kierkegaard, Søren, xv, 9, 191–97, 198, 203

Kingdom of God, 14–15, 17, 32, 46, 55, 71, 76, 198
Kuhn, Thomas, 218

Leloup, Jean-Yves, 78n9
Liberalism, Protestant, xv, 6, 43, 176–89
Loyola, Ignatius, 5, 144
Luther, Martin, 37, 117, 124, 125, 132, 156, 164, 166, 169, 174, 192

Maimonides, Moses, xi
Mani, Manicheism, 42, 58, 59, 118–19
Marcion, Marcionism, 42, 49, 50, 58, 65, 66, 113
    depiction in Irenaeus, 51–56
Mary Magdalene (biblical figure), 76–78
materialism, 88
Maximus the Confessor, 98, 114
May, Gerald, 25, 224
McClaren, Brian, 14
Methodist, Methodism, 168, 169, 171, 173
Mill, John Stuart, 179
Minucius Felix, 47
monasticism, xiii, 114, 130–35
monism, 88
Moravians, 169n6, 185
Mormon, Mormonism, 69n6
Moses (biblical figure), 22, 27–29, 90, 92, 93, 143, 202
mystical spirituality, xiv, 129–52, 234, 235
mystics, mysticism, xiii, xiv, 8, 22, 129–30, 141, 228, 235
    definition of, 129

Nag Hammadi writings, 42n1, 58, 59, 65, 70
Napoleon Bonaparte, 32
nature
    degradation of, x
    as God's garment, xii
    as sacrament, 214–15
Neo-orthodoxy, xv, 43, 197, 199, 200, 201, 205, 207, 208
Neoplatonism, 42, 94–98, 99, 107, 111, 112, 119, 136, 140

Index

New Testament, 20, 21, 22, 27, 31–40, 44, 50, 53
    and the Old Testament, 21–22, 31, 112
    theologies of, 31
Newell, John Philip, xi
Newton, Isaac, 177, 180
Nicaea, Council of, 43n2, 96, 137
Niebuhr, Reinhold, 207
Norea, 63, 75

Old Testament. *See* Hebrew scriptures
Origen (Christian theologian), xiv, 49, 52, 92, 99, 102–14, 138, 141, 144
original sin, 116, 121, 126, 187, 215
orthodoxy, Christian, xiv, 42–56, 58, 99, 102, 113, 114, 125, 155, 185
    definition of, 43n2
    proto-, 43n2

Pachomius (Egyptian monk), 131
Pagels, Elaine, 72
Palamas, Gregory, 137, 149, 151
Palmer, Phoebe, 173–74
Parmenides (Greek philosopher), 84, 111, 184n1
Pascal, Blaise, 25, 150–51
Paul (biblical author), 33, 35–40, 45, 48, 49, 50, 61, 63, 65, 66, 72, 83, 108, 117, 118, 119, 120, 122, 126, 127, 130, 140, 200, 228
    on the church in, 39
    conversion of, 38–39
    and legalism, 37, 45, 66, 122
Payne, Thomas, 181
Pelagius, 121
Penn, William, 161–62
Perkins, Pheme, 79
person(hood), ix
Philo (Jewish philosopher), xiv, 89–93, 100, 108, 111, 143
    view of Logos in, 91, 92
philosophy
    pagan, 82
Pietism, xiii, xv, 5, 162–65
Plato, Platonism, xiv, 42, 49, 60, 63, 83, 84–87, 90, 91, 92, 101, 102, 107, 111, 112, 116, 142, 149
    analogy of the cave, 87
    on body and soul, 85, 86–87
    on cosmology, 84, 85
    on creation, 91–92
    on epistemology, 85–86, 96
    on forms and ideals, 84–85
    on theology, 85, 87, 92, 95
Pleroma, 61, 62, 63, 69, 74, 75, 76, 77, 78
Plotinus (Roman philosopher), xiv, 94–98, 112
prayer, 102, 108, 121, 122, 139, 144, 197, 233, 234, 235, 236
predestination, 116, 125–27, 167, 172, 205–6
Proclus (Roman philosopher), 94, 140
Protestant(ism), xv, 43, 116, 132, 136, 146, 148, 163, 174, 176, 182, 211
    See also Liberalism, Protestant
Reformation, 48, 125, 131, 134, 154–58, 174, 176
Scholasticism, 164
Psalms, book of, 19–20, 27
Pseudo-Dionysius. *See* Denys the Areopagite
Puritans, Puritanism, 156, 158, 215–16, 172
Pythagoras, Pythagorean, 90, 130

Quakers, xv, 157, 160–62, 163, 235

religion, xiv, 1, 14, 24, 129, 183, 203, 211, 214, 224, 135
    definition of, 1–5
    natural, 180
    revealed, 180
Renan, Ernst, 32
revelation, 123, 201, 202, 204, 208
    as event, 199
    general/natural, 200, 201, 202, 203
    special, 200, 201, 203
Revelation, book of, 20
revivalism, xiii, xv, 165–71, 172
Ricoeur, Paul, 10
Rohr, Richard, xv, 218–25, 228–29
Roman Catholicism, 43, 49, 114, 116, 125n3, 134–35, 136, 144, 146, 148, 151, 155, 162, 176, 182
Romanticism, 182–83, 185, 186

sacraments, 159, 161, 163, 171, 214, 234, 235
salvation, 14, 15–16, 25, 46, 54, 66, 76, 77, 120, 122, 126, 187, 204–5, 206
    assurance of, 163, 169
    universal, 106, 112, 189, 206
sanctification, 172, 173, 174
Sartre, Jean-Paul, 191
Schleiermacher, Friedrich, xv, 82–89, 196, 203, 204, 208
Schleitheim Confession, 157
scripture, 111, 112, 113
    allegorical reading of, 82, 90, 103, 112, 119
second journey, 8–14, 108–11, 129, 225
    Jesus Christ and, 32–35
    Paul and, 35–40
Self, Selfhood, xii, 7
    false. *See* ego, egocentricity
    True, xii, xiii, 14, 39, 40, 70, 71–72, 188, 222
Septuagint, 90, 91
Seth (biblical figure), 63, 70, 75
Simon Magus, 52
Simon Peter (apostle), 76, 77, 78, 93
sin, 4, 15–16, 24–25, 44, 46, 55, 109, 121, 124, 166–67, 186–87, 203, 221
    See also original sin
Smith, Huston, 231
Sophia, 62, 74, 78
Sophists, 86
soul, x, 8–9
    journey to God, 76, 78, 86–87, 108–9
Spener, Jacob Philip, 163, 164
spirituality, xi, xii, xiii, 1, 13, 14, 22, 43, 44, 207, 211, 227
    biblical, xiv, 19–40
    creation, 215–18
    definition of, xii, 5–7, 217
    early Christian orthodox, 43
    first-half-of-life, ix, xii, xiv, 7, 9, 13, 21, 22, 43, 45, 56, 80, 120, 126, 129, 155, 187, 188, 209, 220, 221, 224, 225, 227

    goal of, xii
    Jesus and, 32–35
    mystical. *See* mystical spirituality
    orthodox Christian, xiv
    Paul and, 35–40
    personality and, 231
    phases of/types of, 7–8, 109–10, 194–95
    progressive, xv, 214–25
    second-half-of-life, ix, xii, xiv, 8–14, 21, 22, 40, 43, 56, 67, 80, 120, 126, 129, 188, 219, 220, 221, 224, 225, 227
    typology of, 231–36
Stoic, Stoicism, 42, 83, 88–89, 90, 93, 101
    doctrine of the Logos in, 88
    view of happiness in, 89
Streng, Fred, 4
suffering, 60, 220–25
Symeon the New Theologian, 137, 150

temptation/testing, 109
Teresa of Ávila, 11, 135, 144, 219
Theodosius (emperor), 59, 135
theology, 1, 141
    Christian, 46
    crisis, 200
    definition of, 5
    dialectical, 199, 200, 202
theonomy, 209–10
theosis, 111, 120, 137, 141, 149–50, 152
Thunder, Perfect Mind, 75
Tillich, Paul, xv, 4, 207–13
Torah, xi, 27, 37, 46, 60
tradition, 45
Transfiguration. *See* Jesus Christ, transfiguration of
Trinity, doctrine of, 46, 93, 95, 96, 107, 116, 136, 137, 142, 149, 152, 201–2, 204
truth, religious, 51, 54, 123, 124, 145, 196, 200

Unitarianism, 180

Valentinus, Valentinian, 42, 49, 51–56,
    58, 59, 63, 64, 65, 68, 69, 70, 94,
    99, 103, 104, 105, 114
  on *gnosis*, 70, 71, 102
  life of, 42n1, 100
  on salvation, 68, 69, 70, 76
  on sin, 68
  on soul and spirit, 70
Virgil (Roman poet), 117
Voltaire, 179

Wells, H. G., 32
Wesley, Charles, 168, 169, 170
Wesley, John, 117, 167, 168, 169–72
  and holiness theology, 173

Whitefield, George, 168, 169–70
Wilber, Ken, 9
wisdom, 83
worship, 19–20, 122, 234–36
    Christian, 46

Young, William A., 4

Zeno (ancient philosopher), xiv, 88
Zinzendorf, Count Niklaus von, 169n6
Zohar, the, 50
Zwingli, Ulrich, 156

www.ingramcontent.com/pod-product-compliance
Lightning Source LLC
Chambersburg PA
CBHW062011220426
43662CB00010B/1291